STUFFY

The Life of Newspaper Pioneer
Basil "Stuffy" Walters

STUFFY

The Life of Newspaper Pioneer
Basil "Stuffy" Walters

By RAYMOND MOSCOWITZ

IOWA STATE UNIVERSITY PRESS • AMES

To my mother and father,
CECELIA and EDWARD MOSCOWITZ,
who even in death were the
main inspiration for this book

© 1982 The Iowa State University Press. All rights reserved. Composed by Fox Valley Typesetting, Menasha, Wisconsin, and printed by The Iowa State University Press, Ames, Iowa 50010.

First edition, 1982

Library of Congress Cataloging in Publication Data

Moscowitz, Raymond, 1938–
    Stuffy: the life of newspaper pioneer Basil "Stuffy" Walters.

    Includes index.
    1. Walters, Basil Leon, 1896–1975.   2. Journalists—United States—Biography.
I. Title.
PN4874.W287M6   070′.92′4 [B]   82-50
ISBN 0-8138-1896-6   AACR2

CONTENTS

FOREWORD *by John Chancellor*   vii

PREFACE   xi

1. FRONT PAGE: BABY BOY SCHMITZ   3

2. DISCOVERING INK AT AGE TEN   11

3. SILENT CAL, YELLOW ROBE, A SPEECH   24

4. HOOKING UP WITH COWLES   33

5. MR. WALTERS, MEET MR. GALLUP   40

6. TWO PLACES AT ONCE   54

7. THE BATTLE FOR MINNEAPOLIS   63

8. A GOOF, A SCOOP, TWO WARS   72

9. HOOKING UP WITH KNIGHT   88

10. THE BATTLE FOR CHICAGO   97

11. FIGHTING FOR FREEDOM   113

12. SUCCESS PILES UP   126

13. THE HODGE SCANDAL   141

14. EXCLUSIVES FROM THE MIDDLE EAST   149

15. HOOKING UP WITH FIELD   165

16. CONSULTING AND CORN   180

INDEX   191

FOREWORD

THIS is a book about America informing itself, of a country coming of age, of a people learning about themselves and the world around them. It is the story of a magic moment in the history of American newspapers. It is a tale of technology, of change, of modernity, and of a man who had the wit and the courage to understand those challenges and opportunities.

Stuffy Walters lived a life that bridged two worlds: the staid, self-satisfied journalism of the early years of the century, and the wonderful, inventive, innovative years of the thirties, forties, and fifties, when newspapers were the monarchs of the media. It is to his credit that he was one of the people who not only made the passage across that bridge, but led the charge.

I knew him in Chicago and from a very respectful distance. I was a beginning reporter at the *Chicago Times,* and he was the hugely successful editor of the *Chicago Daily News*—the Honorable and Terrible Basil Leon Sir Stuffy Walters, scourge of the opposition, builder of circulation, master of typography and technology, a man we regarded with the utmost gravity and seriousness.

Chicago was his largest stage and his biggest audience. Yet the art he practiced there had been learned elsewhere, and that it succeeded in the deadly, no-holds-barred competitiveness of Chicago journalism showed how well his early lessons had been learned.

He had the one quality that can lead an editor to greatness: the ability to understand change. He was born before the Wright brothers flew, but he was quick to realize the value of airplanes in covering stories. The first newspapers he worked on used photographs sparingly, if at all, but he helped break new ground in the use of pictures and new kinds of cameras. The language of journalism was stiff and formal when he began, but he showed newspaper writers how to put their stories in words and phrases which meant much more to readers.

Stuffy Walters worked for some distinguished publishers, but his real masters, the people on whose behalf he worked the hardest, were the readers.

Some of his efforts to modernize and, indeed, popularize journalism seem old-fashioned today; some of his efforts were hilarious and have made their way into the folklore of American journalism. But he was always pushing in the right direction, and the changes he brought about in the Middle West were noticed and copied across the country.

It would be a mistake to judge Stuffy Walters against the background of early bi-planes, big old Speed Graphic cameras and reporters with press cards in their hatbands who said "Hello, sweetheart, get me re-write." His is the story of a man who was always looking to the future and using what he found there to improve the papers he edited.

Newspaper editors steal one another's ideas constantly, read each other's papers, and are always on the lookout for something new that works.

His greatest accomplishment may have been that more editors stole Stuffy Walters's new ideas than any other editor of his time.

It seems to me that this is the great value of his life. He not only served the people of a number of cities and regions, but through his pushing and prodding, his delight with the new, and the quality of his thinking his influence was amplified nationally (indeed, internationally—his work was followed in the offices of London editors).

Mr. Moscowitz's book serves a greater purpose than biography, than the story of the life of an endlessly interesting journalist. There is a greater lesson in these pages, and it is this: the basic principles of good journalism, developed in this country in the twentieth century, will be the basic principles in the twenty-first, no matter what the technological changes will be.

We know those changes will be great. We know that newspapers as Stuffy Walters knew them will undergo great changes. We know that some of those changes have taken place already, and that they are bad. We know that some other forms of contemporary journalism, such as the shabby practices on certain local television programs, are equally bad. The future is mixed, at best.

Stuffy Walters's principles, however, prove that success need not cheapen; that popularity does not require pandering; and that above all the news itself, the basic building blocks of journalism, can be made relevant and interesting for the average reader or listener.

The world grows more complicated each day. Editors in the future will face complexities unimagined by the contemporaries of Stuffy Walters. But as he found a way, others can find a way to make people understand what is happening to them in their own communities and around the world, to make them want to understand, and to find joy in the understanding.

That was his accomplishment, and the reasons for it are to be found in this book.

JOHN CHANCELLOR

PREFACE

ON a sunny, crisp day in September 1964 when I was a young reporter for the *Frankfort* (Indiana) *Morning Times,* I came to work and found on my desk a letter with a local return address. It began, "Dear Ray: You certainly did a splendid objective reporting job on the Bontrager speech. And you proved that objective political reporting can be interesting. If all the reporting in this campaign throughout the nation were equally conscientious, I would not worry about the critics of the press." The letter closed, "By such standards, I would award you, sir, with A plus. Best, Stuffy"

Pleased but calm, I showed the letter to the veteran city editor, Vance Sappenfield. "Hey, fella," Sappenfield said with a hint of excitement in his voice, "do you know who 'Stuffy' Walters is?"

"Vaguely," I replied. I had joined the *Morning Times* staff only five months earlier. "I think I saw his name in a college text or two."

Sappenfield smiled widely and proceeded to tell his newest reporter, Ray Moscowitz, about "Stuffy" Walters.

I would come to know much more about Basil Leon "Stuffy" Walters. A few weeks after his letter arrived, I was invited to visit him on a Sunday afternoon at his countryside home a few miles outside Frankfort. I arrived at noon and soon sat down to a huge lunch. I departed at 10:30 that night. Minding my manners, I had tried to leave twice earlier, but each time he asked if I could stay. Gladly, I responded—and he continued to pick my mind clean. Each time I tried to learn more about him—Sappenfield had thoroughly whet my appetite—I would get only a few crumbs of information. No, he wanted to talk about tomorrow's newspapers and the course of the nation and Clinton County politics and communism's threat to freedom and the pros and cons of television and books and economics—and how these things affected people's lives. People. They fascinated him. He wanted to know all about them. Who's this woman or that woman? What did I think of this fellow or that fellow? That Lugar fellow, the young mayor from Indianapolis, he will go places, don't you think?

Our relationship grew, even though I worked for the *Morning Times* only seventeen months. And as Walters played a key role in the development of my newspaper career, I learned more and more about him. The crumbs of information began to form a doughnut over the years. I soon realized that I had come to know one of the great editors in the history of American journalism.

Walters's greatness was formed in a combination of ways. To begin with, he had an uncanny feel for what people wanted in their newspapers. He was a colorful, charismatic man with a common touch, who was able to give his newspaper the extra human dimension that drew readers.

He was also fearless. He was not afraid to experiment and innovate, and he boldly forged ahead with investigative stories of great significance. His fearlessness to try new things in writing, editing, photography, content, and typography produced tremendous circulation results—and a host of followers. His fearlessness in exposing abuses and wrongs produced major awards, but more importantly, contributed to the betterment of the society he served.

Walters relied on his own instincts to a large extent, but he knew that research was important, and he became one of the first editors to use it significantly and profitably.

Finally, Walters possessed an indefatigable devotion to freedom of the press. He became one of the Twentieth Century's leading spokesmen and defenders of the First Amendment, constantly asserting that freedom of the press is the core from which all of America's freedoms spring.

I deeply appreciate the help of the following people:

First, members of the Walters family: Mrs. Basil L. (Rhea), sons Thomas and James, and daughter Mrs. Richard (Nancy) Valentine. I was given free access to Basil Walters's extensive papers and records and aided in other important ways.

Also, the late John S. Knight and Montgomery J. Curtis of Knight-Ridder Newspapers, Miami; Kenneth MacDonald, retired editor of the *Des Moines Register and Tribune*; and Angelo Cohn of Minneapolis. Each of these men provided valuable information.

Also, Don M. Nixon, Wabash, Indiana; John E. Mitchell of Nixon Newspapers, Wabash, Indiana; Howard Brown of Kenosha, Wisconsin; Rose and Lou Freedman, Frankfort, Indiana; Robert and Gerry Moscowitz, Encino, California; Ron and Sharon Hasson, Encino, California; and Leon and Barbara Benon, Montecito, California, whose support and encouragement kept my enthusiasm at a high level.

Also, Anita Aungst of North Manchester, Indiana, and Cathy Trump of Wabash, Indiana, for helping type the manuscript and for taking care of other small, but important, chores.

And, finally, my wife, Barbara, who was always there when needed.

STUFFY

The Life of Newspaper Pioneer
Basil "Stuffy" Walters

Front Page: Baby Boy Schmitz

H E came bounding out of his office cubicle toward the city desk, his five-foot-six, two-hundred-pound body resembling a beer barrel lurching down a hill after falling off a delivery truck.

Shirttail loose, sleeves rolled to elbows, tie slightly askew, he clutched a journalist's thick lead pencil in the stubby fingers of his right hand. An ever-present cigarette struggled for its last breath, captured in the left-hand corner of his mouth. Ashes lay in a small pile on his shirt front, caught in the indentation of his chest, unable to fall over a bulging belly. As usual, he was oblivious to them. A smile forced his beefy cheeks to bubble up under glasses that covered eyes wide with curiosity.

As usual, he wore his nervous energy, but his subordinates knew that he was in control, was ready to direct another winning effort in the Minneapolis newspaper war that was growing hotter with the July days in 1936.

Basil Leon Walters was being "Stuffy" Walters—a newspaper editor who disdained the Ivory Tower, whose personality was the opposite of his nickname, whose enthusiasm, imagination, creativity, and drive infected people, whose innovative newspaper mind left imprints of influence, whose powerful empathy for the human condition was like the most sophisticated radar.

Most of all, this was the Stuffy Walters who would always say, "News, news, news. That's what makes a newspaper. Publish all the other stuff, but never forget the news."

And now, on July 18, 1936, the *Minneapolis Star* had a real piece of news—a genuine coup in the days of a non-television society—the kind of news Walters loved to crow about as the *Star,* long the underdog, fought for life and acceptance in a three-newspaper town.

Walters had decided that the high cost of chartering an airplane

3

would be worth what promised to be a "talking story," the kind people talked about for days. And now, as he reached the city desk, Nat Finney, a thirty-year-old veteran reporter, and Robert Fraser, the twenty-four-year-old rookie photographer, laughed and gestured excitedly as they told about their adventure.

It had started when Finney was tipped off by an old University of Minnesota band chum. Over the years, Finney had often thought about the fellow, a small, intelligent chap who played the sax and carried on interesting conversations. After their university days, the fellow had gone on to get a degree in medicine and begin practicing while Finney entered the world of journalism.

Now, in 1936, Finney's friend had called from Graceville, Minnesota, a tiny burg of some 500 people nestled near the state's western border with South Dakota. Walters and Finney discovered that the little community was about 200 miles almost straight west of Minneapolis—a long way to go for a story in those tough depression days. But after Finney's phone conversation, he and Walters knew they had something.

Upon returning, Finney and Fraser confirmed the hunch, telling how their pilot landed his small plane in a stubble field once filled with oats and wheat. It was Fraser's first plane ride, and he excitedly related how the pilot looked for a spot devoid of stumps and logs.

Walters reached the city desk and asked the young photographer, "Can you get me a life-size picture?"

Fraser, trying to establish himself in photojournalism when the term *photojournalism* barely existed, flashed a look of half-belief. But there was a piece of a smile in his face, too, and he nodded yes.

"You're going to play it all the way across page one, aren't you?" Finney said, making more of a statement than asking a question.

"That's what I want to do," Walters replied.

"It won't fit," someone said, thinking in terms of the picture running three or four columns wide by twenty-one inches long, the length of the newspaper page's printing area.

"No, but it will go diagonally," Walters said.

"Sure," Finney agreed.

The others were skeptical, but Walters's and Finney's minds had been on the same wavelength from the beginning. Finney had fiddled with the thought as he sketched his lead paragraph during the return trip from Graceville. Walters, always looking for something spectacular—but honest—had hatched the same thought after reading the first two paragraphs of Finney's story:

> GRACEVILLE, Minn.—Baby Boy Schmitz, weight at birth 15 pounds, 15.2 ounces, height 24½ inches, head 16 inches, chest 17 inches, across shoulders 8 inches, July 16, 1936, Western Minnesota hospital.
> In such laconic scientific terms, without a word about Mrs. Veronica Schmitz, the mother, medicine records the birth of the largest baby ever born alive in Minnesota—as far as a day's check of doctors and records shows.

When the *Minneapolis Star* hit the streets that afternoon, its front page froze almost everyone whose eyes caught a glimpse of it. There, stretched out full length on his left side, lay Baby Boy Schmitz, adorned in king-size diaper, hands tucked in close to his chest, right leg slightly bent over his left leg, at peace with the world.

The photo was turned on a forty-five degree angle and, below it, the *Star* had placed a yardstick, chopped off at twenty-two inches, to dramatize the baby's huge size.

The baby's head rested just below the *Minneapolis Star* nameplate, to the right of small type carrying the dateline. To the right of the baby's head was a three-line, all-caps headline, set flush right, that read:

LIFE-SIZE PICTURE
OF MINNESOTA'S
BIGGEST BABY

Below the headline, in smaller type that also angled flush right, was a terse caption giving the basic details and ending with this sentence: "Pictures of Baby exclusively in The Star in the Twin Cities."

Slightly below the front-page fold, readers got the full story under a two-column, two-line headline that read:

State's Huskiest Baby
Tips Scales to 16 Lbs.

Finney reported that the child was what doctors call a nine-and-one-half month baby. The bulk of his story jumped from page one to page two. Writing in the conversational tone that Walters advocated, and for which he would later receive much national attention, Finney wrote:

> The doctor in charge (you can't use his name because of the ethics of the medical profession) is a tall, young chap. He started the delivery with one nurse assisting him, Miss Rose Boylan. Half an hour later, he called desperately for another doctor and nurse. They came as fast as they could.
>
> Another half an hour and an emergency call for another doctor and another nurse was sent out. They came. Then for another hour and one-half the six of them worked to bring Baby Boy Schmitz into the world alive. Mothers will understand that. There isn't much that a man can say.

The huge infant wasn't able to breathe on his own. The doctor told Finney, "They have to cry, you know. You have to make them cry."

Finney told *Star* readers about the "extreme prairie heat in the delivery room" as the doctor worked another ninety minutes to urge life into the baby, using the prone pressure method of artificial respiration. "I breathed for the baby with my hands," the doctor explained, adding that his arms became exhausted. He explained, too, how he used hot and cold baths—quick changes—to help shock the baby into life. Still, the baby did not fully respond. Finney wrote: "[The doctor] used a drug called coramine. He spanked Baby Boy Schmitz. Slapped him. Jounced him." Almost three hours later, the infant finally began breathing on its own and settled into a peaceful slumber.

Finney's story wasn't finished. It reported that Mrs. Schmitz, a farm wife, had twelve other children . . . that her husband, Jacob, stood six-foot-four . . . that Mrs. Schmitz was a medical oddity, herself—a twin born in nine months, three months after her sister who quickly died . . . that earlier Mrs. Schmitz had twins of her own, a son weighing eleven pounds, fifteen ounces, and a daughter weighing nine pounds, fifteen ounces—a near-record birth that prompted President Franklin D. Roosevelt to send a letter of congratulations.

The front-page picture enthralled Minneapolis that day—so much so that the *Star*'s two rivals ridiculed the effort, calling it a case of journalistic bad taste.

Still alert as 1980 dawned and living in a retirement home in Silver Spring, Maryland, Finney recalled, "There was carping criticism of us. But what the hell. . . . Our motto in those days was, 'Raise hell and sell newspapers.' Some people said we embarrassed the Schmitz family, but we didn't. Really.''

Jacob Schmitz, who eventually moved to nearby Wheaton, Minnesota, confirmed Finney's words. His memory still sharp at eighty-five, he told how he and his late wife were "real proud of that child—so proud we agreed to show him off at a county fair. Some people disagreed with what we did, but we didn't care.''

The child was named Jacob, Jr. He grew to normal proportions —six feet, 175 pounds. And he died young, at age thirty-one in 1967, from encephalitis, which he first contracted at age four. At his death, his height at birth—twenty-four and one-half inches—was still a record. It stood until 1979. His size at birth had, indeed, been a Minnesota record. And a records check at Johns Hopkins, the noted Baltimore hospital, disclosed that he is the largest American baby born alive since 1895.

The birth of a record-sized baby was hardly significant news in the context of a struggling depression economy, a looming presidential race, President Roosevelt's new social programs, and the creation of John L. Lewis's CIO late in 1935.

Basil Walters knew that. But Basil Walters, unlike the vast majority of editors, knew something else—that for newspapers to remain successful, they had to change from mostly gray type, stodgy headlines, and dull writing into less forbidding, brighter packages with livelier writing that was easier to read.

Not that Walters wasn't a serious man. He was. He had been a debater in high school and college; he had read widely; he had thought considerably about his community, his country, and his world; he had spent countless hours in formal and informal academic discussions. He would thoroughly agree that newspapers had the greatest responsibility for putting crucial events into proper perspective by reporting them accurately and honestly. In fact, he demanded that the editors and reporters who worked for him do so or find other employment.

But Walters was also very human. While he was serious about his work and took a no-nonsense attitude toward it, he did not, at the same time, take himself too seriously. He had come out of a world of simplicity and soil, had become a man of hearty appetite and hard work, of God and family, of patriotism and freedom, of hope and optimism, of joviality and gregariousness, of humor and good cheer, of justice and honest government, of fearlessness and the will to fight for his beliefs, of thrift and a strong distaste for waste.

Out of that mix, out of his lack of pretentiousness, out of his gut feelings for what people wanted, Walters came to preach,"Make the significant interesting.'' He believed newspapers should be "human,'' personal. Newspapers, day after day, should not wear unsmiling faces that report mainly war, poverty, crime, and other social ills. Newspapers should climb into the bowels of life and report with relevance and meaning.

In a world constantly changing, newspapers had to change, too, he insisted—not just from year to year, but from day to day. While the birth of a record-sized baby might top the news one day—despite its lack of significance—the news of a major new industry in Minneapolis might be dominant the next day and, on the following day, the report of a powerful earthquake in South America might receive the greatest front-page treatment.

Newspapers could never remain static, Walters asserted throughout his life. They had to search for new ways to attract and hold readers, had to explore new forms of writing, had to use photography and other graphic devices to a greater extent, had to try new typographical approaches—had to be, at times, bold, breaking out of worn-out molds and using a life-sized picture of a record-sized baby.

Walters practiced what he preached—with gusto. His boldness and innovative techniques kept working, his newspapers kept growing, his stature kept increasing until Nat Finney would say years later, "He was one of the very great editors because he knew what a newspaper was all about.''

Walters knew what freedom was all about, too. And he knew that without a free press nothing else counted, within or without journalism. Freedom and independence had been drilled into him as a young man growing up in Indiana and, very quickly, he realized that the First Amendment was central to all liberty. His devotion to a free, unencumbered press pushed him to the forefront of the cause.

Throughout Basil Walters's entwining journalistic and personal lives ran a thread from which were attached strong, basic beliefs: humanize the news; don't sacrifice honesty and fairness for sensationalism; don't be afraid to innovate; never be satisfied with what you've achieved; audit the affairs of government closely; make the newspaper appetizing throughout; and always be aware of threats to erode freedom, especially the people's right to know.

Unlike many great editors, Walters did not practice those beliefs from a cloistered position of power and influence. Instead, he devoted most of his time to the newsroom, where he loved the excitement and camaraderie. His mind worked quickly and his chunky body was reminiscent at times of a ball in a pinball machine, bounding from desk to desk. He would throw out ideas and help write stories, playing the major role in producing newspapers that proved to be among the most successful in the history of American journalism.

SIDEBAR*

He Was Never Bored

Ask a newspaper editor what he looks for in hiring reporters and "curiosity" will probably top the list.

For James Walters, the youngest of Basil Walters's three children, curiosity "was the thing that crystallized everything that Dad meant to me. It didn't matter where he went—and I was with him so many times—there was something for him to be curious about. There was always something to be fascinated with and to be excited and enthusiastic about. And it could be something simple."

When his father retired and left Chicago, Jim Walters recalled, some people asked him, "Aren't you going to be bored down in Frankfort (Indiana)?" And Walters replied, "No, Frankfort has more to offer than any place in the world." Part of that was talk for the people who jabbed him a bit, but not entirely.

"He could be in Timbuktu and that would be the most fascinating place in the world, because he would see it," Jim Walters explained.

He would look around and pick up something. . . . Or he would say, "By golly, I wonder how that got there," or "I wonder why it's that way." He'd look for somebody to talk to about it. And most of us, well . . . we just didn't get that interested or excited.

* A sidebar is a story, usually shorter in length, relating to the main story. Often it is given special typographical treatment, such as being boxed, typeset on a different column width or having a shaded or colored background. Basil Walters was a master at using sidebars.

I never saw my father bored. People go through life and say, "Oh, I'm bored." People go to New York and Paris, all over the world, and they say, "I just don't know what to do, I'm bored." Dad could be anywhere and he wouldn't be bored.

When his father died, Jim Walters asked the minister to read a paragraph in a book published in 1969 by IBM, entitled *Not Subject to Change*. Walters felt the paragraph, written by William Sheldon, fit his father perfectly. It reads:

There are those much more rare people who never lose their curiosity, their almost childlike wonder at the world; those people who continue to learn and to grow intellectually until the day they die. And these usually are the people who make contributions, who leave some part of the world a little better off than it was before they entered it.

Another attribute high on an editor's list is storytelling. Jim Walters said:

Dad was a good storyteller. I think that to him, newspapering—after all the statements about social responsibility and mirroring of society—newspapering was storytelling. He liked to go around and listen to stories and tell his own. And he liked to get those stories in print. I think the newspaper people he admired the most were the ones who could take little vignettes and make fascinating pieces of news out of them. He always said that people like to know about other people, about their friends. Worldwide news is important, he'd say, but it's not what really excites people. The local news was the big thing, and yet he ran big papers.

CHAPTER TWO

Discovering Ink at Age Ten

To some people it sounded strange when Basil Walters talked about retiring to an Indiana farm and eventually starting a new career—raising pigs. After all, his life had been spent in a journalism career rooted to such cosmopolitan centers as Chicago, Detroit, Miami, Minneapolis, Milwaukee, Indianapolis, and Des Moines.

But people who knew Walters well were not surprised at all when he chose to live out his later life in a farmhouse surrounded by rich soil in the open prairie country of Clinton County, Indiana. That's where his family roots were. They nourished him during his years in urban America, and he was often described as an "Indiana country boy" or a "country-cousin kind of editor."

His daughter, Nancy, remembered that in the forties he got enthusiastic about a little English magazine called the *Organic Gardener* and started growing earth worms in the backyard, twenty years before health foods became the vogue. By the sixties, when retirement loomed, that interest in the soil had grown even stronger.

Walters's American roots began with grandfather Frederick, who was born of German stock in Duncannon, Pennsylvania, on November 21, 1833. Basil Walters would inherit many of his grandfather's genes. Frederick, like his grandson, was a small man of five feet, four inches. But Frederick passed on more than physical characteristics. He was a man who believe deeply in freedom—as his grandson did—and who felt that it was important to fight for what was right. Slavery was not right and so at twenty-eight, Frederick Walters volunteered on September 15, 1861, for the Union Army. A government record lists him as Frederick Walter—without the *s*—and shows him serving at Duncannon for three years before being discharged in the fall of 1864.

Frederick Walters had entered the Civil War as a family man. He was married to a Pennsylvanian named Barbara Gross and had two sons, born in Pennsylvania in 1857 and 1859. Basil's father, also named Frederick, would come along next, arriving on October 18, 1865, in Clinton County, where his father had acquired farmland shortly after the war. Another son and a daughter would follow.

Situated in west-central Indiana, Clinton County's flat terrain provided rich soil for farming. But the area was isolated from important markets, hindering early settlers. It wasn't until 1870, when young Frederick was five years old, that the railroads began to build lines through the county. By the time he grew into adulthood, Clinton County had become a key rail center and rich in agriculture. If all of this wasn't enough to keep him down on the farm, Nancy Christina Fisher was. Although only seventeen, more than ten years younger than he, she captured young Frederick. He saw in her a petite, energetic woman whose red hair matched a fiery personality that contrasted with his rather easy going, gentle demeanor. They had come to know each other well. She was raised just a mile-and-a-quarter down the road, one of eleven children born to James Shield and Nancy Heaton Fisher.

Young Frederick and Nancy were married in December 1892, and began farming ground owned by Frederick's father. Their first child, Basil Leon Walters, came along May 3, 1896. He was bright from the beginning. By the time he was two years old he had a working vocabulary. Ambitious, hard-working, and deeply religious Nancy Walters wasted no time teaching him to speak out, preparing him at age three to make miniature talks in Sunday school at the Morris Chapel Church. Eventually, Nancy took her son to such county towns as Antioch and Boyleston—distant places in those horse-and-buggy days—to appear at special community gatherings.

Young Basil received wide exposure in those days when community life revolved around the school and church. By speaking before large groups at such an early age, he developed an extrovert personality, one completely void of shyness, wrapped in warmth, earthiness, and a fundamental liking for people. He oozed friendliness. Years later, after strenuously arguing with him, people walked away with a smile and a good feeling toward him. He had developed, in his early life, a quality that made it hard for people to dislike him, even when his views hardened as he grew older.

A sister for Basil came along in 1905. Her name was Wilma. By then, he was attending the Walters School, named after his grandfather. It stood across the road from the farmhouse—a small, red brick building.

The joy derived from Wilma's birth was dampened a year later, when Basil's father died on March 7, 1906. A combination of typhoid fever and pneumonia took his life at age forty-one. Basil was not quite ten years old—and suddenly the man of the family.

At first, his mother chose to remain on the forty-acre farm, where she received assistance from her brother-in-law, John, and her father. But Nancy had a strong sense of independence; she was determined not to lean on them. She began learning more about farming and, as she did, her strong-willed nature caused her to dislike a federal government that periodically told her what she could and could not do. She was dedicated to hard work, believing that the work ethic was crucial in leading an upstanding Christian life. She cherished her independence and toiled long hours to preserve it. Like many farmers, she possessed an energetic and optimistic spirit, wrapped in a conservatism that sparked a touch of narrow-mindedness—a spirit bolstered by the belief that God and her Methodism would guide and protect her.

Basil saw those traits in his mother and they, in turn, became his. He would later contend that government should stay out of people's lives. He thrived on hard work—Saturday was never a day of rest with him. He always felt that things would turn out all right. He fought for individual independence. He called on his God . . .

Nancy wanted her son to become a teacher. She didn't want him to become a farmer, fearful that the independent mind he was acquiring, through her, would cause him to tell her what crops to grow and how to market them. She'd manage them fine herself, thank you.

Teaching and farming never really had a chance. Shortly after his tenth birthday, Basil began delivering the county-seat daily, the *Frankfort Morning Times,* and discovered that he had ink in his veins. His career decision thus was made early. Years later, he would address circulation managers' meetings and recall memories of rolling out of bed at five in the morning so his papers could be delivered by seven.

Delivering the *Morning Times* was possible because Basil's mother moved the family into Frankfort, some five miles from the farm. She had decided that a city environment would be best for raising her two small children. She took in roomers at her big house at 257 South Jackson Street and did sewing to make a living. Those funds were supplemented with money from the farm, which her father and brother-in-law, John, agreed to look after. But she insisted on writing all the checks and managing the finances, taking advantage of her strong mathematical ability.

Basil grew closer to Grandfather Fisher, who had retired early from farming and moved into town. There his grandfather's interst in politics grew. In later years, Walters talked about tagging along with Grandfather Fisher when he visited farmers in a horse and buggy and talked politics.

A Democrat, Fisher would exclaim, "You're not going to vote for William Howard Taft, are you?" leaving the farmer either thoroughly irritated, unsure, or with a change of mind before the visit concluded—and giving young Basil an education outside the class-room.

Like today's farmers, they were unlike the dumb image long associated with them. Like now, when they gathered at the grain elevators or in the fields or in each other's homes, they talked long and intelligently, having read widely in the idle hours when the land could not be worked and only Mother Nature was in charge.

Grandfather Fisher so thoroughly immersed his grandson in politics—and ideas about life in general—that Basil's interest in speech and debate enveloped him by the time high school arrived. By then, too, the values that had come from his mother—who led an honest Christian life, in which hard work, fairness, and obeying the law were uppermost—were locked in. Those ingredients, mixed with the thorough liking of people that Grandfather Fisher helped to nurture, heightened Walters's interest in life's complexities, emotions, twists, and turns. They pushed him toward newspapering, where the outlets for becoming involving with the panorama of life are numerous.

By age eighteen, Walters had developed a fine mind and an abundance of confidence. Buoyed most of the time, he developed a philosophy of not looking back. His intelligence, which especially showed in his debating activities, led to the nickname "Shark." Paul Meifield, a very close Frankfort classmate, recalled, "Basil was such a good thinker, excelling in all studies, that the nickname was a natural."

One thing Walters did not excel in was basketball, a sport that Hoosiers consider sacred. Despite his diminutive stature, however, Walters played for the 1914 Frankfort High team. Walters did not excel in baseball, either, but it played the key role in eliminating

"Shark" as his nickname. Playing in a Frankfort sandlot game one afternoon, Walters was stationed at first base, despite his small target. When an opposing batter hit a stinging line drive over his head, Walters leaped high and made a sensational grab. This reminded on-lookers of John Phaelen "Stuffy" McInnis, then a star first baseman for the old Philadelphia Athletics.

"Yea-a-a-a-a, Stuffy!" went the crowd. "Stuffy" stuck. "I liked it, and I encouraged it," Walters said years later. "I wanted it always as a reminder that I could get to be stuffy."

Although his nickname was inspired by a sports hero, Walters wasn't much of a fan. His size, perhaps, discouraged dedication to athletic endeavors. A chauffeur's license issued to him in 1914, at age eighteen, showed he stood five-foot-five and weighed 135 pounds. He would grow another inch in height and several pounds in weight. At times, he hovered around the 200-pound mark, resulting in a forty-four-inch belt by the time he retired—a testament to his joy for good food. (At the 1937 Associated Press Managing Editors convention in New Orleans, he and four other managing editors were asked, "What is a managing editor?" Walters replied, "They try to look wise. Their hardest job is attending civic luncheons and dinners every noon and night. Next to that, their hardest job is keeping their waistlines down.")

Walters acquired the chauffeur's license because of Finton A. Crull, who owned Flora and Crull Clothiers for men. Basil went to work for Crull part-time when he was sixteen, and the proprietor took a liking to him. When Crull said he needed a young man to periodically drive his parents to different places, Walters was glad to earn a few extra dollars. (Oddly, several years later in Minneapolis, former associates recall that Walters was such a bundle of nervous energy he preferred not to drive and was taken to and from the newspaper by fellow staffers who lived nearby.)

When he wasn't working in his spare time, Basil was editing the high school paper and participating on the school's debate team. Debate was an extremely popular school activity in those days. Oratorical contests were as popular as high school basketball is today in Indiana—which means the debating team was the number one extra-curricular outlet. Rivalry was so intense that special trains took fans from one community to another. When Walters won second place one year at the Central District contest at Noblesville, he was looked upon as a high school hero. (Once, in later years, when he was asked if he would describe himself as a muckraker, he said no, that he saw himself as a gadfly, questioning and debating the day's issues.)

After Basil was graduated from Frankfort High School in 1914—the imposing, three-story stone building still stands on East Clinton Street but no longer houses classes—Walters, with Crull's help, managed to scrape together enough money to enroll at Indiana University in the spring of 1915. He went right into journalism. The masthead of the *Indiana Daily Student* for the 1915 fall semster lists him as a reporter, along with Eugene J. Cadou, who would go on to become one of Indiana's great political writers before retiring from United Press International.

Walters's first year at Indiana University provided him with a friendship that would develop over the years—a young man named Wendell Willkie. Raised in Elwood, a town thirty-five miles east of Frankfort and roughly the same size—about 10,000 people then—Willkie would go on to become the 1940 Republican presidential candidate and run against Franklin D. Roosevelt. Walters and Willkie were on the 1916 Indiana University extension debating team. On August 17, 1940, when an estimated 250,000 people jammed Elwood for the formal notification of Willkie's candidacy, Walters, now a noted editor, would be a special guest of Willkie, now a noted politician and thinker.

After Walters completed his freshman year at Indiana University, the newspaper itch was so strong he decided to take a cub reporting job on the *Richmond* (Indiana) *Palladium* in the summer of 1916. The itch had been caused, in part, by a professor who stressed that a good newspaperman must see stories where other fellows see blanks.

Walters agreed. So when Hassal T. Sullivan, an Indiana University alumnus who was the *Palladium*'s city editor, offered to put him on the payroll, Walters accepted.

After seeing his stories in print, Walters admitted that some difference existed between theories taught in school and demands made by a real city editor. He was able to hold down the job, but was unable to "put across" the stuff the professor said marked a good newspaperman. "Sparkling stuff, written from a new angle, centering about a brand new idea, is what we want," he heard almost daily.

Walters began to worry for one of the few times in his life. He began to classify himself as a failure. But his sense of humor, one of his best assets throughout life—a gurgling laughter easily identified him in a crowd—helped him weather the periodic disappointments. In fact, it led to an idea that eventually got attention throughout the state.

Walters decided to form the young "failures" of Richmond into a club for the purpose of trying to discover the "way out." He had no trouble finding members and organizing the group.

He entered the newspaper office one morning and casually informed the staff that he had organized a "Get Out and Get On Club." He asked how much he should write about the organization.

"What 'ell's that?" asked Ramsey Poundstone, the veteran political writer. "Cub, just forget everything they ever told you at Bloomington (where Indiana University is located) and write that story," the old hand advised.

Walters wrote about young fellows who had ambition but had not moved to the front. He wrote about how they intended to ask the big business and professional men of Richmond to tell them "how to do it," and how the man that made good would be expelled from the club after he told the other members how he did it.

The story scored big. Walters began forming other clubs in Indiana cities. The Indiana City Editors' Association boosted the movement. Basil Walters had taken a step forward. It was not the only step forward he took while in Richmond.

Walters was nearing a year on the job when Indiana's tornado season struck with full force on Sunday, March 11, 1917, ripping into New Castle (spelled Newcastle at that time), thirty miles to the west. Looking around for a "warm body" on his small staff, the editor spotted Walters. Years later, it was easy for Walters to remember the one-word command: "Go!"

Walters was not only "warm," he was eager and resourceful. Extravagant, too—which would surprise some old-timers who say he was stingy with a buck. While other reporters caught a relief train on its way to New Castle, Walters hired a taxi. It was a bumpy ride, but Walters arrived before the relief train despite having to help the driver remove trees and other debris from the road in order to get through.

It was almost evening when Walters arrived. The earlier calm of that late-winter Sunday had turned into howling winds. The dark funnel cloud had followed, hitting just west of the city, moving southeast, and then veering northeast. The twister had struck town at 3

P.M., killing nineteen people outright, destroying 250 homes, and leaving another 75 badly damaged. The death toll would eventually reach twenty-two.

The staffs of the two newspapers, the *Courier* and the *Times,* were off duty, like most other folks on a Sunday afternoon, but all troops were immediately called in. The two newspapers decided to combine for a "Monday Extra"—and Walters took big advantage of that decision.

Walters found the combined newspaper office coming alive as reporters began writing their tornado stories. He soon realized that those stories were bottled up in New Castle because the violent storm had knocked down transmission wires. Reaching for his wallet, Walters bought carbon copies of the stories being written by the local reporters for six dollars—all he had. Then he hustled home, scoring a scoop for the *Richmond Palladium,* which gave the outside world the first complete report of the New Castle disaster.

Not long after the tornado story, Walters terminated his Richmond experience. It had lasted only a year. He told Richmond staffers and friends he was going to return to Indiana University, claiming membership in the "failure class" and holding his title as president of the "Get Out and Get On Club."

The return to Indiana University was a short one, however. On April 6, 1917, the United States entered World War I. Some college men enlisted almost immediately. He had just been named managing editor of the school newspaper, the *Indiana Daily Student,* before his deep-seated patriotism—he wore it on his sleeve throughout his life—compelled him to join Uncle Sam's armed forces. Before April turned into May, Walters volunteered. His call-up was not immediate. He was able to edit a few issues of the *Daily Student.* And he was around long enough to meet a captivating young woman.

Returning to Indiana University in 1917, Basil Walters found himself among a shrinking group of men working on the *Indiana Daily Student.* As the United States entered World War I, young men moved from the nation's campuses to battlefields overseas. The *Daily Student* asked various departments to dispatch coeds to the *Daily Student* office.

Among those who went was an extremely shy freshman from Anderson, Indiana, named Reah Elizabeth Handy. She had convinced her mother that she should attend college and study social work instead of remaining at home and working. Miss Handy had never considered studying journalism and, when a professor asked her to visit the *Daily Student* office, she replied, "Oh, no, I can't do it." The professor responded, "Yes, you have to go."

She recalled years later, "A friend and I ventured into the office. Stuffy was managing editor and he interviewed me and, of course, I got the job because there wasn't anyone else. My work was very poor because I was no newspaperwoman at all."

Journalism's loss was Basil Walters's gain. He dated Miss Handy until school ended in June—a very short time, but long enough to provide the foundation for an eventual marriage that lasted until his death—almost fifty-two years.

Walters had enlisted with the Indiana University army ambulance unit and was awaiting assignment along with twenty-five other volunteers. Sent to Allentown, Pennsylvania, the men were promised quick transfers overseas after training. They arrived in Pennsylvania on June 21—so quickly, they were quartered in the horse and cattle barns of the Allentown Fairgrounds before their uniforms were ready. They began training for the newly created United States Army Ambulance Corps (USAAC) in civilian clothes. Their excitement at the thought of going overseas slowly evaporated, however, when it became clear that there would be no rush overseas.

Walters and others, including another Hoosier, Cliff "Fizzy" Warner of Danville, convinced the brass that the flimsy *Ambulance Service News,* established exactly one week before they arrived, would ease the men's restlessness if improved. Walters became city editor and Warner, who had been an editor of the *De Pauw University Daily,* became assistant city editor. Later, Walters became the news editor and Warner the city editor. They were part of a six-man editorial board headed by editor William W. Faries of the University of Pennsylvania.

Published each Saturday morning for five cents a copy, the *Ambulance Service News* grew to sixty-four columns of editorial material full of features, camp news, and cartoons of the ambulance service. The paper's popularity was helped by a whacky cartoon strip called "Buck Jones." When camp football games were played Friday afternoons, the paper published an "extra," carrying the story and play by play, usually less than thirty minutes after the contest.

The paper's slogan read: "If it isn't fit to print, it isn't news."

20 STUFFY

One suspects that Lt. Col. C. P. Franklin decided what was fit to print. He was listed as the newspaper's censor. In a letter written in January 1918 to the Indiana University journalism department, Walters told about *Ambulance Service News,* which, by then, International News Service hailed as a pioneer of its kind. Walters wrote that "strict censorship on military secrets and news which would tend to destroy discipline and morale gives a deskman something to think about."

He noted with great pride in his letter that the *Ambulance Service News,* which later was named the *Camp Crane News,* "is one of few operated entirely by the soldiers" among those that began to appear throughout the country. Walters showed an intense interest in circulation even then—later, as editor of the *Minneapolis Star,* he would achieve amazing results—such as when he wrote about how the camp had less than 3,000 men, but the paper had a circulation of 3,000. "Circulation among parents is growing steadily," he said. Other parents received their soldier sons' copies as a "letter home."

Walters got his first taste of publishing problems at Allentown, providing a foundation that later would help him in Italy, Minneapolis, and Chicago. He wrote, "The paper is published in a plant which puts out two dailies. The (military) draft has taken many printers. This may give you an idea of some of the difficulties under which we work. The other papers have a habit of taking type from our forms when head material runs scarce. The printing company reads the proof, but the war has also struck this department pretty hard. The elimination of typographical errors is the greatest problem."

Down through the years, Walters never forgot his military experience with the ambulance corps. His pride in the unit mixed with the ink in his veins. Throughout his life he attended alumni functions, exchanged correspondence with fellow members, and wrote glowingly of the USAAC for various publications. His patriotism became even stronger once the United States achieved victory. It was still evident years later, when the United States entered World War II while Walters was the editor of the *Minneapolis Star.*

Walters wrote part of the introduction to the *History of the United States Army Ambulance Service,* published in 1967 to celebrate the USAAC's fiftieth anniversary. He recalled that the Ford ambulance was as new to World War I as the helicopter ambulance was in the late sixties of the Vietnam War. Not everyone could drive those ambulances, he noted. Volunteers had to be able to both drive and make automobile repairs.

Horses and mules were only gradually giving way to the truck and the tractor late in the war. Tanks and airplanes were in their infancy and, on the Italian front, cavalry was still horse-mounted. Wrote Walters, "Horseshoe nails were a constant peril to thin automobile tires, especially on skids at a crossroad under enemy artillery fire."

In Italy, he continued, much driving was done on mountain roads and "gasoline was fed to engines from gravity tanks. On steep grades it was frequently necessary to drive backwards in order to get the gas flowing into the engine. Brakes were not built for moutain driving and frequently gave way to wear. The wise driver watched for well-placed trees that could be used for an emergency stop on the way down."

Walters observed and wrote those things as editor of a "trench newspaper" in Milan, Italy, where he was sent a year after arriving in Allentown. By then he was editor of the *Camp Crane News* and the war was winding down. It would end a few weeks later in November 1918.

Editing an American military newspaper in Milan proved to be an unusual experience from the very beginning. Shortly after arriving, Walters was ordered to report to the ambulance service's commander. "We are going to have an American newspaper for the Yanks in Italy," the commander said. "You are the editor."

Walters remembered that incident years later and, as he told about it, his infectious, gurgling laugh punctuated his narrative. "You know," he smiled, "a colonel can be more tyrannical and unreasonable at times than a city editor.

"I said, 'But, sir, there aren't any English-speaking printers in Italy.'

"The commander replied, 'That doesn't matter. We want the first edition out in ten days.'"

Never mind that the war was about to end any day. The paper was needed to boost morale and, Walters was told frankly, as a propaganda tool. He found a Milan printing firm, Societa Editoriale Milan, willing to undertake the assignment. A bundle of American dollars was strong incentive. Never mind that not one person in the company spoke English.

Walters and others went to work. All copy, including heads, was typewritten. The Italian printers followed copy to the letter. To

Walters's surprise, they made fewer mistakes than the average American printer. Corrections were also made on the typewriter. American page make-up, which differed considerably from Italian newspapers' typography, was accomplished through an interpreter.

The first edition came off the presses on November 21—on time. The new Milan newspaper continued to be delivered weekly to American servicemen scattered over 500 miles in Italy and Austria. An explanatory article in the first edition said the paper was for the "folks at home" as well as the service men. The article explained that correspondents from every contingent were to supply news of their organization, and army posts were to be given all the space they wanted. Today's editors, most of whom must scramble to print all the news in the limited newsholes that are left after the ads are put in, would have a space orgy with the government's don't-worry-about-the-cost policy Walters enjoyed.

Walters, who learned the virtues of industriousness in his formative years, had discoverd two things: (1) that, in fact, almost anything can be accomplished if one tries hard enough, and (2) Italian compositors who can't speak a word of English can do an excellent job.

An Education in Different Ways

After retiring, Basil Walters received an honorary doctorate from Indiana University in recognition of his journalistic contribution. It partially took the place of the bona fide degree he never received because, when the war ended, he did not return to Indiana University for a third time. Instead, he plunged into the world of professional journalism.

"I got my education after I finished school,' he told George Brandenburg for an *Editor and Publisher* magazine story that appeared March 8, 1952. "I'd get in on these over-my-head jobs and then I'd learn what I had to know for the job in hand. If there was a war in China, I'd hustle over to the library after a day on the desk and read everything on China I had time for. The same for political campaigns, tornadoes and other news events."

Not that Walters didn't believe in formal education. He did. He believed in correspondence courses, too, and took them in 1918 while receiving military training at Allentown, Pennsylvania. Receipts in a battered scrapbook show that he took courses from the International Correspondence Schools in Scranton, Pennsylvania. One course was "Local and Retail Advertising," dealing with "punctuating and editing," "type and type measurements," "correct and faulty diction," and "copy for advertisements, part one."

The "Designated Editor"

The United States Army Ambulance Corps—the embodiment of Walters' patriotism—became imbedded in his life. Long after World War I ended, Walters kept in contact with survivors. He continued to be USAACs "designated editor," and was the first editor of the *USAAC Bulletin.*

Walters was actually a one-person staff for the quarterly publication. One-dollar subscriptions covered publishing costs, made easier because Walters worked out of his home. As in his army days, Walters urged people to send in items. "Chicken dinner" stuff rolled in—items about about who was doing what, letters from members in foreign places, who had visited whom. The publication also carried a detailed report of the group's annual convention.

It was, in short, the kind of newsy publication Walters strived for all his life, the kind that concentrated primarily on dispensing information rather than esotericism. For example, readers of the November 1920 issue learned that there is "quite a USAAC colony among the movie folks."

A fellow named Adolphe J. Menjou, formerly Captain Menjou with the Italian contingent that later moved to France, had written to Walters and included that information. Then-actor Menjou noted that he had just completed "Head Over Heels," with Mabel Normand, and "The Faith Healer." Menjou knew that was news. After all, he and Robert Hutchins, who had become University of Chicago president, helped edit the Milan base newspaper.

CHAPTER THREE

Silent Cal, Yellow Robe, A Speech

THE nation was on its back at 3 o'clock in the morning on November 11, 1918, when the Associated Press sent a "flash" across its wire: the Germans have surrendered—World War I is over.

It had been a costly United States victory. Of the 4,355,000 troops mobilized, 126,000 were killed, 254,300 were wounded, and 4,500 were listed as either prisoners or missing. Basil Walters was not one of those statistics. And in May 1919 he was discharged, having earned something of a reputation for his efforts in military journalism.

Now twenty-four, Walters decided to forego completing his college education and instead weighed offers for his services. He chose the *Indianapolis Star,* where he would be just forty-five miles south of Frankfort. It was a good choice—by the time 1920 dawned, he was promoted to telegraph editor of the 120,000 circulation morning daily. He was moving up quickly for someone so young.

But Walters stayed only a year, finding an offer from the highly regarded *Milwaukee Journal* too good to refuse. He had not sought the job; the *Journal* had come to him. Joining the paper in 1921, Walters wasn't in Milwaukee very long before the paper sent him to New York as its correspondent there. It meant long-distance correspondence of another kind—with Reah Handy. She had taught school for three years at a time when a college degree was not required and now was finishing up at Indiana University.

This long-range correspondence lasted only a year. Walters returned to Milwaukee. By then, Miss Handy had graduated with a degree in social economics and was employed at the University of Michigan Hospital in the summer of 1922 as a welfare-type case worker. The romance was strong, but marriage waited until 1923. Miss Handy's social work career ended with her move to Milwaukee.

Walters spent most of his seven-year career in Milwaukee—from 1921 to 1928—as telegraph editor, selecting and editing stories from the wire services. A speech in that city in 1925 about the handling of Associated Press copy brought him his first national attention.

Walters also got attention in Milwaukee for his ability to teach young reporters and to extract good writing and reporting from them. He was like a great football coach who, despite not having exceptional ability as a player, possessed tremendous ability to bring out talent in his players. "He wasn't a writer, but he could guide people," his wife said after his death. "He was an idea man. And he was patient with people—part of his nature, to a certain degree."

Walters sensed, however, that his editing career was stagnating on the *Journal*'s news desk. He decided to mix in some reporting. Although his work was solid, it did not achieve the acclaim his editing prowess had brought him.

It would not be accurate, however, to portray Walters as a writer and reporter of limited ability. On the contrary. As his overall journalistic success brought him greatness and acclaim over the years, his relatively few writing and reporting efforts were shoved into the background.

Walters couldn't have succeeded as an editor without first possessing talents needed as a reporter. This included the innate, almost special sense of what is news. When young reporters in Milwaukee asked him what constituted the essentials for a successful reporter, he replied, "Tell something new, something novel, and tell it in an interesting manner."

Simple advice. He followed it in June 1927 when he was sent to cover the visit of President Calvin Coolidge to Rapid City, South Dakota. The event drenched the Bad Lands in the most excitement since the days of Sitting Bull, Calamity Jane, and Wild Bill Hickock.

Walters's reporting and writing caught the color—and novelty—of the event. His stories, at times, dragged; but, for the most part, they captured the presidential visit fever. The stories were so descriptive and zesty, the excitement that enveloped the Black Hills before and during Coolidge's visit can still be felt upon rereading them in the eighties.

Walters had fun with Smoky Thomas, who owned a grocry store at the foot of Hangman Hill. The hill got its name after three men were hanged as horse thieves on June 20, 1877. Fifty years later, Walters reported that the chief topic of discussion in Rapid City from that date was whether or not one of the men hanged was innocent.

But Smoky was the story, and Walters knew it as he wrote:

> He is preparing for summer tourists who will be
> attracted by the coming visit of President Coolidge
> to the Black Hills. Smoky is so old he totters, but be
> it known that Smoky learned his cuss words. True
> gems they are in the literature of blasphemy and vul-
> garity, from Wild Bill Hickock, who had 38 notches
> on his pistol before he was assassinated, and from
> Calamity Jane. These notorious Black Hills' charac-
> ters were his pals and townsmen. Jane was his sweet-
> heart. . . .
>   Smoky ducked into a room and reappeared with
> a wicked looking pistol. "I'd like to tell Mr.
> Coolidge the history of that gun," he butted in as
> Lin (Smoky's wife) was explaining what a fight she
> was having with people, "ignorant people; well now
> some of them are not ignorant either, but anyhow
> they don't read . . ."

Her anger was directed at those, including Walters, who complained about and questioned how much the president's visit was
going to cost the taxpayers. But Smoky was paying no mind to the
missus and Walters was obviously having difficulty concentrating on
her words as Smoky flashed the pistol. Walters wrote:

> Smoky began whirling that wicked looking
> "cannon" on his finger, a true mark of a pioneer
> "shootin' fool," and the muzzle on every round
> passed in true aim down the entire anatomy of your
> tenderfoot correspondent. "Ain't no danger, I'm an
> expert," Smoky explained, but your correspondent
> asked no more questions about how they felt about
> Mr. Coolidge's coming.

In another story shortly before Coolidge's arrival, Walters wrote
about how Rapid City and the Black Hills found a new "gold" vein—
"the vein that lines the pockets of tourists."

> "We don't deal in pennies in this section,
> stranger," is heard once again.
>   Silver dollars—the natives seem to despise
> paper money, although they will accept it from tour-
> ists—are the media.

Gold, that magic word of the Black Hills, has again been struck and everybody knows the gulch. Its name is Calvin Coolidge. The excitement is almost as great as in the days of Sitting Bull, Calamity Jane and Wild Bill. Spare beds are nuggets. There are almost as many rooms for rent signs as there are flags. The Indians in this instance are vigilantes. Who they are nobody knows, but they may be lurking behind almost any tree and they have sworn to do dire deeds to profiteers. The vigilantes have the situation well in hand at the moment, but this is only the "grub stake" day of the 1927 gold rush. The prices at a favorite restaurant jumped approximately 15 percent Monday night (eight days before Coolidge's expected arrival).

The town is full of secret service men, and, gosh, how the people like it. The secrecy, the mystery—men walking swiftly but with sleuthlike tread through the hotel lobbies provide a thrill better than many paid $10 for when the Ku Klux Klan was selling memberships here. There is no official word whether secret service men play poker or not, but there appears to be quite a number of "secret conferences."

In a third story, Walters wrote how elaborate plans to welcome Coolidge were shelved after Colonel E. W. Starling of the secret service told the welcoming committee, "Gentlemen, the President is coming here for a vacation." There would be no cannon salutes, no parades, no speeches. The president would be in Rapid City for only a minute after leaving the train and getting into an automobile that would take him to his Black Hills lodge.

But Silent Cal's visit—vacation or not—had overwhelmed the natives. And Walters caught the color:

Chief John Kills a Hundred, Chief No Flesh and Chief Crazy Horse, proud remnants of the royalty of a proud race that has been shunted away on a reservation, once more are mixing war paint. In front of their teepees, they are preening their headdress. With trembling fingers they are fashioning a new headdress, a headdress for the chief of them all, the President of the United States.

Some evening after President Coolidge arrives here, the winds of the Black Hills, which once stirred

the manes of their racing ponies as these chieftains
whooped into battle or into the hunt, will bring to
the President a great welcoming cry. The Sioux are
going to go to his lodge and adopt him.

Chauncey Yellow Robe, disciplinarian of the
Indian school and nephew of Sitting Bull, will have
charge of the adoption. . . . He says the adoption of
President Coolidge will herald the death knell of the
Indian race as a race. Within 25 years there will be
no Indian race, all will be Americans, he says. He
believes it best for the Indians to lose their identity as
a race and throw their lot into the great American
melting pot.

Walters got more than just stories on Coolidge's visit. He chatted
with Chauncey Yellow Robe long enough for the Indian to refute a
story that had recently appeared in a popular magazine. The article
claimed that General George A. Custer took his own life after the battle of Little Big Horn in Montana on June 25, 1876.

In a full-page article in the *Milwaukee Journal* on August 21,
1927, accompanied by sketches of Sitting Bull and General Custer,
Walters wrote:

Two of Mr. Robe's uncles, Iron Plume and
Non-Butcher, took part in the final battle against
Custer, and Mr. Robe heard the story of the fight
from their lips. Often, when he was a child, they sat
with him by the campfire under the stars after the
day's buffalo hunt and taught him, while he committed to memory the history and traditions of his
people.

The Indians had taken precautions to prevent any soldiers escap-
ing at Little Big Horn, but one did break away, Walters reported. He
quoted Iron Plume's story, as told by Yellow Robe:

We galloped our horses in pursuit and fired as
we went. The fleeing man returned our fire. He outdistanced us and we knew we could not catch him.
We were ready to abandon the chase when to our as-
tonishment the lone survivor of the battle drew rein,
raised in his saddle, placed his pistol to his temple
and killed himself. Why? We do not know. We
found that he had used his last cartridge to end his
own life."

But, Yellow Robe told Walters, his extensive research "definitely established that this man was not Custer. Custer died where his five companies fought and fell. Two hundred and six bodies were buried on the field."

Walters's article then told the background of Little Big Horn. At times, Yellow Robe sounded like Indian leaders of the American Indian Movement that came out of South Dakota in the seventies. Yellow Robe told Walters:

> It is disgraceful to confine the unnaturalized ones on reservations. Through all history the large nation has ignored the rights of the weaker one. . . . The white man wanted the gold in the Black Hills and he ignored treaties with the Indian and invaded the hunting grounds which had been set aside for the Indians. Forgery and trickery were resorted to by the representatives of Washington. Was it not natural that the Indians should fight this invasion? You would do the same today if America were invaded.

The Speech That Propelled Him

There was something for almost everyone to chew on. Basil Walters talked about dry writing and how dangerous a scissors could be in the hands of an unskilled copy editor. He lashed out at sensationalism, particularly the playing up of crime news. He urged cooperation among members.

The speech propelled Walters into the national spotlight. Delivered to the Wisconsin-Upper Michigan Associated Press Editorial Association in 1925, the wide-ranging talk was sent across the AP wire as a piece of in-house copy. Excerpts were printed in AP's *Service Bulletin* for September 1925, and correspondents were invited to comment.

"Our first duty is carefully to edit and head The Associated Press report so as never to distort the true facts or make it appear that The Associated Press is prejudiced," Walters told the gathering of editors who subscribed to the AP service.

Walters was referring to incompetent and/or lazy copy editors who mar stories when they are told to cut an eighteen-column-inch story in half. Often, the copy editor simply chops off the bottom nine inches on the basis that newspaper stories are written in inverted pyramid style—the most important information first, the least important last. That method often works but, at other times, information at the end of the story is vital. Thus, copy must be cut in other parts of the article. As Walters put it:

> The Associated Press frequently delivers stories in great detail in order that individual members can choose the amount that limited space conditions will permit. This is no job for the scissors, because part of the sheet clipped off may be needed to make the story truthful and fair. Rather, it is a job for a pencil in careful hands so that some parts of the story that are of no particular interest to our particular communities can be eliminated. In doing this, extreme care is necessary so that in no way are the facts altered.

Continuing in an editing vein, Walters tactfully indicated that he thought Associated Press writing was dry, saying:

> In years gone by, the comment has often been heard around telegraph desks that The Associated press report is too dry. "You get the story, the A.P. will get the facts," has been the jest to reporters. In an effort to be accurate, the report was almost solemn. . . . The A.P. could always be relied upon to get in the facts but often the stories were devoid of color.

That criticism was offset by a plea for cooperation. Walters thought there was "a tendency . . . in some cities to hold back flashing important news to The Associated Press to make possible a scoop over some other member paper that has limited circulation in the community." Everyone in the room could relate to that. Although AP is a cooperative, in which members are supposed to phone a state bureau with breaking news of wide interest in their community, members do not always cooperate. A member paper often lets a news cycle elapse before making the call, insuring exclusivity for at lest one edition.

"Suppose all the brother members of the service adopted such a selfish policy," Walters said. "It would cripple The Associated Press report that you receive and make it less valuable, because The Associated Press has been built on a standard of unselfish cooperation."

Then Walters turned his attack from selfishness to one on sensationalism. Again, AP won praise as Walters aimed his criticism at the individual newspapers. AP, he said, has "remained steadfast during America's (crime) spree of the last few years and has maintained itself above all things else as a decent news service whose dispatches we would desire our children to read. . . . The A.P. daily now is providing stories of daring adventure, not useless adventure, but deeds of daring and achievement that will benefit all mankind. Play up this kind of news and make these men the heroes of your readers, particularly the young."

Walters asserted that "American newspapers must lead the people, and particularly the young people, back to the lanes of common sense and sane thoughts. If we must print crime news, let's picture the criminal in his true light, as a sickening, selfish weakling, not as a daring adventurer."

The invited reaction rolled in, and much of the January 1926 *Service Bulletin* was devoted to it. Walters won strong backing, with the crime/sensationalism aspect of his speech drawing the most attention.

AP correspondents throughout the country and in some foreign bureaus praised him for his attack on sensationalism. "There is no doubt that the press is largely responsible, as Mr. Walters says, 'for the great loss of the sense of morality that prevails,'" wrote Rome bureau chief Salvatori Cortesi.

W. A. Wells, in San Francisco, wrote, "It was a pleasure to have his judgement in support of a news style of standards in which heroes are not made of cheap criminals and in which the constructive happening of the day is kept to the fore."

But while he won majority support, Walters caught some opposition. D. A. Russell, Jr., of Atlanta, wrote:

"He makes mention of the fact that too many times the criminal is played up as a 'hero.' I do not ascribe to this method; on the other hand, I think the criminal should be styled in his true light, but even then there are certain dashes of bravery that even the thug can make, which, to say the least, is daring. I do not think it contrary to the best interests of journalism to credit the hold-up man with a daring chance, for necessarily that is part of the news. . . .''

Comments were also made on Walters's remarks dealing with editing and writing, and his call for greater cooperation among members was praised. They all added up to debate within and outside the Associated Press organization—and Basil Walters derived much attention for being a thought-provoking catalyst.

Hooking up with Cowles

BASIL WALTERS, thirty-two years old, was locked in. He had to sever his Milwaukee ties. He had been thinking of buying a small weekly in Red Key, Indiana. The situation didn't look especially good, but it had some possibilities. He'd give the *Journal* two weeks' notice and prepare to return to Indiana.

Walters had just returned from Red Key when he received a letter addressed to "Basil Walter, Telegraph Editor, Milwaukee Journal, Milwaukee, Wisconsin," dated January 9, 1928. It arrived from Des Moines, Iowa, where the Gardner Cowles family had just acquired the *Register* and merged it with the *Tribune-Capital.* Walters read:

> I am attempting to find a new News Editor for the Evening Tribune-Capital. You have been very highly recommended to me by several newspapermen. The position affords, I believe, an unusual opportunity for someone.
>
> If you are at all interested, I would be very happy to discuss the matter with you personally. I expect to be in Chicago on either Friday or Saturday of this week at the Hotel Blackstone. I would be glad if you could come to Chicago at my expense to meet me on one of those days. If you are interested, please let me know immediately the hour most convenient for you, and I will arrange my plans accordingly.
>
> I will keep the entire matter private so that there will be no embarrassment to you if you decide you do not care to leave the Journal.

The letter was signed by Gardner Cowles, Jr., known as "Mike." His father, Gardner, Sr., had made the *Des Moines Tribune* an outstanding paper, and his older brother, John, was the associate publisher. Mike, only twenty-six years old, was managing editor.

Once again, Basil Walters had not sought a job; it had sought him. But the letter created a dilemma. The Walterses had decided to buy the small Red Key weekly.

Before visiting Red Key, Walters evaluated his Milwaukee situation. He had been there seven years, mostly as telegraph editor. He was anxious to get ahead and his chances for promotion were not good. He wanted to move up to news editor, but a good friend held that position and Walters would not sacrifice friendship for office politics in a bid to "steal" the job. Rather than search for another job, he wanted to run his own paper, he told his wife. She agreed. Thus, the Walterses gave serious consideration to moving to Red Key, Indiana, on the Indiana-Ohio border.

"Neither one of us was impressed, but we decided to buy the paper," Reah Walters recalled. "I was always ready to move, because I had a great deal of faith in him and his work. I knew that he knew what he was doing. We put down quite an amount of earnest money for a young married couple."

Still, Walters felt he had to meet Mike Cowles. He knew it never hurts to be interviewed for another job when you're already employed. Besides, Milwaukee was less than two hours from Chicago. And who knew what Des Moines might hold?

It held a lot, Walters decided after talking with young Cowles.

"What shall we do, go to Des Moines or not throw out our earnest money?" Walters asked his wife of five years.

"I don't care," was her simple reply. So Walters made what proved to be a major decision in his life—Des Moines. Soon he and his wife were on their way to Iowa, where the roads were in such horrible condition the young couple had a difficult time getting their furniture moved from Milwaukee. Taking along little daughter Nancy was much easier.

Mike Cowles was glad to see Walters arrive. Among the people from whom he solicited recommendations were Kent Cooper, the Associated Press's general manager who had earlier recognized Walters's ability in Milwaukee, and Robert Bender, a key United Press executive. The Cowles family wants quality people, these men were told. The Cowles family will get a quality person in Stuffy Walters, the two men replied. That was good enough for Mike Cowles, who had grown up in a world of success.

It was a world created by his father, a fiscal conservative who advised young people to never depart with their last dollar.

Born on February 28, 1861, in Oskaloosa, sixty miles southeast of Des Moines, Gardner Cowles grew up in a deeply religious home run by his Methodist minister father, William Fletcher Cowles. He grew up, too, with a love for the railroad, but when he could not find railroad work, he turned to teaching. By the time he was twenty-one, he was seeking a school superintendent's job. He got one in 1882 at Algona in northwest Iowa for $720 a year.

A year later he was still superintendent, but journalism drew his interest. He bought half of the weekly *Algona Republican.* Cowles had hardly put away his ownershp papers before Harvey Ingham, writing for the *Upper Des Moines,* also in Algona, attacked him in a front-page editorial, charging a conflict of interest. The Algona pupils were being neglected because Cowles had bought into a "second-rate newspaper," Ingham asserted.

If the students were, indeed, neglected, it was for only a year. Cowles made money, but he sold his share of the *Republican* in 1884. Despite Ingham's strong editorial attack, he and Ingham became fast friends.

Cowles left newspapering to join his father-in-law, Ambrose Call, in a successful Algona business that operated mail wagons from railroad stations to Iowa communities not served by trains. Cowles would earn more than a living with his father-in-law—he would get an education on mail delivery that would serve him well later in Des Moines journalism.

First teaching, then journalism, then business—Gardner Cowles still wasn't sure what he wanted when an interest in banking developed. Using money he had carefully saved, he acquired an interest in a chain of ten banks in Kossuth and Emmet Counties, Iowa, while remaining in Algona.

Politics continued to be an avocation, as it would be for his sons, John and Mike. Gardner, Sr.'s minister father was the cause. His involvement in politics was so deep he had taken dangerous and courageous stands against slavery. Thus, it was natural that Gardner, Sr. plunge into Republican affairs and, by twenty-seven, he was drawing enough attention to be elected secretary at the 1888 Republican State Convention. Eleven years later he would be elected to the Iowa Legislature from Kossuth County.

Ingham, meanwhile, found trouble. He had purhcased the *Upper Des Moines,* a weekly, and spoken out boldly in his editorials. His endorsement of Cowles for a second term in the legislature drew opposition. Anti-Ingham sentiment, in general, encouraged the establishment of a fourth weekly newspaper, the *Advance,* according to veteran Des Moines reporter George Mills in his book *Harvey Ingham*

& Gardner Cowles Sr. Like Ingham's paper, the *Advance* was a Republican publication—giving the community three GOP papers. Its goal of cutting into Ingham's profits bore fruit. That and other troubles, along with an offer to be editor of the *Des Moines Register and Leader,* prompted Ingham to sell out in the spring of 1902.

But according to Mills, Ingham's troubles didn't end. Sixteen months after moving to Des Moines, he was distraught, feeling he had failed to reestablish the *Register and Leader.* When he heard the paper was about to be sold, he called good friend Gardner in Algona. The two men had earlier discussed acquiring the paper, with Gardner taking control of the business end and providing much-needed cash while Ingham looked after the news/editorial operation.

Banker Cowles had to move quickly after Ingham's call, according to Mills. Three prominent Iowans, including F. L. Maytag, then a farm machinery manufacturer, later an extremely successful appliance manufacturer, had agreed to buy the paper. But there were some technicalities, Ingham wrote to Cowles. If Cowles could come up with $50,000 to $75,000, the two men could gain control.

Cowles wound up paying $67,000 for 1,500 shares—fifty percent of the outstanding stock, according to Mills. The Cowles publication dynasty in the upper Midwest was born.

Drawing on his experience with his father-in-law's mail wagon business, Cowles preached two keys to circulation success: (1) concentrate on subscriptions and take whatever street sales you get, and (2) a mediocre paper with a strong circulation department can defeat a strong newspaper with a poor circulation department.

Still, Cowles knew that editorial excellence was a necessity. In Ingham he had a powerful editor who fought for his views—civic improvements, greater human rights, the elimination of gambling. These were views that Cowles shared.

Ingham allowed editors and reporters to experiment in an effort to create a more readable product—a philosophy that would rub off on Basil Walters years later and play a vital role in his success.

One of Cowles's and Ingham's earliest editorial acquisitions was Jay Darling, who would become a Pulitzer Prize-winning cartoonist, a forty-year institution, an employee given great latitude in his work, and a man of cold steel when angered. At times, he and the Cowleses would disagree, causing them to stop talking to each other.

Mills's book tells how the silence between the Cowleses and Darling "sometimes forced the late Basil (Stuffy) Walters, managing edi-

tor of the 1930s, to serve as a mediator and information conduit.
'There would be differences of opinion about the views expressed in
Ding's cartoon,' Walters recalled. 'I would not say the Cowleses were
mad at him, just uncomfortable. Ding would say: 'Would you please
tell Mike (Gardner Jr.) this or that?' ''

The senior Cowles was stubborn and tough about any story un-
favorable to someone connected directly or indirectly with his newspapers. He wanted those stories published and given proper news
play. Mills tells about Cowles learning on the street that a family
member of a high *Register* official was arrested on a driving charge.
Walters, who had moved up to managing editor when the alleged incident occurred, told Mills, "Mr. Cowles really let me have it because
we had not printed the story. But we had nothing to go on. There was
nothing on the police records. That was as close as I ever came to getting fired." Police officials, Mills writes, insisted no such arrest was
made and no story ever appeared.

Mills also writes of Cowles's careful eye for money—an eye that
Walters inherited. Mills writes:

> As in most business and professional operations, periodic anti-waste
> campaigns sprang up. In the 1930s . . . Walters ordered editors and reporters
> to bring back to the office all the newspaper pencils they had accumulated at
> home. It is one of the characteristics of reporters and editors that they ac-
> cumulate clutches of pencils at home, in pockets, in purses, in desk drawers.
> After Walters took the customary ribbing for his "returning the pencils"
> edict, he said he had done it on Gardner Cowles' orders.

Walters savored the ribbing. He made it clear he just wanted to be
one of the guys, bumming cigarettes and getting in his own jibes. His
energy was infectious. People knew he'd work a twenty-five-hour day
if needed. While everyone did not agree with his ideas—as expected—
he commanded tremendous respect. He displayed strong loyalty to the
Cowleses and, in turn, achieved his staffers' loyalty by defending their
actions.

In short, Walters in Des Moines became known as an enthusiastic
little fellow who demanded that people do their best, as a firm but fair
editor full of ideas, as a man hard to dislike even if he didn't agree
with your position.

Even Frank Eyerly, who would eventually become managing
editor of the Des Moines papers, had kind words in later years, though
it was well known that Eyerly didn't think much of Walters's overall

ability. Eyerly saw in the adrenalin-drenched Walters "an under-educated windmill." But Eyerly admitted Walters was "an extremely competent deskman" and "dynamic" newspaperman.

Walters knew that Eyerly saw him as too much of a down-home type, lacking intellectual skills needed to deal with serious problems. But Walters adjusted to Eyerly's feelings toward him and, even when Eyerly's name was mentioned years later, Walters described him in favorable terms.

Red Key's loss would be Des Moines's gain for nine years, a period that resulted in strong growth for both the newspapers and Walters's career.

Two years before Walters's Des Moines experience ended, a *Time* magazine story about Cowles Sr.'s success, said:

> Basil L. (Stuffy) Walters, 39, short, barrel-shaped (200 pounds) and genial, is managing editor of both the Register (morning) and Tribune (evening). Between his two staffs, entirely separate for each paper, has grown a genuine news rivalry, essentially in a city where there is no other local competition.

It was a busy, active nine years . . . years that would see the introduction of the "machine gun camera," the great reporting of Richard Wilson, the development of an outstanding editor in Kenneth Mac-Donald, the first major steps toward readership research, the snow-storm scoop, the fire that Walters and dynamite couldn't stop from destroying a downtown, the carrier pigeons who were briefly "hired," the kidnapping of a famous baby, and regular trips between Des Moines and Minneapolis.

Never Underestimate the Written Word

As a kid, Vernon Pope hung around the post office at Delmont, South Dakota, where his mother was postmistress. He read all the newspapers and magazines that poured in for delivery.

Later, he matriculated from South Dakota to Drake University in Des Moines, where his money ran out. The result: an office boy's job at the *Des Moines Tribune*—and the beginning of a journalism career.

In 1927, a year before Basil Walters's arrival, Pope received a top assignment as rotogravure editor. The *Tribune,* like many other newspapers, was entering the new Sunday magazine supplement field using the slick-art form.

Pope performed so well that he was tapped again ten years later for a picture magazine Mike Cowles decided to launch. Within eight months, circulation of the new venture—*Look* magazine with Vernon Pope as editor—surpassed 2,000,000.

Pope's work became so well known many people termed him the father of photojournalism. Pope, however, would never underestimate the written word—thanks to watching Basil Walters.

In a March 1969 interview with *Editor and Publisher,* Pope told how Walters approached a new reporter after a few days and asked about the news in the paper.

"You had ought to know," Pope told the magazine. "Because if you didn't know, you were out of there. Fired!"

By 1969, Pope was busy with his own Rockefeller Center public relations firm, but not too busy to talk about newspapers and magazines. They could be better, he asserted, if more editors adopted Stuffy Walters's attitude about the young people they hired—by looking for omnivorous readers.

Pope recalled what Walters often said in Des Moines: "Nothing is going to come out of a head, unless somebody has taken trouble to put something in it."

Mr. Walters, Meet Mr. Gallup

BEFORE the night was over, there would be anger, occasional shouting, and argumentative exchanges. One young professor and several pros would go at it. An innocent copy boy would get caught briefly in the crossfire.

The professor entered the *Register*'s city room for what appeared to be another routine visit to see how two of his copyreading students were faring under the tutelage of the Des Moines professionals. Basil Walters, having been promoted to managing editor shortly before 1930 dawned, waved to the professor and flashed the smile that was automatically part of his greeting. Walters like the professor. They had exchanged ideas on how newspapers could be improved, sometimes getting into friendly debates. Walters genuinely liked the man. And vice versa.

Walters met him through the Cowles boys, Gardner Jr. (Mike) and his older brother, John. They met him in the late 1920s, when he was at the University of Iowa at Iowa City, and persuaded him to head the journalism department at Drake University in Des Moines. They told him he could send his copyreading class, two students at a time, to work nights on the *Register*'s desk. The extra bait hooked him. The professor moved to Drake and initiated his *Register* copyreading program.

That night the professor initiated an exploratory program of newspaper readership research. He approached Walters near the horseshoe-shaped copy desk, around which copyreaders edited stories and wrote headlines. In general, he asserted, the *Register*'s banner line story, normally national or international in origin, was the poorest read in the newspaper.

Walters and the others flinched. The anger and arguing began. Holding his ground, the professor said he had assigned some of his students to ring door bells and ask people about their reading habits. They found a large percentage of readers who didn't know all the words used in the banner line—words used to give the paper an intellectual tone. The readers, in fact, devoted their time to local and state news written in simpler language.

The telegraph editor, who played a major role in selecting the national or international wire story that normally received the banner line, challenged the professor. "Why, the copy boy knows all the words used in our banner line!" he half-shouted.

Walters beckoned to the copy boy and asked him about a particular word in a banner line. The copy boy said he had no idea what it meant. Not convinced—after all, what did a lowly copy boy know?—the copyreaders said they'd show up the young professor at dinner across the street in Thompson's Restaurant. They'd ask some diners about the banner line's meaning.

The copyreaders barely dug into their food before they began to choke on it. The food was fine—but customer after customer couldn't comprehend the banner headline. The professor's food went down smoothly. His point was proven—with flesh-and-blood readers.

The professor had been confident of the result. He had formed his theories after an earlier visit one night with Walters and he had already found them correct.

The professor's theories were recalled one summer afternoon in 1973 by Walters as he sat inside the screened back porch of his Clinton County farmhouse and chain-smoked Lark filters.

He asked me that night how we selected the banner story. I told him we got a nightly headline schedule from the *New York Times* that was distributed by the Associated Press. A lot of times we selected a particular banner story because the *Times* judged it to be the most important world or national story. It didn't make any difference that the rest of the paper was devoted, for the most part, to Iowa and local stories.

He asked me if other Des Moines-area editors used the same method. I didn't know, but I was curious to find out. So he and I began asking other editors and we found out that many of them also used the *Times* as a guide. Others made their judgment on the basis of AP wordage, figuring the more words, the more important the story.

The professor sensed that the professionals were making news judgment errors. He launched his student door-bell survey—and he discovered that his two basic hunches were correct: (1) readers wanted stories that touched them, the closer to home the better, and (2) readers wanted stories written in simple, easy-to-follow language. As the professor's initial claims proved correct, Walters discarded his anger and asked himself, "Just who is this Professor George Gallup?"

He was, of course, the George Gallup who would eventually leave journalism to form the American Institute of Public Opinion, better known as the Gallup Poll. His firm would receive notoriety in 1948 for predicting that Thomas Dewey would defeat incumbent Harry Truman for president. Over the years Gallup achieved great respectability as his firm built a record of accurately polling public opinion on critical questions of the day.

Walters was among the first to learn how correct Gallup could be. The professor proposed that he select a story from the reject pile and print it in the *Register* as a test. Many editors would have allowed their egos to get in the way and politely declined. Walters not only agreed to the polling, but volunteered copy boys to help out if needed. The results of Gallup's readability experiments astonished Walters. The professor repeatedly outdid the professionals—and the word spread to Gardner, Jr. He convinced his banker father to finance a wider, more sophisticated survey on what people read, to be directed by Gallup. Gallup had not yet developed his balanced, scientific system of interviews but he was able to have interviewers ask people in almost every Iowa county what they read in newspapers.

The system was rather simple, Gallup recalled. "I would have people go through the newspaper, page by page, column by column, with the interviewer to learn exactly what stories had been read, skipped and just how far the reader went into the stories."

The results formed the first Gallup survey of newspaper reading habits— and in turn, helped revolutionize the techniques Walters used to edit the *Register and Tribune.* The techniques went beyond story selection. They also involved writing and copy editing, leading to clearer prose, simpler sentence construction, and brevity.

Gallup's research eventually involved eye researcher Dr. Herman Brandt, who supported Gallup's hunch that many people were not reading much of the *Register and Tribune.* Brandt placed a camera behind a hole in a curtain at the University of Iowa and photographed the movements of a reader's eyes as he or she shopped over a page for something of interest, skipping what remained.

As Gallup perfected his survey techniques, requiring the tricky and intelligent use of statistics in assembling the material and interpreting its significance, Walters's interest grew sharper.

J. Montgomery Curtis, a man with a brilliant newspaper mind who finished his career as a vice president for the widely respected Knight-Ridder chain, remembers those Walters-Gallup days: "I first heard of Stuffy in Des Moines. He had Gallup do a stint on the telegraph desk. Talk-making stories found their way into the paper and dull stuff was spiked. Readers talked. And circulation climbed."

In the October-November 1941 issue of *Quill* magazine, Walters wrote about his early days with Gallup: "Reporters were encouraged to write their stories in the same way they would tell the story to a friend. First person was used when it added anything to the story."

Walters told reporters, "Tell your story, don't *write* it." He and Gallup noted that a good storyteller does not speak in a monotone but, rather, puts inflection in his voice and gives color to his ideas. They pointed out that people fall asleep listening to a person who talks in the same tone, particularly if the person speaks too long.

Among the young newsmen who benefitted from Walters's teaching was Ken MacDonald, who landed a copy desk position on the *Tribune* despite being a 1926 University of Iowa journalism graduate. Such credentials were looked down upon in those days. MacDonald eventually became editor and then editorial chairman for one year before retiring in 1977, after fifty years with the *Register and Tribune,* stamping his name alongside Harvey Ingham, Walters, and a few others in the annals of great Des Moines newspapermen.

MacDonald learned quickly from Walters that a newspaper's most important job is to produce news and write it with a human touch. Others, like Angelo Cohn, who would later take part in Walters's revolutionary typography and editing experiments in Minneapolis, got the same message pounded into their heads.

When asked in the summer of 1978, MacDonald and Cohn described in overlapping ways Walters's voracious appetite for digging out news that best related to the human condition—news that the person on the street could easily identify with.

Cohn remarked, "He had empathy for the reader and the common touch. He represented this human dimension in the American newspaper as well as anyone . . . and perhaps better than anyone. He really knew how to relate humanness to the news. . . ."

MacDonald agreed, and commented:

He understood that newspapers are a mass medium and he wanted to appeal to masses. He was not interested in the abstract. Long stories of political analysis bored him. So did speculative stories about what might happen in the future. He was interested in today. "Don't waste space speculating on what's going to happen next week," he would say. "When it happens we will cover it."

It was the so-called human interest aspect of the news that fascinated him, and in every story he searched for that element. For young editors he often recalled the conversations he overheard on the streetcar when, as a young man in Milwaukee, he was riding home after work. The other passengers, reading the paper he had helped edit, rarely mentioned the long, top-of-the-page, "hard" news stories that had taken most of his editing time, he said. It was the short items at the bottom of the page that they mentioned, perhaps about a baby who had fallen out of a third-story window and landed unhurt in a pile of leaves. It was not that he wanted only superficial news in the paper. He wanted the substantial news, too, but he wanted it with a human interest touch so the ordinary reader would be interested in it.

Gallup's survey results alone didn't influence Walters's thinking about printing stories that touched readers' hearts and minds. On a day-by-day basis, research is limited as stories break; Walters leaned heavily on his intuition, sensing that if a story interested him, it would interest others. Walters believed that if a story didn't prick his own curiosity, it probably would stimulate very few others.

Walters thought "ahead" of the news, too. When a presidential train crossed Iowa during a political campaign, Walters knew the "hard" news—the issues, the charges, the countercharges, the promises, the trial balloons—had to be covered, and he assigned political reporters accordingly. But he felt the readers wanted more than just the political maneuvering. So, keeping the human touch in mind, he boarded the train and wrote about what it was like on one of those special vehicles. He described the accommodations, the staff, the food, the handling of guests. He wanted the readers to feel they were along for the ride, seeing the candidate's dinner table and sleeping berth and "sitting in" on informal press conferences as the train chugged through Iowa hamlets.

Walters knew that truth, indeed, is stranger than fiction. He would not countenance stories with inaccurate information. Sensationalism was sternly avoided.

"He would cross-examine reporters on how they knew that their account of what happened was true," MacDonald noted, saying:

He often recalled the time during the early days of trans-Atlantic flying when a news service, through an identification error, reported that a flyer had landed in Paris when, in fact, he was still miles away over the ocean. "Touch the plane before you report it has landed." he would say. No scoop was worth risking an error. "If you're right, people will soon forget it. If you're wrong, they'll never forget it," he would advise. The still-remembered *Chicago Tribune* headline proclaiming Dewey the winner over Truman in the 1948 presidential election illustrates his point.

Walters's stress on accuracy, however, did not dampen his desire to be first. Indeed, in a day when electronic news hardly existed— there was no television news during much of his career—more newspapers were around, striving to hit the streets first with the latest. Walters's enthusiasm and energy became his trademarks. Staffers, competitors, and fellow journalists learned that when his chunky body rolled into extra-high gear, there was no stopping him. Raw energy and impatience consumed him when a major story broke or new developments occurred, producing a nervousness that caused him to frequently dart from desk to desk to check out information, scratching his buttocks along the way. Staffers would openly make jokes about the scratching, and he'd respond with his gurgling laugh, loving the camaraderie.

Nervous energy propelled him around the newsroom and also caused his fingers to fly on a typewriter. MacDonald recalled:

He often would begin typing a sentence before he had thought how he wanted to end it, and if he changed his phrasing he didn't waste time crossing out what he had written. He merely left a few spaces and began again with a new sentence. This produced fast copy; it also sometimes puzzled the person who edited it.

Walters's go-go style and enthusiasm burst forth in June 1931, when a devastating fire broke out in Spencer, Iowa, population 5,019. Des Moines veterans reminisced over the incident for years—and, of course, embellished it each time they told the story.

The story goes that Walters, concerned for the town's safety and future, put the Des Moines fire chief on an airplane, hoping he had enough expertise to direct the Spencer firefighters to effective measures. Legend has it that Walters also got the idea of shipping lots of dynamite to the scene. With the dynamite, buildings that lay in the fire's path could be blown up, allowing the blaze to burn itself out.

Supposedly, the fire chief found early air travel to his disliking, and by the time he arrived in Spencer, he was too sick to give a single directive. What's more, by the time a reluctant trucker delivered a load of TNT the fire had already burned itself out—along most of Spencer's business district.

There is much truth to that account, but a story in the July 4, 1931, issue of *Editor and Publisher* sounds more accurate. It reports:

> For a few minutes late Saturday afternoon, June 27, news editors of the *Des Moines Register and Tribune* were trying to buy, beg, borrow or steal all of the dynamite in the entire northwest quarter of Iowa.
>
> Here is the reason.
>
> The telephone rang in the office of Basil Walters, assistant managing editor [actually, he was then the managing editor, not assistant]. A voice said:
>
> "This is the dispatcher's office of the Milwaukee railroad. We have a message for you. It reads:
>
> 'Town is burning. Send plane with dynamite and fire chief. Leo C. Daily, secretary, Spencer, Iowa, Chamber of Commerce.'"

Editor and Publisher reports that the message was received at 5:02 P.M. and that by 5:30, *Good News II,* the *Register and Tribune* plane, and two hired planes were "roaring northwest from Des Moines toward Spencer 130 air miles away. The planes carried reporters and cameramen from the paper, the Des Moines fire chief and two of his assistants, and explosive experts."

That account fits Walters perfectly—Walters, the small bundle of human dynamite hanging up the phone and immediately issuing orders.

The *Editor and Publisher* account reports that *Good News II* left Spencer "just as dark fell over the ruins and landed at Des Moines airport at 9:30. An hour and a half later, trucks were pulling out of the *Register and Tribune* loading docks with Sunday *Registers* containing the first pictures of the fire [that] destroyed the greater part of the business district. More than 70 places of business were wiped out.''

Good News II returned to Spencer Sunday morning, carrying a load of the latest city edition with pictures of the fire, the story continues. (Oh, yes . . . the Spencer fire all began after a boy dropped a ten-cent sparkler into a stock of fireworks in a drug store, setting off hundreds of small explosions.)

The trips to Spencer were nothing new for *Good News II, Editor and Publisher* readers learned. The magazine reported that the plane's trips that weekend "climaxed a spurt of activity in which *Good News II* flew 3,950 miles on nine consecutive days," most of which involved editorial department picture assignments in Illinois, Minnesota, Nebraska, Missouri, and, of course, Iowa.

Even with *Good News II* at his call, Walters, like other editors, was hampered in his desire to get nonlocal news photos into print quickly. The transmission of wirephotos by the Associated press, United Press, and International News Service wasn't perfected. Pictures involving distant events arrived in the newsroom long after stories about those events.

Always seeking a photo edge in particular, Walters listened when a reader who raised carrier pigeons told him pictures could be delivered faster by pigeons than any other means of transportation. Convinced the man was serious, Walters decided to test the claim. He chose the hanging of a much-publicized criminal at Fort Madison, Iowa, nearly 200 miles from Des Moines.

"A somewhat incredulous photographer found himself dispatched to Fort Madison along with a crate of carrier pigeons," MacDonald recalled. "He hurried out of the prison after completing his gruesome assignment, and small capsules of his film were attached to the legs of the pigeons. They were released for the flight to Des Moines where Stuffy was eagerly waiting, hoping to have pictures in print before any other papers in the area. Unfortunately, the pigeons never made it back to the newsroom, but the incident remained part of newsroom lore long after the event which prompted it had been forgotten.''

Despite Walters's affinity to act on instinct, he only shouted "Stop the presses!" once, according to oldtimers at the *Register and Tribune.* That was the afternoon Walters received a flash over the phone that the University of Iowa was suspended from the Big Ten

Athletic Conference for rule infractions. No one can remember whether the presses were actually stopped, MacDonald said, "but there is no doubt that Stuffy's shout alerted the staff that an important story was breaking and the managing editor expected instantaneous coverage."

As is the case now, being first with a truly important story didn't happen often. So Walters sought to capture readers by producing a newspaper that looked different, featuring an exciting front page that was easy to read. Flexibility reigned as editors put together pages with a variety of type. Stories featured short paragraphs and stories were short enough to allow as many as twenty on the page. And, of course, stories and photos were loaded with human interest.

It was in Des Moines where loop-the-loop—a typography term that has never been fully described—was born. Many editors in the 1970s moved toward a magazine approach—only three or four large stories and perhaps two large pictures on the front page. They would scorn Walters's thinking. Walters, in retirement, did not scorn theirs. He preferred not to discuss his thinking in the thirties, forties, and fifties. He wanted to talk about where newspapers were going tomorrow. Trying to learn about loop-the-loop from him was like eating one potato chip and then being denied the rest of the bag.

"He was convinced readers have a brief attention span," MacDonald said, adding:

A front page with only six or eight stories disappointed him; a page with two dozen delighted him. To him a front page was a buffet table. If there were only a few items on it, some persons might find nothing appealing. It there were many items, the odds were that every appetite would be satisfied. A long column of gray type depressed him.

It was hard not to have fun with loop-the-loop makeup. A journalism student won't find pure loop-the-loop discussed in textbooks because it had no rules, no formula, no uniformity.

Walters thoroughly enjoyed editing. He liked to demonstrate to young copy editors like MacDonald how to cut a ten-inch story to two inches without losing essential facts. MacDonald explained:

If a story couldn't be short, he wanted it broken up typographically to lure readers into it, and he devised typographical tricks to do this. He used many subheads. He set some paragraphs in bold face and others in italic. He might set a key sentence all in capital letters.

Not everyone agreed with Walters's methods. Some editors argued that frequent changes of type were disconcerting to persons reading through a long story. Surveys conducted in the fifties and sixties revealed that there is validity in the argument. But Walters's ideas got results even so. And while some subordinates fight editors' ideas despite positive results, the majority of the editors who worked for Walters did not. He enjoyed the deep loyalty and respect of his staff because he was always willing to debate with those who disagreed. "He was affable and good-humored," MacDonald recalled. "He didn't demand; he tried, instead, to persuade. He was a popular editor. It is doubtful if any other editor in recent times has had as many friends throughout the newspaper world."

Walters earned respect, too, because of a genuine love for the newsroom's atmosphere. Unlike most editors who imprison themselves in ivory towers and/or administrative offices, Walters searched for time to spend in the newsroom. His presence was infectious; it was clear that he wanted to be just one of the boys who rolled up his sleeves, loosened his tie, drank his coffee, smoked his cigarettes, and put pencil to paper.

As managing editor of both the *Register* and the *Tribune,* he would frequently work a full day on the afternoon *Tribune,* eat supper at home, and then spend several hours at night supervising the morning *Register.* There were standing instructions that he be called at home at any hour of the night if a major story broke. MacDonald explained:

He often said he wanted to be on the scene, not because he didn't trust the staff to cover the story without his personal direction, but because he wanted to help with problems that might otherwise distract the editors, such as arranging for additional press crews when needed for an extra edition or rearranging delivery truck schedules to get later news to far-away readers.

That was demonstrated when the Lindbergh baby was kidnapped on the night of March 1, 1932. Walters was away from home on the evening the infant son was abducted.

The kidnapping announcement stunned the public. Charles Lindbergh was an immense public hero after his solo trans-Atlantic flight; his wife, Ann Morrow, was a much-admired daughter of a U.S. ambassador and later became a noted author. Walters didn't hear about the crime for several hours. When he did, he raced to the office, literally running into the newsroom. "Some staff members think he slid the last few feet to the news editor's desk,'' MacDonald said with a smile.

The first edition was already put together, but Walters wasn't about to leave. He eagerly participated in headline conferences for later editions. And, though tempted to help edit the stories, he didn't, sticking to his dictum of "keeping out of the way," when his staff worked under pressure.

"He stayed in the newsroom all night that night," MacDonald recalled, adding:

Shortly after midnight he phoned the key members of the *Tribune* staff, most of them asleep and unaware of the story, and summoned them to the office to begin work on the next day's paper. Occasionally he went into the newspaper library in an adjoining room and slept for a few minutes on a long metal table. But periodically he would hurry back to the newsroom to see if there had been new developments.

In 1933, a year later, the country was still talking about the Lindbergh abduction—as it would for years—but the major story now was President Franklin Roosevelt's New Deal. Launched shortly after he took office, when the nation was mired in the depression, the New Deal affected several areas that touched people's lives: agriculture, energy, welfare, stocks, housing, roads, banking.

Walters, noting that Iowa was "no longer being run out of the Statehouse but out of Washington," sent Richard Wilson to the nation's capital in 1933 as the *Register and Tribune*'s first fulltime Washington correspondent. Wilson, twenty-eight, proved to be an outstanding choice. He produced exclusive stories and won numerous awards, including a 1954 Pulitzer Prize, during a distinguished Washington reporting career that ended in 1975 with retirement.

As George Mills noted in his book, *Harvey Ingham & Gardner Cowles, Sr.,* Wilson ignored the routine wire stories being sent by AP, UP, and INS and concentrated on reporting Iowa-related issues in depth. Mills wrote:

Wilson was first with details on the New Deal's proposed farm program—a matter of great interest to Midwestern farmers—and he forecast the defeat of F.D.R.'s Supreme Court-packing plan when the U.S. Senator Clyde L. Herring of Iowa was a key figure in Roosevelt's controversy with the Congress over the plan. . . .

Early in his bureau career . . . Wilson set two goals for himself: To build up his contacts by seeing at least two news sources each day and to write two stories daily, one with an Iowa angle and a second of national scope.

It is easy to see why Walters chose Wilson for Washington. Walters knew Wilson was a "see and tell" reporter, a leg man who dug for news and, at the same time, could untangle the government gobbledygook for the average Iowan on the street. Walters didn't want someone who sat around in an office all day making a few phone calls and rewriting news releases. He wanted someone who would get among 'em, who would listen carefully, and ask pointed questions. In Wilson, he had that person.

The "Machine Gun" Camera

King Alexander of Yugoslavia was dead. Assassinated. His dictatorial rule, which had suppressed all opposition since 1929, was over suddenly in 1934. Basil Walters and chief photographer George Yates were impressed with the photos sent from Marseilles, the exotic port city in southern France where King Alexander was shot. Described by some as "play-by-play" shots, the dramatic photos showed a mounted soldier cutting down the assassin, King Alexander gasping for his last breaths, and French Minister Louis Barthou, also shot, bleeding to death.

"Could you have bagged photos like that?" Walters asked Yates.

"No, I couldn't have changed plates fast enough," Yates admitted, explaining that the pictures before them were from a newsreel camera. The "stills" were blurred, he said, because a newsreel camera has a slow shutter. In newsreels and movies, the blurs melt into each other. "I'd need a new kind of rapid-fire camera to get good sequence pictures of fast action," Yates added.

"Well," Walters challenged, "you're one of these ace news photographers, why don't you get it?"

"Because," Yates replied, "no such camera exists." But the challenge remained—so Yates decided to de-

velop his own camera. Only a few weeks passed before
Yates proudly announced to Walters that he had developed what became known as the "machine gun camera" with a "lightning-fast shutter." It was capable of
freezing every piece of action into beautifully focused
pictures. The Yates creation was made out of a movie
camera revamped with a long range lens, shutter step up
to 1/1000 second, and the ability to frame sixteen shots
per second.

Yates saw the sports picture potential immediately.
"Now we'll be able to show the way a winning play puts
the ball over the goal line, motion by motion," he
gushed. "Sports fans can see the interference clearing
the roads, tackles missing by a hair, the ball sailing
through the air from one gridster to another. We'll take
thousands of pictures and use only the best."

Walters's joy matched Yates's: "This will make'em
sit up. We'll take the whatsit to games by our plane."
His mind computed the distance to the University of
Iowa: thirty-eight minutes for the hundred-mile trip to
Iowa City.

So as the 1935 football season got under way, the
"whatsit" that became known as the "machine gun"
made its major debut amid much promotion in the
Register and Tribune—which long believed in its ability
to sell anything through its advertising. It wasn't long
before 2,000 pictures of a single football game were being shot by Yates and his fellow *Register and Tribune*
photographers. It was all worth it. Fans and readers of
the Sunday morning sports section responded with overwhelming praise, justifying Walters's and Yates's time,
planning, and decisions to put money into a project that
greatly advanced newspaper photography.

A year later, Walters didn't need a sophisticated
camera to help him score a personal scoop. It began
when a Rock Island passenger train became snowbound
near McCallsburg, Iowa, a pebble on the map. The train
drew national attention as it became trapped in a bliz-
zard that left fifty-one passengers stranded for twenty-
seven hours. One of those passengers was Stuffy Walters.

Walters, who had become a regular weekly com-
muter between Des Moines and Minneapolis, wasn't
about to stay trapped aboard the Pullman coaches.

After interviewing several passengers, he pulled out his basic little Jiffy camera, got his pictures, and then trudged three miles through snow, howling winds, and fourteen-below-zero cold to the nearest telephone. The *Register and Tribune* got a vivid on-the-scene report of the stalled train. Walters was half frozen by the time he reached his destination, but he had his scoop—and once he thawed out he was talking about it on the radio.

Back in Des Moines, Reah Walters called to daughter Nancy, "Come quick, your father's on the radio." Indeed he was, loving every minute of it, frozen ears and all.

Two Places at Once

I F the Cowleses could have cloned another Basil Walters, they would have. That not being possible, they did the next best thing—they put him in two places at once.

Seeking to stretch the family's journalistic holdings from Des Moines, the two brothers bought the *Minneapolis Star* in June 1935, despite Gardner Sr.'s doubts that the struggling afternoon paper could survive against tough competition from the *Journal and Tribune*. The elder Cowles, then seventy-four years old, had reason to be pessimistic. The *Star* had been founded in 1924 by the Non-Partisan League with more than 6,000 stockholders. It was hailed as an excellent example of cooperative ownership—only to go bankrupt and be reorganized four years later.

No matter. John Cowles, then thirty-six, and a friend from his Harvard days, Davis Merwin, had discussed expansion for three years. They wanted a newspaper that had achieved solid reader loyalty, where home delivery—the key to Gardner Sr.'s circulation success—could become stronger. In Minneapolis they saw a city troubled by underworld elements, but, at the same time, a community of high literacy and an even distribution of purchasing power. The liberal *Star,* shunned by the silk-stocking elite and dominated by unions, fit the bill. The Cowleses bought the *Star* for $1,000,000; Merwin purchased a minority interest.

Like the Cowles brothers, Merwin, then thirty-five, had grown up with newspapers. His family had long owned the *Bloomington* (Illinois) *Pantagraph,* and young Davis had succeeded his uncle in successfully running the operation. John Cowles installed him as the *Star*'s publisher. Twenty-eight months later, Merwin resigned because of ill health. John Thompson, who had been with the *Star* since its inception, moved from general manager back to his former post as publisher.

Circulation growth in those twenty-eight months was tremendous —from 80,000 to 135,000. *Time* magazine, in a November 1, 1937, item on Merwin's resignation and other *Star* changes, praised Merwin's efforts. He deserved this praise to some degree. But insiders knew that it was Basil Walters's editorial genius that got the *Star* moving. "Stuffy deserves a lot of credit for the growth of the *Star* in the early years. He had a world of enthusiasm and imbued the staff," John Cowles recalled.

Walters did not go to Minneapolis immediately but eventually he was spending as much time in Minnesota as in Iowa. For a brief period he functioned as managing editor of the *Star* and the Des Moines paper at the same time. John Cowles recalled, "Stuffy was ambitious and could not get used to the idea of having anyone other than myself have authority over him."

Walters was a dedicated family man—"wonderful, absolutely marvelous," Reah Walters said—but he agreed to the unique commuting assignment because of his loyalty to the Cowleses. He generally would spend Monday morning through Thursday as editor in Minneapolis, then return home to Reah and his children—ages ten, four, and two—for three days. Sometimes he would forego the train for a private plane. He carried a small, tan, canvas duffle bag that was just big enough for three shirts, an extra necktie or two, and a clean suit of B.V.D.'s.

Although he had spent most of his life in the Midwest, where winter can sometimes be extremely severe, Walters was not prepared for the exceptionally harsh Minneapolis winter. One morning, as he left his hotel for the *Star* office, the doorman stopped him, saying, "You better not walk today, Mr. Walters, you'll freeze your face." It was thirty-three below.

The bitter winter and the bitter newspaper situation he found at the *Star* didn't bother him. He had always been a man with an optimistic outlook, a man who didn't stay down very long after a setback, a man who possessed a rugged individualism. At the same time, he sensed the personal opportunity before him, knowing that he could initiate a different brand of journalism and live or die with his own ideas, theories, and efforts.

On February 20, 1959, Walters, as executive editor of the *Chicago Daily News* and the Knight Newspapers, returned to Minneapolis to speak before the Minnesota Editorial Association. He talked about those early days:

> It was here as most of you know, that I had my first big opportunity to try anything and everything. . . .
> We didn't have much money or prestige. We couldn't buy the Associated Press. Even the undertakers refused to call us on important deaths. The city editor could see the flagpole at the Minneapolis Club from his desk. When the flag went to halfmast, he'd call without identifying himself and ask, "Who's dead?"
> Our only advantage on the *Star* was that we were so scared that we parted with past traditions and tried almost anything that came into anybody's head.

Walters began to give the *Star* greatness, and, in the process, his innovative ideas and uninhibited editing became known as the "Stuffy Walters School of Newspapering." It was an influential school—and with good reason. Figures released by the Audit Bureau of Circulation showed the *Star* had topped 158,000 through July 31, 1939. By then, Walters had become the *Star*'s fulltime editor.

The human element played a powerful role in Walters's thinking. "News creativity" was a favorite term. Angelo Cohn, who worked on the copy desk in those days, talked about it:

> Reporting and covering the things that were happening—the flow of life, the changes. One day your headline is the fact that we've blown an atomic bomb for the first time and it's history in the making. The next day, you forget about the atom bomb, because Russia has declared war on China. The fact that life is not working in a pattern, like an assembly line. Stuffy would try to capture the human element and influence in the news—the fact that it's a lot of different people with different ideas and looking at the same thing in different ways.
> Obits were extremely important to him. He wanted them to have a little spark of something, and if somebody in the city who died was prominent, somehow he wanted you to get that right into the lead. And he would try to weave city history into the obit.

Not everyone was influenced by the Stuffy Walters School. Some editors accused Walters of practicing "upside-down" journalism when he introduced writing and typography innovations to achieve what he called "a change of pace." Walters was criticized for allowing reporters considerable latitude in interpretation. He was derided, too, for not saving all of the best stories for page one. Instead he scattered them throughout the paper to create "reader traffic."

But upside-down journalism worked, compensating for a tight

money supply. Still, it wasn't cash that prevented the *Star* from obtaining Associated Press service. Angelo Cohn explained:

> At the time, the *Minneapolis Tribune,* for some crazy, historic reason, was the strongest, most powerful voting member in the AP setup. The *Tribune* had three separate franchises. One was for the morning *Tribune,* which at one time had been a separate paper, one for the afternoon *Tribune,* and one for the extinct *Minneapolis Times.*
> We were told that no other paper at that time had three votes on the AP council. The *Journal* also had a franchise. It's my understanding that the *Journal* and *Tribune* went to the AP meeting and said, "Look, there are four franchises in this town. How many do you need?"
> And then the *Tribune* group also had INS (International News Service, which later merged with United Press to become United Press International). They controlled King Features with INS.

That's not all. The *Tribune* and the *Journal* worked with the St. Paul papers to form a miniature news cooperative for the area called the Northwest News Bureau (NNB), Cohn recalled. NNB was connected with other papers in the state, "and they had a powerful cooperative covering a lot of the court material that was routine, plus the Minneapolis Grain Exchange, which was a great thing in those days," Cohn said. "Here was a great flow of economic news going through there, and they controlled it. The *Star* couldn't get it."

One advantage of being unable to buy AP and most of the better syndicated features was that Cowles money could be spread elsewhere, including the new *Look* magazine.

Louis Cook, in a *Detroit Free Press* article on August 21, 1971, recalled how difficult that time was. *Look* began in the old *Des Moines Register and Tribune* building in January and February of 1937, he wrote. Noting that the depression was still hard upon the nation, Cook wrote that Walters not only issued the return-the-pencils edict, but "cut artgum (erasers) in half. He made regular tours of the newsroom to collect paper clips that might have been left around."

Some people complained at his actions, but Walters wasn't bothered. He knew upon arriving in Minneapolis that dollars were scarce and the profit-and-loss statement was showing a deficit. He had long since been a fiscal conservative, because of his childhood years when he had watched his mother struggle with finances to keep the family going.

Cohn, too, remembers that Walters was never very liberal with money. But he felt the Cowleses contributed to the situation. He said, with a wide grin, "After a Des Moines reporter arrived in the North Africa war zone, the other correspondents amused themselves by trying to figure out ways to pad his expense account so he could come out alive." He paused, then continued:

Stuffy never hesitated to compliment somebody if he did a good job, but he didn't hand out money. When Carroll Binder came over to the *Star* to become editorial page editor, after Stuffy left Minneapolis, he started a little system of paying a small bonus or extra payment for something a reporter might write for the editorial page on something he was covering. It might be only five dollars, but Stuffy would never have stood for something like that.

Monty Curtis illustrated Walters's high regard for careful spending.

Stuffy went with a group of newspapermen to Havana in 1949. Some of us went shopping. My wife and I were standing at a leather goods counter in a department store. A clerk was trying to sell my wife a hideous alligator skin purse. The clerk began to lower the price. I interrupted, "If you want the thing, buy it. If you don't want it, don't even let the clerk give it to you!"
Stuffy was standing right behind and heard this. Every time I met him in subsequent years, he always recalled this and said that the phrase saved him a lot of money when he was shopping with his wife.

Leroy Keller, a newspaper broker and consultant who represented United Features Syndicate in those days, recalled a situation involving Walters.

He needed good comic strips and other features. United Features had brought out only the year before the highly popular "L'il Abner." Stuffy wanted it, because it had not yet been placed in Minneapolis.
The problem was he felt he could not pay the going rate in Minneapolis. We hassled around for a full week over the price he could afford. Finally, I proposed a compromise. I would give him a low starting rate, but add to it a certain amount for each 10,000 circulation gained.
The *Star* took off like a rocket and soon he was paying way above the normal rate. Naturally, he screamed about this and he finally settled for a new satisfactory rate on a long-term agreement. It was one of the rare times in Stuffy's career where he underestimated his ability as an editor and circulation getter. What he accomplished in Minneapolis is now history. The glory and credit belongs eternally to this superb craftsman.

The money pinch was for real. Cohn supplied an example: "Northwest Airlines had an accident; lost an airplane in Duluth. And we were short of money. Dave Silverman (managing editor) and

Stuffy went around the newsroom borrowing money so we could send a reporter up there. The paper just didn't have access to money that quickly.''

Walters overcame his money problems by simply whipping the opposition on the news, by handling local and wire stories better, by presenting "hard," day-in-and-day-out information more attractively and more excitingly. He took his "superb craftsmanship," as Leroy Keller put it, to the copy desk. As in Des Moines, he hovered over the desk operation. He made sure the newspaper was edited for "the common people, knowing what would appeal to them," said Frosty Jenstad, who worked the desk in those days. "As as result, he pulled off some great tricks in circulation through the years," Jenstad added.

Jenstad finished his Minneapolis career as a *Star* editorial writer. Like others, he did not see Walters as a highly intellectual editor, but rather as someone "right out in the newsroom smoking his cigarettes, with sleeves rolled up and punching a typewriter or passing out ideas to rewrite men who were combining two or three wire stories into one.''

Citing Gallup's research, which was more scientific and accurate, Walters pushed his ideas on tight, crisp, bright writing. Louis M. Lyons, who was curator of the Nieman journalism fellowships for several years, described a Walters writing "trick" that became famous. In a 1954 lecture entitled "The Business of Writing," Lyons said:

> One of our most successful newspaper editors, Basil Walters—"Stuffy" Walters—used to have a conviction that most writers overwrite. To get them out of it he required a reporter returning from assignment to come in and recite the story to him before he wrote. In his oral report, the reporter tended to give a natural, rapid narrative, leaving out nonessentials. Then Walters would tell him to go and write it just as he'd talked it.

In a May 1938 article for *Editor and Publisher,* Walters wrote:

> On the local level we are trying to get reporters to write their stories more the way they talk. We're forgetting the rules of who-what-why, etc. in leads when necessary.
> You've heard about the sitting up exercise for writers, haven't you? A fellow just sits down at a typewriter, looks around and keeps writing anything that comes into his mind. Sounds crazy, but it works.

Another Walters "trick" became equally well known. He experimented with a stenographer surreptitiously taking down the reporter's story as he recited it. Then, after the reporter submitted his copy, Walters would haul out the stenographer's transcript and tell the startled writer, "That's the way it should have been written." The "secret steno" method often produced an outstanding story.

Short sentences were the key, no matter the writing method. Walters's clipped style became even more famous years later at the *Chicago Daily News*. The word around the newsroom was that Walters would toss out any sentence of more than fourteen words.

A *Daily News* reporter once wrote an eight-word first paragraph on an economy story. It read, "Will there be a boom or a bust?" Too long, Walters said. The reporter returned with, "Boom or bust?" Too long, Walters said. The reporter boiled the lead paragraph to one word, "Boom?" The next paragraph followed with, "Bust?" The third paragraph read, "Those are the questions." Walters loved it.

Tony Weitzel recalled Walters's writing requirements in a 1973 column he wrote for the *Naples* (Florida) *Daily News*. Weitzel, a former Chicago staffer, wrote: "The guys on the rewrite desk used to sit and strain to meet Stuffy's exacting specifications for short lead paragraphs. One perspiring newsman swore once in Billy Goat's Tavern that there was only one lead paragraph in all literature that meets Stuffy's requirements. It's the line in the New Testament that says, 'Jesus Wept'."

Walters's stress on terseness is shown in the *Chicago Daily News* of Monday, October 11, 1954, after flooding wracked Chicago. The first ten paragraphs of the *Daily News*'s main story are an exercise in brevity and completeness:

> Cloudy Monday—rain Tuesday.
>
> That's the weather forecast Chicago faces as it bails out after its wettest weekend in 69 years.
>
> The city is still partly paralyzed.
>
> The rain started about 4:30 P.M. Saturday.
>
> By Monday morning even the skyscrapers had wet feet.
>
> The official rainfall recorded at Midway airport for the 38-hour period ending 6:30 A.M. was 6.24 inches.
>
> Some 700 persons are flooded from their homes, most of them in 14 suburbs.
>
> Outgoing and incoming trains were cancelled in two of the city's great railroad stations—the Union station and the Dearborn station.
>
> In Chicago alone, damage was estimated at a minimum of $10 million.

> No one was in a position to say immediately
> what it might be for the entire area of about 62 sur-
> rounding towns that were flooded.

That kind of writing, first encouraged in Des Moines and more so in Minneapolis, inspired a 1955 Walters spoof by Hal Tribble, editorial page supervisor of the Knight-owned *Charlotte Observer*. After one of Walters's visits as executive editor, Tribble wrote and published the following editorial.

> Stuffy Walters dropped by Charlotte the other
> week.
> Visiting.
> Nice fellow.
> One of the boys.
> One of the really great boys.
> Big.
> Almost a legend.
> Maybe strictly a legend.
> Who's to say?
> Stuffy grew to size as managing editor.
> It's a title.
> Means "boss."
> Nowadays they call it "executive editor."
> New age.
> Same meaning.
> Stuffy does most of his bossing around the
> Chicago Daily News.
> Nice, nonetheless.
> A little peculiar, maybe.
> Likes short sentences.
> Terse.
> Gets 'em.
> We're glad he came by.
> Glad.
> Honestly.

Newsweek reprinted it word-for-word on May 6. Walters calmed the slightly nervous Tribble with a note: "Dear Country Cousin, I know when I'm licked. Stuffy."

Walters won numerous followers who agreed that his ideas helped their papers gain readability. There were, of course, those who disagreed. They argued that the reform went too far, that the two-line lead paragraph, the elimination of jargon, and the boiling down of the most complicated news to man-in-the-street terms could make a story about the economy, for example, sound like a nursery rhyme.

Getting Exposure

By 1937, Walters was seldom called Basil. It was "Stuffy." He had gained much nationwide publicity with his ideas, flair, personality, and success. He did not take himself too seriously. But he liked the publicity.

He got excellent exposure in a February 25, 1935, *Time* magazine advertisement placed by the *Register* and *Tribune*. The one-column ad was headed "Scribes," and in much smaller type above that it said, "An advertisement About Iowa." The ad, in fact, was about the *Register* and *Tribune*, and there, in the only picture, was a half-column photo of Basil Walters. The caption read, "Managing Editor Walters Explores Iowa Coal Mines." Walters wore a miner's hat and coat along with his usual grin.

But most of Walters's recognition was serious in tone, not puffery. He was elected chairman at the 1937 convention of the Associated Press Managing Editors association, which remains today one of the country's foremost press organizations. The convention was held October 14 through 17 in New Orleans; less than a month later he resigned after the Cowleses moved him permanently to Minneapolis. The organization did not forget him. It elected him chairman in 1941, and, at the same time, he served as secretary of the prestigious American Society of Newspaper Editors.

Walters had become accustomed to living out of suitcases by 1937. Good thing. He repeatedly found invitations to speak all over the country. In November 1938, he went to his alma mater, Indiana University, to speak on "An Editor Looks at the News." His speech centered on George Gallup's readership research, which Walters was putting to even greater use in Minneapolis. By then, Gallup had gained national recognition for his political forecasts.

There would be much more travel and recognition for Stuffy Walters in the years to come.

The Battle for Minneapolis

Basil Walters was pooped. Happy, but pooped. He had achieved outstanding success in Minneapolis, but after some two years of commuting, he wanted off the exhausting Des Moines-Minneapolis shuttle.

He marched into Gardner Cowles's Des Moines office and told the elder statesman of northwest journalism, "I'll stay here and work for you in Des Moines—or else you can do whatever you want about it —but I'm not going back to Minneapolis."

The commuting stopped. But Walters was going back to Minneapolis. Shortly after making his feelings known, Walters was summoned by Cowles. "John will move up to Minneapolis with his family, and you move up there, too," Walters was told nicely, as if there was no doubt in anybody's mind that Walters would agree.

Walters did not agree on the spot. He checked with his wife, as was his custom. On the way home that night he worried. The children were young, Minneapolis had some rough elements, Rhea might be affected by the extreme cold and snow. After getting settled that evening, he told Rhea about Cowles's request. "Oh, it's all right with me," she responded, noting she hadn't been feeling well in Des Moines.

The move came on Veterans' Day, November 11, 1937. The Walters family moved into a big house with five bedrooms, a three-car garage, and a big yard. The Walterses paid a whopping rent for those days—$100 a month. The Walterses' three young children took a quick liking to Minneapolis. They tobogganed in a park two blocks away. They frolicked around Lake Harriet, two blocks in another direction. They ice skated and played hockey on a "rink" their father made by flooding the huge back yard.

Life wasn't immediately pleasant, though, for Basil and Rhea

Walters. They had moved into a house at 46th and Bryant, the edge of the "Silk Stocking" neighborhood, where the wealthy looked down upon the labor-dominated *Star*. The *Journal* was the newspaper of their neighbors, and the neighbors weren't bashful about letting the Walterses know it.

Walters was not surprised by the hostility. He had felt it even before moving his family to Minneapolis. Gardner Cowles and his fearless Des Moines editor, Harvey Ingham, had long fought gambling interests. Cowles wanted Walters to extend that crusade to Minneapolis, where underground elements were operating rather openly at the time. Walters agreed that such a crusade was needed and, in turn, felt heat in various threatening ways. Some people at city hall intimated they would run the new editor out of town—a challenge Walters relished. As the threats occurred more often, Rhea Walters became fearful, remembering that not long before they moved, the editor of a Minneapolis weekly was killed.

She recalled those days: "Stuffy always said, 'You do what's right and fair, and they are not going to bother you.' He never showed much fear about anything. He always looked around to see what was happening—he was cautious, but he wasn't afraid. He was pretty even-tempered most of the time; he never really got shook up. You would think with all the experiences he had that he would. I can't say he never was upset. There were any number of times when he would come home and be very sick to his stomach. Pressure."

Pressure, of course. Walters not only faced competition in Minneapolis, but also from the twin city, St. Paul. The *Pioneer Press*'s managing editor was Russ Wiggins, who later became editor of the *Washington Post*. Mrs. Wiggins called Walters "the friendly enemy"—and, in fact, the Walterses and Wigginses were friends despite the competitive situation.

In September 1953, Walters gave a speech before the Rotary Club of Minneapolis. He said:

Sixteen years ago, when John Cowles practically forced me to leave Des Moines and move my family here, I thought I was being banished to Siberia. I was fearful lest my family would perish in the severe winters. I was soon to learn, of course, that while winters are sometimes severe here, people adjust quickly to them. . . . Whenever things look pretty hazardous in this dangerous world of ours, I remind myself of my foolish fears about moving my family to Minneapolis. Fears are so often worse than reality. When I was a kid and became frightened by some strange sound or shadow, my dad always insisted that I search out the source.

Walters adjusted. He searched out sources. And he had fun.

Disdaining the "That's the way we've always done things" syndrome, Walters's unique use of typography resulted in doing something different every day. Remember Baby Boy Schmitz?

Walters's thinking was so unorthodox in the late thirties, it drew mocking guffaws. Not from circulation manager W. D. Parsons, though. In a January 27, 1940, interview with George Brandenburg of *Editor and Publisher,* "Pars" said circulation success at the *Star-Journal* (by then, the Cowleses had bought out the *Journal*) was not based on "high-pressure tactics, nor on magic. . . ." It was directly attributable to the editorial department, he explained, saying:

> It goes back to 1935 when the Cowles brothers purchased the paper. At that time the *Star* began experimenting typographically, pictorially, and in a "fresh" treatment of the news content. . . . It made the paper "Page One" all the way through. . . . As Basil Walters, the editor, has pointed out, the paper was designed for eye-traffic up and down every page, not just the front page alone. . . . The town and the Northwest took to it. The change was so startling that at one time our circulation leaped almost 10,000 subscriptions in a single month.
>
> That's the reason I say our circulation success rests with the editorial department. That part of our organization puts out a product that is easy to sell. We have sold it by stressing our newspaper, not by premiums to our readers. The keynote of the entire story is cooperation within the organization.

That same issue of *Editor and Publisher* carried a long article on Walters's appearance at a weekly Nieman Fellows' dinner January 18 at Cambridge, Massachusetts. As was tradition, a gabfest followed dinner, rather than the guest giving a speech. The Fellows, themselves, chose their dinner guests.

His roast beef dinner tucked away, Walters lighted a cigar and opened the session by frankly admitting that his copy and makeup techniques may be a brand of "quack journalism," but they were clicking. A "new journalism," he dubbed it.

It was, more accurately, "pragmatic journalism"—if it worked, if it clicked, use it. If something didn't work, or stopped working, drop it. If his "quack journalism" failed, newspaper doctor Walters would have buried it.

His philosophy was illustrated years later in a visit with Monty Curtis, who was then a major figure with the highly respected American Press Institute (API). An API seminar group had just finished meeting with the *New York Times*'s publisher, editor, and other executives. Walters, in New York at the time, went along. Curtis remembered:

> As usual, the then rather stilted *New York Times* type and makeup came in for heavy criticism. No one liked those skinny, condensed gothic one-column headlines. No one liked the severely symmetrical makeup. But the fact remained that the *Times* was a great success.
>
> On the way out of the building, I asked Stuffy what he thought of the recommendations that the *Times* re-jigger its type and makeup. I will never forget his answer: "At this stage of development, I would be inclined to leave grandma exactly as she is. She is awfully healthy right now. The time for changes may come later but this is not the time."

Never mind that the appearance of the *New York Times* sharply contrasted with the one Walters's papers had. It worked. And that's the message he continually threw out at the Fellows that January night in 1940.

When his use of bold-face paragraphs drew criticism, Walters reminded the group that "the circulation sheets are proof of the pudding" and, therefore, readers must be pleased. Paragraphs are not necessarily bold-faced to emphasize the more important thoughts in a story, but to fluctuate the "inflection of voice" in telling the story, he said.

"It's no sin to be interesting," he continued. "(I) refused to listen to newspapermen" in the process of pepping up the Minneapolis newspapers.

Walters talked about RPU's—"Reader Pulling Units." In short, he explained, "a good newspaper should have enough RPUs on each page to make the reader examine the paper from cover-to-cover every day. Obviously, this is a good selling point to advertisers." (And— what Walters didn't tell the Fellows—sufficient advertising revenue is an absolute necessity if the newspaper is to maintain quality and remain editorially strong.)

Walters told the Fellows that his paper bought more columnists and syndicated cartoons than they could use each day. (By 1940, those good advertising dollars had made such possible.) If a columnist is interesting throughout his entire piece, it runs intact, Walters said. But a day or two later, the same columnist might be slashed to three or four paragraphs—or entirely, if substance is lacking. What Walters didn't tell the Fellows about columnists is that he thought little of them, in general. An exception was Raymond Clapper, whose brilliant career was cut short in February 1944 in a navy warplane accident.

"I'm not over-enthusiastic about commentators," Walters said in a June 1940 *Quill* magazine article. "I think a great newspaper is built not on special features, but on the day-to-day work of a capable staff."

To produce the kind of newspaper Walters spoke about that night required an exceptionally talented copy desk and expert picture editors. Walters didn't have time to explain how the copy desk and picture editors worked together. If the Fellows had read the May 21, 1938, issue of *Editor and Publisher,* however, they would have known. In it, Walters wrote a story entitled "Heads and Text Loop-the-Loop and Readers Flock to Watch." He quoted Bill Bade, then a member of the copy desk:

> Everybody on the *Star* has a hand in the type of paper we are working out. Rim men on the copy desk write a headline, then scan the type chart to see what it will fit in, with an eye to type contrast and harmony. In many cases, the composing room is consulted (for that is the place to learn about type) and the most enthusiastic men about the unique type displays are those in the composing room.
>
> The whole thing is taken as a lot of fun—whistle while you work.
>
> Actually, because of the complete cooperation of the composing room and the enthusiasm these men are putting into the "laboratory work" of working out something new in newspapers, the costs have not risen as a result of the experiments.
>
> Copy editors are urged to try something new. But the rule is that if an attempt is lousy, don't try that type of headline again.

Instead of using pictures as primarily filler material—the standard practice then—Walters scheduled photos into the paper the way he scheduled news. "Stress is placed on picture editing, and a copy desk has been established to handle pictures in much the same manner that printed copy is handled," Walters wrote. "The chief picture editor sits at the city desk and has charge of the photographic department as well as the picture copy desk. Maps are used extensively. This aids in placing related news together and makes it easy for the readers to grasp the entire situation."

Walters, of course, had long been impressed with the power of news photography. He wrote, ''In case of doubt, we kick out what we regard as a five percent news interest story or a one percent reader-interest story and get in a ninety percent reader-interest picture.''

Frosty Jenstad remembered those experimental, flexible, wild days:

We had four or five different type faces available to us for headline purposes, and frequently the copyreader was given carte blanc to write a one, two, three, four, five—up to eight-column headline over a story and use Cheltenham or Futura or any other type face we had around. Even Cooper (a thick-faced type used primarily for ads). We had no typographic plan and it amounted to the appeal of the paper; the paper never looked the same two days in a row. It was just a complete surprise everytime you picked it up.

There were a few occasions when a copyreader wrote a three-line head in which the top line was one type size, the second another, and the third still another. Jenstad recalls, ''As a copyreader, I would write what I thought would be a good headline for a story and then I would go backward and figure out what letter count it would fit in, what type size it would fit, and how many counts. . . . We had a great deal of freedom.''

One of Walters's disciples put it this way: ''We use type the way a musician uses stops on an organ.''

Newsroom personnel and printers generally haven't cooperated very much over the years. Did Walters and the composing room actually have the esprit de corps he and Bill Bade talk about? Said Jenstad:

Yes, as I recall. I got down on makeup fairly soon after I came aboard (walking around the composing room and helping finish pages with problems). The printers used to make a little fun of Stuffy. When he first came aboard, I'm told, he would show up in the composing room and try to get buddy-buddy with the printers. He'd start to recall how he did this maneuver in Des Moines. So it got to be a standing joke in the composing room when Stuffy would show up for the printers to say, ''Hey, Stuffy, come over here and tell us how you did it in Des Moines.'' So I think he kind of got out of the habit of going into the composing room.

The flexibility in headlines produced a loose, undisciplined atmosphere of makeup around the copy desk—the thinking being that the slot man, who laid out the pages, would eventually find a place for everything here and there. There was no policy of grouping similar stories together. And the packaging of news, so prevalent today, was seldom done. There was, as Jenstad recalls, "a lot of seat-of-the-pants makeup in the composing room."

Despite the looseness in planning, Walters and his cohorts sought to create traffic through the inside pages and up and down them. In *Editor and Publisher* he wrote,

> . . . [we are] forgetting the old printing rule of putting art and big heads at the top of the page and coming down gradually to smaller heads lower in the page. We deliberately dummy black heads and art in the middle of the inside pages and at the bottom in order to create eye traffic right past and into the ads that appear on the page.

Walters, who championed the "little man" all his life, had the small advertisers in mind when he planned inside eye appeal. The *Star,* struggling when Walters first arrived because the large advertisers were not in the fold, depended on the smaller merchants for survival. When the *Star*'s success took hold, Walters sought to protect the small advertisers by trying not to bury their ads. He reasoned, too, that if the small advertisers grew, their ads would also grow. And if ad revenue grew, there would be more money for the editorial department.

Pressure created by Walters's flexible approach fell on the slot man. Angelo Cohn sat in that key position most of those years, surrounded by copyreaders like Otto Silha, who would go on to become president of Cowles Communication, Inc., Harold Chucker, who would become associate editor in charge of the editorial pages, and Jenstad, who would become an assistant managing editor before moving to the editorial pages.

Cohn rolled with the punches, and, years later, said he didn't think "our planning was that loose. . . . If you had a reason for doing something, you could."

As an example, Cohn recalled a feature story about a youngster who had an eye problem that caused him to see things upside down, similar to dyslexsia. The story was played on page one, with a kicker headline above the main headline. The kicker line read: "Roger Would Like This." It was printed right side up. The main headline was printed upside down and read: "Headlines Are upside down to Inversionist"—inversionist being the medical term used to describe the child's condition.

The headline idea was Cohn's. Cohn recalled that when Walters saw the paper in his office:

He came storming out—the paper was hardly out of the hands of the copy-boy—and he ran to the desk, saying the headline was upside down. Then he realized what he was seeing and he got a great bang out of it. You know, there aren't a great many papers where you could have done that kind of thing.

Body Snatching

The young *Frankfort Morning Times* reporter asked the retired Basil Walters if he could help him move on to a larger newspaper. "Yes," he told the young fellow. "I'm a body snatcher. I snatch sharp young people from small papers and put them on large papers." His smile, as usual, was deep, wide.

Walters "snatched" his first body in Minneapolis. He discovered Cedric Adams—a Mike Royko-Matt Weinstock-Jimmy Breslin of his day. Like those three outstanding columnists, Adams achieved greatness by writing a column that captured the flavor and essence of his community—Minneapolis—as Royko caught Chicago, Weinstock Los Angeles, and Breslin New York.

Fresh out of the University of Minnesota, Adams worked for the *Shopping News,* a weekly throwaway. Shortly before moving to Minneapolis, Walters noticed the young man's column of chit-chat. Talking story stuff. Walters told news editor Dave Silverman that Adams had a way of saying things that hooked people, and the *Star* should try to hire him.

Once settled in Minneapolis, Walters made Adams a high priority. He suggested to Earl Gammons, who was managing radio station WCCO, that they acquire Adams's services for both the *Star* and the station. Gammons agreed. Adams made the move—and never moved again.

Walters and Adams took to each other like peanut butter and jelly. Adams's column took off, helping boost circulation immensely. Frosty Jenstad remembers being told by a key Cowles executive that John Cowles said two people must never be fired: Richard Wilson in Washington and Cedric Adams in Minneapolis. "It was said that if Cedric ever left the *Star* he would automatically take with him 25,000 of our circulation," Jenstad said. "I think that was entirely possible."

Adams was the epitome of what Walters sought in reporters. He was excellent at digging out information and had a keen sense of what was news. When he got the homespun stuff he knew people wanted, he wrote it entertainingly. Bradley L. Morison, in his book on the *Minneapolis Tribune,* described Adams's column as a collection of "country cousin observations on everything from death to girth control."

Rhea Walters remembers Adams as

very easy going and very naive. You couldn't believe it. He could write such an interesting, funny column. People would always wait for the 10 o'clock news and retire with Cedric Adams. He was the last news in the evening.

One day he wrote a column about four-leaf clovers. And then one of the theaters said through Cedric's column that if someone brought in a four-leaf clover, the bank would give that person a ticket—and the line was almost a mile long.

The Walterses weren't in Minneapolis very long before the telephone jarred them from sleep at 3 o'clock in the morning. It was Cedric. He had been arrested.

"Okay, don't worry about it," Walters responded. "I'll be right down."

Adams arrested? It was an early case of a reporter refusing to reveal his source. Adams had reported that a certain man would be murdered. But someone else had been the victim. Where did Adams get his information? The police wanted to know. Adams wouldn't say.

Rhea Walters remembers:

"He doesn't have to tell," Stuffy told the police. "Besides that, I've just been in touch with the FBI and this is going to be the end," he told them. He then turned to Cedric and said, "Cedric, come on," and they walked out. The police really didn't have anything to hold him on.

Angelo Cohn, who wrote a book about Adams, was assigned to write his obituary in 1955. He called the *Chicago Daily News,* where Walters already knew about Adams's death, and Walters's first comment was, "He's the most human guy I have ever known."

CHAPTER EIGHT

A Goof, a Scoop, Two Wars

BASIL WALTERS had the enemy on the run. He had overcome the early community hostility toward him by plunging into civic affairs, attending some fifty meetings a month. His involvement ranged from the Aquatennial Board of Directors to the Minneapolis-St. Paul Joint Airport Commission.

How he found time for newspapering is hard to grasp, but he did. His loop-the-loop had readers talking—and not knowing what to expect from day to day.

Walters's drive for credibility also played a winning role as the town sought to cleanse itself of crime. His civic involvement was a factor externally. Internally, staffers saw it—by not seeing John Cowles in the city room, save for rare occasions. Walters had insisted that Cowles stay out, lest there be any hint that the chief business executive and part owner was interfering with news department affairs. John Thompson also agreed to Walters's rule. A baseball fan, Thompson innocently wandered into the city room one summer day to check the wire machines for scores. Walters chased him out. Thompson was flabbergasted—but left with a smile, Angelo Cohn remembers.

And then there were the numbers. The opposition couldn't ignore them. *Star* circulation hovered around 160,000 as 1939 opened. This meant Cowles, Walters, and company had doubled the paid distribution in four years. And there were no signs that growth was slowing. Meanwhile, the afternoon *Journal* in the same period had gained just 20,000, while the *Morning Tribune* grew by only 14,000. The *Evening Tribune,* the *Morning Tribune*'s weak sister, fell to just below 70,000.

So, yes, the enemy was squirming. As Bradley L. Morison wrote in his *Sunlight on Your Doorstep,* an authorized account of the *Minneapolis Tribune*'s first 100 years:

In the role of competitor Walters was more than a source of mild annoyance to the Tribune; he goaded it into dark moods of exasperation as his flashy and unorthodox news techniques helped to send the Star circulation soaring. . . .

. . . if the Star staff was having a "whale of a lot of fun" under Walters, the Tribune staff didn't exactly share in the merriment. As Walters' "loop-the-loop" style of front page makeup continued to attract readers with its flamboyant headlines and brash juggling of type, Tribune editors became increasingly contemptuous of the competition.

Then Walters goofed. The mistake—one of judgment that was out of character for Walters—occurred in May 1939, and was a shot of much-needed joy for the *Star*'s competitors. The error also caused deep embarrassment for Walters and, for one of the rare times in his life, Walters's bouncy enthusiasm was momentarily absent the morning after the debacle.

England's King George VI and his wife, Queen Elizabeth, were going to tour Canada. When Walters learned about the tour, he conceived the idea of an "International Good Neighbor" demonstration in Winnipeg, Manitoba, Canada. Backed by the *Star*'s management, Walters explained the affair would emphasize to the world the harmonious relationship between Canada and the United States. *Winnipeg Free Press* executives worked with Walters, and provincial officials toured Minneapolis and surrounding areas.

The event's highlight was scheduled for May 24, 1939, when the King and Queen were to arrive in Winnipeg. Governors from seven surrounding states took the first—and last—"Good Neighbor" train to the Canadian city. Some 15,000 Americans from nearby towns poured into Winnipeg. It appeared the *Star* had pulled off a tremendous promotion success. The paper figured the crowning glory would come when Minnesota Governor Harold Stassen shook King George's hand.

Stassen addressed about 400 people the night before in Winnipeg, stressing friendship and cooperation. On the morning of the twenty-fourth he appeared before 135 members of the Winnipeg Board of Trade at a goodwill breakfast. The breakfast concluded, Stassen was ready for the big international moment.

The *Star* thought it was ready, too. Wanting to get the handshake story and picture in an early edition that day, Walters and others decided to write the story in advance. No problem—so long as the event went as planned. Getting a picture for the early edition was another matter—and here Walters brushed aside ethics for one of the few times in his life. After acquiring a picture of Stassen shaking hands a few days before the event, the *Star* went to its files for a photo of King George shaking hands. The *Star* then merged the two photos for an "historic" handshake picture. Once the actual handshake took place, an honest photo would be inserted in later editions. No one worried about something going wrong. After all, hadn't the State Department processed the whole event in advance?

Walters went to Winnipeg along with Cedric Adams, chief photographer Wayne Bell, a second photographer, and reporter Ben Holstrom. Holstrom's first story, of course, had been written in advance—in typical Stuffy Walters style. The headline over the story read: **"Governor, King Shake Hands at Winnipeg."** The story began,

> WINNIPEG—A governor and a king shook hands to-day.
> The governor was Harold E. Stassen of Minnesota.
> The king was George VI of England.
> The quick, warm gesture was symbolic of everything that has happened here in the past two days . . .

Unfortunately, that's not what occurred in Manitoba's Parliament building. The June 5, 1939, edition of *Time* magazine, reported that what took place was ". . . a newspaperman's nightmare—the awful thing that sometimes happens to newspapers that jump the gun."

As Stassen and his wife moved forward in the handshaking line, a guard asked them to step aside. Stassen produced a card, showing he was in his rightful place, but the guard simply sent the card to Manitoba Premier John Bracken, next to the King and Queen.

Murphy's Law struck. Before the card reached the Premier, an aide took it, glanced at it, laid it aside. The presentation ceremony ended shortly—minus the quick, warm gesture reported in the *Star*'s first edition.

Walters frantically called managing editor Dave Silverman and broke the horrible news. The next edition's new headline read: **"Governor Has Place of Honor Near King,"** and the story began:

> WINNIPEG—A governor and a king sat side by side today.
> The governor was Harold E. Stassen of Minnesota.

The king was George VI of England.
The gesture was symbolic . . .

Angelo Cohn remembers "all hell broke loose" when the international handshake didn't take place. "Wayne Bell called, and I happened to get the call. He said, 'Jesus Christ, something went wrong! We never got the çhance to take the picture for real.' "

Walters came into the office the next day with his chin not far above his pear-shaped belly. And the razzing began. But aside from being unusually quiet, he showed little emotion, Cohn remembers. "He didn't blame anybody. He said, 'We blew it.' We carried a retraction and apologies. And Stuffy said, 'I suppose that's one of the risks of this business, and it can happen to anybody. It should teach us all to be just that more careful.' "

The *Tribune*'s newsroom oozed with happiness as this headline was prepared: **"Mixup Keeps Stassen From Royal Reception."**

The Stassen goof was part of a double punch that struck the *Star* that day. In a six-column headline, the *Star* reported that all aboard were safe after the U.S. submarine *Squalus* sank. The *Tribune* correctly reported that twenty-seven were feared dead.

The *Tribune* produced a public relations brochure that ridiculed the *Star*'s flamboyant treatment of the news, using the two big bloopers as examples. "If this is the new streamlined editorial technique, we'll stick to the old," the *Tribune* sniffed. But by then the *Star*'s exciting look had scored heavily and the paper's reputation for being dependable and responsible was solid.

While there was momentary joy at the *Tribune,* there was none at the *Journal,* whose death was imminent. Three months after the *Star*'s Stassen goof, the *Journal* succumbed, selling out to Cowles in August 1939. Walters became editor of the *Minneapolis Star-Journal*—and a week later faced new afternoon competition when the *Tribune* launched the *Times-Tribune.* The three-way war Walters walked into in 1935 was now a head-to-head affair: Cowles versus the heirs of William J. Murphy at the *Tribune.*

Walters scored a victory in the spiring of 1940. As the *Star-Journal,* now the circulation front-runner, and the *Tribune* put together their Sunday, May fifth, editions on Saturday night, AP moved a story of major significance out of New York. Only Walters, however, recognized the story's importance.

Over at the *Tribune,* the city desk took charge of the story when it was discovered a local man was involved. An assistant city editor summoned Arthur Naftalin, a young reporter, handed him the AP story, and told him to localize it. There was ho-hum in the air as Naftalin called the local man, Professor Alfred O. C. Nier, and asked if he could come out to his house. He could.

Naftalin remembers the visit:

We talked rather casually about the project he was involved in, something to do with nuclear energy. Complex stuff. Nier gave no hint about how important it was. It was all so new.

I came back to the office and wrote a story. The *Tribune* ran the story routinely in the lower left-hand corner of page one. Nobody got excited about it.

Over at the *Star-Journal,* however, Walters was excited, sensing he had a big story with important local connections. Others around the copy desk weren't very impressed, but Walters charged ahead. He ordered a two-line banner headline using type almost an inch in size. The headline read: **"U. of M. Man's Discovery Opens Vast Power Source."**

More than half of page one was filled by two stories and a picture of Nier. The crux of the stories: a new chemical substance promised to revolutionize all methods of power production and to usher in atomic power.

The Associated Press wrote:

> The substance U-235 has been known for some time, but its power potentialities were first suspected within the last three months, since a minute fraction of a gram was isolated in February at the University of Minnesota physics department, under the direction of Prof. Alfred O. Nier.

The *Star-Journal*'s local story began:

> A University of Minnesota physicist has found a way to release in harness the terrific energy of the atom.
>
> He is 27-year-old Prof. Alfred O. C. Nier, specialist in research using the atom smasher.
>
> Of such terrific importance is his discovery that the soberly factual scientific journal, The Physical Review, says in the article in which the discovery is announced:
>
> "Thus the process would be the nearest practical approach to a form of perpetual motion." [Paragraph set in all caps.]

Oddly, while the *Tribune* was able to reach Nier, the *Star-Journal,* for some reason or other, was not. The *Star-Journal* turned to a Nier colleague, Dr. J. H. Williams, who explained Nier had found that "only the isotope 235 has the characteristics of combining with water to produce terrific energy."

Had Walters been tipped? Frosty Jenstad, for one, thinks so. If he was, Walters probably learned that Nier was from St. Paul, had graduated from the University of Minnesota and completed a post-doctoral fellowship at Harvard from 1936 to 1938. While there he developed a type of mass spectrometer—an atom weigher—which lent itself to accurately measuring uranium. In the fall of 1938, he returned to the University of Minnesota to join the faculty and continue his research.

Early in 1939, nuclear fission of uranium by slow neutrons was discovered in Germany. Physicists took great interest because it meant that if a chain reaction involving uranium could be started, huge amounts of energy would be released. An atom bomb might be possible—a matter of much interest and no little fear as war clouds gathered over Europe.

When the American Physical Society met in Washington in April 1939, uranium fission received much attention. Nier was introduced at the meeting to Enrico Fermi, who would become one of the most famous physicists of all time. Fermi and a Columbia University col-league, Professor John Dunning, felt it was important to definitely determine which kind of uranium atom—U-235 or U-238—was re-sponsible for the fission property of uranium. They felt Nier's mass spectrometer, developed for measuring the relative masses of isotopes, could separate large enough amounts to see which would give fission particles if bombarded with slow neutrons.

Nier, Fermi, Dunning, and a few others discussed a possible joint experiment. They agreed that Nier should try to separate small amounts of U-235 and U-238 on separate targets which would be shipped to Columbia University to be bombarded by neutrons from the Columbia University cyclotron.

But Nier had "many other irons in the fire, and I did not seri-ously tackle the problem until the fall of 1939." A letter from Fermi in October, urging him to proceed with the experiment, was the catalyst.

In February 1940, Nier perfected a new instrument that made the separations possible and, on Friday, February 29, he mailed the tiny samples to Dunning. The Columbia group went to work immediately after receiving the samples on Saturday. Early Sunday morning Nier received a call. The target on which his instrument had deposited U-235 gave off fission products when bombarded with slow neutrons. Fermi wrote in his October letter to Nier that he was convinced that using the mass spectrograph was the best way to decide whether the slow neutron fission is or is not due to the U-235 isotope. Fermi was correct. And it was now known that if U-235 was to be used in practical ways, nuclear plants would need to be built to enrich the substance. One result was the large separation plants in Oak Ridge, Tennessee, to accomplish enrichment.

Some scientists said later they knew U-235 was the key agent. But Fermi, who understood the field better than almost anyone, wasn't sure. His letter to Nier indicated that. Nier, in fact, had scored a major scientific success—and Walters had followed with a journalistic success.

Naftalin eventually gave up journalism for politics, becoming a Hubert Humphrey protégé and serving four terms as Minneapolis mayor, from 1961 to 1969. But he still remembers that Saturday night-Sunday morning in 1940:

We hung around waiting for the *Star-Journal*'s final Sunday edition, which came out around 2 a.m. But it didn't arrive. So I went home. The next morning, when I saw the *Star-Journal* at home, I thought, "Why didn't somebody tell me how important this was?" Some of our people said the *Star-Journal* was just being sensationalist, but that wasn't true.

There were doubts at the *Star-Journal,* too, Jenstad recalled. "It wasn't until later that we realized Stuffy was right. The story was a biggie and, of course, it had much bearing on the war that was getting underway." Jenstad told of a coincidence that occurred years later:

Some of us were reminiscing in the city room one afternoon, and I decided to haul out the bound volume that had the isotope 235 story. We had barely opened the bound volume when Stuffy popped into the newsroom. The timing was really something. He had been in Chicago many years, but was in town for something. We all got a big laugh when he saw what we were talking about.

What Jenstad, Walters, and the others saw that day was a front page that represented some of Walters's thinking about typography. Below the big banner headline was a three-line drop head over the two left-hand columns. Below that headline, in smaller type, was another three-line, two-column drop head. The story ran two columns wide down the left side of the page.

To the immediate right of that story was the Associated Press dispatch out of New York. The type was set in "bastard" measure to run four columns across the remainder of the page. The four-column headline, in half-inch italic type, bumped up against the main drop head for the local story. The four-column italic headline read: **"Pound of New Substance Reported to Carry Explosive Strength of 15,000 Tons of TNT."** Over that headline was an all-cap kicker, set in Roman type, which read: **"REVOLUTION IN POWER?"**

Throughout both stories, some paragraphs were set in boldface, others in italic. And star dashes—three tiny stars in a row—appeared between every three or four paragraphs. Some paragraphs were set in caps. Other paragraphs were indented so that an extra margin of white space lined each side of the column. Indeed, the entire page was laid out with white space in mind. Some modern-day editors would say the page lacked simplicity and cleanliness. They would say the page was hard to read. But they would probably admit that the page was put together with thought and purpose.

The complex hard news of the important U-235 stories was offset by two soft elements at the bottom of the page. One was a story reporting that the owner of the Kentucky Derby winner formerly lived in the Minneapolis area. The second element was Cedric Adams's column, "In This Corner." Set two columns wide, it ran down the right-hand side of the page, offsetting the main U-235 story. Cedric Adams was his usual cornpone self that day. Among the six items in his column was this one:

> Down in beautiful Lake City, the Tennant & Hoyt Company manufactures flour. Adjacent to their flour mill is a modern, air-conditioned office. But every year at this season, the front door is locked and callers are instructed to use the entrance at the rear. And here's the reason: Annually a robin builds her little nest on one of the ledges near the front door and Mr. Hoyt immediately orders the door closed to remain closed till the bird's family has been raised. Industry has a heart—in Lake City, anyway.

The readers loved it. Walters couldn't get enough of it.

To some readers, perhaps, Adams's item about a robin bringing life into the world was not news. Particularly compared to the U-235 story or the world war that would soon monopolize front pages. But Walters saw "news creativity" in that mother robin—and on one occasion, when "Mrs. Robin" had twins, Walters trumpeted the birth in an eight-column headline across the top of page one: **Mrs. Robin Has Twins.** Four photos helped capture the event. The page was often re-produced later in discussions about loop-the-loop makeup.

Walters never stopped listening to what the common man around him was saying. Says Angelo Cohn:

I saw any number of times when a copyboy would tear off stories from a wire machine and throw a batch of copy on the desk—undifferentiated stuff—and the kid might say, "Gee, there's a good story in there. This fancy race horse broke its leg." The copyboy's opinion meant more to Stuffy, for instance, than if John Thompson, the publisher, had come out and said, "How's General Motors stock doing?"

Walters knew the condition of General Motors stock was important—sure—but he also knew that it would run far behind Sister Kenny. He knew, too, that if the *Star-Journal* didn't do something on her behalf, she and a great service would be lost to Minneapolis. Having struggled for thirty years to receive recognition of her treatment of infantile paralysis in Minneapolis, Sister Elizabeth Kenny, a former Australian bush nurse, found that her passport was expiring in 1941. Walters made Sister Kenny's woes widely known and, in the course of helping her win passport renewal, played a big part in the construction of the Elizabeth Kenny Polio Institute in Minneapolis.

The March 22, 1943, issue of *Newsweek* reported, ". . . Walters won thousands of new readers and nationwide acclaim by publicizing Sister Elizabeth Kenny's infantile paralysis program in time to save her expiring passport."

Said Sister Kenny, at the institute's dedication, "I have found true people in Minneapolis to whom I can pass on my work for crip-pled children."

While Walters was helping Sister Kenny win her battle, America was edging toward one of its own. The "flow of life" that Angelo Cohn talked about earlier took an ugly turn on Sunday, December 7, 1941, when Japan launched its surprise bombing attack on Pearl Harbor. Monday's front page couldn't accommodate Mrs. Robin. It could only reflect the somber, straight, serious tone of an event that would leave an indelible mark on American history.

Because the *Star-Journal* was an afternoon paper, the news department was shut down on Sunday. Once the attack was an-nounced, though, Walters began bringing in the troops. They pre-pared a front page that was almost entirely devoted to the bombing, leading off with a seventy-two point all-caps banner headline, "U.S.

DECLARES WAR ON JAPAN." A sixty-point type headline, preceded by four sets of six stars each, read: "**3,000 Killed or Injured in Attack on Hawaii, 2 American Warships Sunk.**"

The *Star-Journal*'s treatment of Pearl Harbor had a flair to it, yet preserved a tone of seriousness. Walters was saying, no matter how somber events might be, they did not have to be told in dull, flat fashion—only with responsibility and honesty.

The additional oomph given the Pearl Harbor story shouldn't have surprised anyone. Two years earlier, also in December, the still-new *Star-Journal* rejoiced when the British Navy scuttled the German battleship *Graf Spee* in the harbor at Montevideo. The *Graf Spee* had been enjoying a "sea day" with the British, knocking out vessel after vessel. Finally three smaller and outgunned British ships trapped her. The victory at Montevideo was England's first. When Winston Churchill, who headed the British navy, heard the news, he danced a jig. Stuffy Walters would have danced with him, judging from the strong play he gave the British victory.

George Crim headed the *Star-Journal*'s promotion department in those days. He referred to Walters's techniques as "Stuffy's Roman Candle and Fireworks School of Journalism." Crim's job was to "try to match Stuffy's relentless ebullience in the *Star* with its sound version: in as many as five radio shows a day over the top three radio stations in the Twin Cities. We did a daily newsarama show (Kevin McCarthy, with the circulation department, was one of the actors)."

Walters's "school" had the *Tribune* hating the *Star,* Crim remembered. "When we bought them—never mind all other mush-mouth words about it, for that's what we did—and some of their staff came over to live and work with us, it was like inviting the Hatfields and McCoys to the same lunch table."

That might be stretching things, but it's close. T. J. Dillon, the *Tribune*'s managing editor then, described Walters as "one of the hardest and at the same time swellest competitors a newspaperman ever had." In a picture of the two men that appeared in the *Bulletin of the American Society of Newspaper Editors*, the caption read: "Until the papers go to press, they both make it plain, 'We'd like to cut out each other's gizzard.'"

The *Tribune* sale took place in May 1941. Crim recalled weekly promotion meetings that soon occurred:

with Stuffy excitedly telling what was coming so I could yell about it all with the actors and actresses on the radio. Some of the *Tribune* people sat around the conference table in glazed disbelief. And every week, we gleefully toted up the gain in circulation. To many of the old *Tribune* crew, at least for a time, it was like somebody setting off a stink bomb in the Union League Club.

Bradley Morison was a *Tribune* editorial page staffer. He recalls in his *Sunlight on Your Doorstep*:

> I was sitting at my typewriter in the Tribune's editorial offices when the news of the merger came.
> Shortly afterwards, Basil L. "Stuffy" Walters, the Star's executive editor, loomed in the doorway.
> "I wonder if I could have your editorial page proofs," he asked politely. "We're planning to publish tomorrow's Tribune in our Star-Journal plant."

Morison writes that the Tribune staffers' curiosity was centered sharply "on the Star-Journal's dynamic, hard-driving, bustling, imaginative executive editor . . . with (his) solid bulk of a linotype machine and the enthusiasm of a Little Leaguer."

Walters was not particularly happy with the *Star-Journal* copy desk, and thus one of his first moves after the acquisition was in that direction. "I want the entire *Tribune* copy desk," he said when personnel was discussed.

Walters, meanwhile, fought America's enemies the same way he fought his newspaper competition—all out. His dedication, cheerleading, and patriotism, wrapped in his army ambulance experiences of World War I, were illustrated in *Star-Journal* and *Tribune* pages. The papers pushed scrap metal drives in the autumn of 1942. A nationwide contest was underway then. Walters took to the airwaves to say that "the editors of the nation are vitally interested in the success of the Minneapolis campaign for scrap metal collection. They know we will be right up front when the poundage is tabulated."

Walters also played a role when a special financing program was created by American newsmen and the Treasury Department on a $13 billion second war loan drive. Active in that effort to raise war funds was John S. Knight, then vice-president of the American Society of Newspaper Editors. Knight would later team with Walters in a long, successful venture at the *Chicago Daily News*.

In 1943, Walters represented both the American Society of Newspaper Editors (he was the group's secretary) and the Associated Press Managing Editors' Association (he was that group's chairman for the second straight year) in a six-week tour of the United Kingdom. Some fifty editors had been invited by the British government. Much of the visit focused on the air war being carried out against Germany by American and British pilots.

Walters did some of his best writing and reporting from London. The Sunday, August 8, 1943, *Tribune* carried a long dispatch which began:

> A continuous series of catastrophies to German cities caused by a rain of death and destruction from Allied planes is opening the battle of Germany.
>
> Destined as it is to be one of the crucial battles of all time, it may not be a short battle. It will be a battle which brings into play everything science and propaganda and politics can devise.
>
> The success of the battle of Hamburg is increasing the stature of air war enthusiasts. These men are becoming more convincing in their claims that this is a bombers' war, just as the one before was a trench and tank and machinegun war.
>
> Frankly, as you stand around the airfields in England you become convinced you are in a revolution in warfare as decisive as that which saw a switch from crossbows to gunpowder.
>
> The crossbow boys couldn't believe it then, and only the bomber boys believe it now. But how they believe it.

Walters practiced what he preached—the "local angle." In "Brief Notes from Britain" he wrote:

> Corporal Bernard Duff, who worked for Snyder's at Duluth and whose mother lives near Mankato, is cook for the post famous for food as well as Thunderbolt fighters.

And:

> Harry Pihl, 672 Ivy Avenue, St. Paul, who has three brothers in Minneapolis, is happily married to an English girl. He and his pals were lost in a blackout. They asked three sisters the way to the station and thus started a romance.

And:

> Technical Sergeant George Latourell of Madelia is the crew chief of the Thunderbolt which holds the record of being in the air more hours than any other.

His plane is named Sweet Pea and the insignia shows
the Popeye character in a baby carriage bristling
with guns.

Another dispatch reads, in part:

U.S. Soldiers Behave Well
in England, Walters Finds

This is a special report to wives and sweethearts
of boys stationed in England.

Your men folks are behaving pretty well. The
fact is I think they're doing better than their dads did
in 1917.

English girls are attractive, and many of them
are not adverse to serving as a cure for homesick-
ness.

But in general, the boys are mostly interested in
the girls back home and in winning the war at the
earliest possible time so they can get back to
them. . . .

My advice, girls, is that a letter a day will keep
the vamps away.

By the time Walters returned from England, his national stature
was immense. Only five months before making that tirp, the March
22, 1943, edition of *Newsweek* devoted most of its media department
to Walters in a story headlined: "Unstuffy Stuffy."

The story described Walters as "a managing editor's managing
editor" who has "influenced the contents and style of newspapers far
beyond his bailiwick. . . . Walters is virtual arbiter of what Minneapolis' 487,000 citizens read in their papers."

Outside of journalism, too, Walters's recognition grew. The prestigious Indiana Society of Chicago, which restricts membership to
Hoosiers who have gained prominence and distinction in a particular
field (or two), had approved him for membership in September 1940.

Despite professional and non-journalistic honors, praise, and
recognition, despite all he had accomplished under and for the Cowles
family, despite the security he had for his family in Minneapolis—
Walters would leave the community. In style.

On May 3, 1944, Mayor Marvin Kline proclaimed "Be Kind to
Stuffy Week."

Advice from J. Edgar Hoover

Basil Walters fought a lot of wars in his Minneapolis days. One battlefield was Minnesota's highways, where people were slaughtering each other. Walters launched a peace offense on September 1, 1940— but only after talking with FBI Director J. Edgar Hoover.

After being in Minneapolis permanently for three years, Walters saw how the gangster element there operated. A "gangster alley" was evident, running from Texas, through Arkansas, Missouri, and Iowa to St. Paul, where the police chief provided a sanctuary—providing the outlaws behaved.

Walters went to Washington to ask Hoover for advice. A surprised Walters was told that a good start would be to support the excellent citizens traffic safety movement sponsored by the Minneapolis Automobile Club. Hoover felt it would be relatively easy to get people interested in working together for civic improvement through traffic safety. From that small beginning, a healthier interest in all civic affairs would develop.

"This seemed like a rather sissy approach, but I decided to give it a whirl," Walters recalled years later. "After a few months I learned there's really a science to this highway safety business."

He learned it, along with other editors, at a traffic safety course in Duluth, where the Three E's were emphasized: Education, Engineering, and Enforcement. When the editors returned home, they found that local safety councils already had educational machinery in place. Walters figured that all the local communities needed was good reporting of the mounting auto deaths and destruction, plus "a little sound and informed editorial support."

He found Minnesota "was blessed with a fine and far-seeing highway engineering department. What these public officials needed most was a medium to get their information across to the public so it could become a part of the debate through which a sound public opinion is formed.

"Only in this way could the public be certain that public monies were spent wisely instead of being wasted on political boondoggles. And so the second E—engineering—was found. . . ."

Finding the third E—enforcement—was harder. Walters and the other editors learned that, with a few notable exceptions, "the law enforcement officials of Minnesota—sheriffs, police chiefs, patrolmen, prosecutors, judges—were living in the horse and buggy age mentally and were determined, by god, not to modernize."

That's when Walters found Franklin K. Kreml. A young police official in Evanston, Illinois, Kreml was gaining recognition by reducing traffic deaths there.

Walters summoned him for consultation. At the same time, police, prosecutors, and government officials began realizing they had community support for enforcing traffic laws. Hoover's advice was paying off—and eventually, the Twin Cities would lose their reputation of being great gangster hangouts.

While Frank Berry of the Minneapolis Automobile Club was pulling almost every significant organization together to participate in the traffic safety council, Kreml was doing his thing in enforcement.

"He was just the proper mixture of diplomat and tough guy," Walters said. "It would be an overstatement to say he cleared away all the roadblocks. But he did get a number of rails off the fence and paved the way for constant improvement."

Minneapolis's program was a lead other communities could not ignore. Minnesota's "Save 100 Lives" campaign, aimed at reducing fatalities by that number in one year, began on September 1, 1940. The results were impressive. A hundred was not reached the first year, but after twenty-eight months, fatalities were reduced by 202. Thousands of Minnesotans were more educated in the principles of safe driving. Walters led the effort that first year.

Fifteen years later Walters spoke at a Traffic Safety Clinic for Newspapermen in Evanston, sponsored by the Inland Daily Press Association, the Medill School of Journalism at Northwestern University, and the Traffic Institute, also at Northwestern. "This whole highway safety program . . . got a setback during the war,'' he said, adding:

The high regard for human life and suffering got an awful setback. Somehow we just seemed to take for granted that there is going to be a frightful slaughter on our streets and highways. Our sense of values has become dulled.

Somehow we don't seem to realize that a guy is just as dead if he is killed by a gun or by polio, cancer or heart disease. Yet we all know that families suffer the same grief and hardship.

Walters, now the executive editor of Knight Newspapers, based in Chicago, told the editors:

instead of dictating public opinion, our job is to serve as a gadfly stinging into action the public conscience and in creating and reporting debate.

As a result of my experience years ago in Minnesota, may I be so bold as to recommend that on your return home you seek out those folks who are already interested in highway safety and that you tell them you want to cooperate with them in making your community the safest one in the state? Share with them and with your public officials the things you have learned here.

They did. A similar program was launched in Illinois in 1958 after Walters helped found the Illinois Editor and Publisher Highway Traffic Safety Seminar in Peoria on January 10, 1958. The seminar became an annual event, moving to different cities each year.

After retiring to his Indiana farm, Walters spoke to editors and reporters at a Hoosier State Press Association meeting in Indianapolis and called for a traffic safety program. Editors gave his speech and ideas wide support, but a program never got off the ground.

CHAPTER NINE

Hooking up with Knight

H E had achieved a brilliant journalistic triumph with the Cowleses. He had taken a sad third-place newspaper and not only toppled the leaders, but gobbled them up. He had introduced new ideas which received national recognition—ideas that some editors initially scorned and eventually adopted. He had become prominent in prominent organizations, holding high offices in the Associated Press Managing Editors association and the American Society of Newspaper Editors. He had, in short, become a leading figure in American journalism by 1944.

But Basil Walters, now forty-eight years old, had no thoughts about slowing down. In fact, he was beginning to feel restless. As executive editor of all the Minneapolis newspapers, he was required to concentrate more on management duties, meaning less time in the newsroom where he was happiest and at his best.

Thus, when John S. Knight offered Walters an opportunity to become more active in the newsroom—at a considerably larger salary than what the Cowleses were paying him—Walters happily accepted.

Some Minneapolis oldtimers say that it wasn't just Knight or more money that caused Walters to move on. They say Walters's ultimate authority as editor eroded after Gideon Seymour joined the *Star* as chief editorial writer. They say that Seymour—serious, straight-forward, highly intellectual—was winning John Cowles's favor.

George L. Peterson, who worked closely with Seymour on the *Star* editorial pages, agreed with others that a rivalry had developed between Seymour and Walters. "Looking back on those days, I feel Seymour had the inside track with John, despite Stuffy's fine service," Peterson said.

Peterson is correct. John Cowles confirmed it:

Stuffy was ambitious and could not get used to the idea of having anyone other than myself have authority over him. I thought Gideon Seymour was far better qualified than Stuffy to have charge of the *Star*'s editorial pages. Stuffy was far superior in circulation promotion. He had a flair for it, but Gid had superior overall judgment. There was ill feeling between Gid and Stuffy. I think Stuffy simply sensed that Gid was going to eventually take over the editorial page job.

Walters was not forced to leave Minneapolis. This is clear, although some oldtimers don't agree. An exception is Peterson, who said he was "quite certain that Stuffy was not invited to leave Minneapolis." Cowles, again, confirmed that view: "I think Stuffy would have stayed in Minneapolis if I had offered to make him the editor with full authority, but I did not want to do that as I thought so highly of Gid. But Stuffy was not forced to leave. I would have liked to have kept him."

Rhea Walters also said her husband could have stayed in Minneapolis, "but Mr. Knight's offer was too good; the salary was much greater than what the Cowleses were paying Stuffy."

Publicly, at least, Walters certainly left Minneapolis without any bitterness. Privately, he might have felt the Cowleses treated him a bit shabbily and didn't pay him enough, considering all that he had achieved. But Walters practiced what he preached to young reporters and editors: "You can't fire the publisher."

Rather than burn his Minnesota bridges, Walters expressed loyalty toward the Cowleses. He displayed it after a big staff dinner that was arranged as a send-off for him and official designation of Seymour as the new executive editor.

After a fine meal at the Covered Wagon, a popular restaurant on Fourth Street where journalists often congregated, people began drifting their separate ways. Most of them drifted toward Seymour, Angelo Cohn recalled, although the emphasis on the occasion was supposed to be Walters's farewell.

Walters, who did not like to drive, had been taken to the affair by sports editor Charlie Johnson, who helped organize the dinner. Now, the festivities complete, Walters wanted to go home. Johnson wanted to remain. The sports editor knew Cohn and Walters lived in the same neighborhood. Could Angelo give Walters a lift? Angelo could.

"That was the last time we were really together before he actually left Minneapolis," Cohn recalled, adding:

He said two things that I remember well. One, he was very curious to see what kind of people he would have to work with in the Knight group, because it was very large, and the first thing he always did was to see what his staff consisted of.

And then, about the last thing he said to me, which I thought was most impressive—when we really said good night—was: "Well, so far, how do you like Cowleses' jounalism?" In other words, it wasn't Walters's journalism. He was working for John Cowles. Hell, it wasn't any Cowleses' journalism. It was strictly Stuffy's stamp on the papers. But his sense of loyalty was such that, to the last minute, he said, "How do you like Cowleses' journalism? It's fun, isn't it?"

Walters's departure caused concern among some Minneapolis executives. They worried about staff depletion, recalled Paul Swensson, who worked on the *Tribune*'s copy desk and later became managing editor. World War II had cut deeply into the quality of news people. Walters, however, promised not to hire Minneapolis's best people, and he kept that promise, as Swensson learned obliquely.

"I left the Minneapolis newspapers in the summer of 1944 for the *San Francisco News,* a Scripps-Howard paper," Swensson said.

Several months later, I heard from Stuffy, but not in the genial voice of many years of close association. He dressed me out severely for not letting him know that "I was available." I was offered successive appointments as Sunday editor of the *Detroit Free Press* to be followed as understudy to Ev Norlander, managing editor of the *Chicago Daily News.*

Walters had moved to Chicago, via Detroit, after developing a close friendship with Knight—a friendship that was cemented in London in 1943.

Knight, whose father made the *Akron Beacon Journal* successful before his death in 1933, had bought the *Miami Herald* on October 15, 1937, from Colonel Frank B. Shutts. A vigorous, intelligent man who was then eleven days short of his forty-third birthday, Knight liked challenges. He saw one in the *Herald,* which he felt did not equal the *Beacon Journal*'s quality but had strong potential.

The potential was there, all right. By 1943, Knight and his brother, James, made the *Herald* a winner. Along the way, in 1940, they had added the *Detroit Free Press* to their organization.

John Knight's next challenge was issued in the spring of 1943 by President Franklin D. Roosevelt. Accepting the recommendation of Byron D. Price, who headed the Office of Censorship, Roosevelt appointed Knight as Chief Liaison Officer in London. Knight worked closely with British censorship officials and scrutinized mail, cables, and related material which provided information connected with World War II.

Walters, with other journalists, would also go to London in 1943, as secretary of the American Society of Newspaper Editors and chairman of the Associated Press Managing Editors Association. Included in that entourage were such outstanding editors as the *Atlanta Constitution*'s Ralph McGill and chief officials representing the Associated Press and United Press. They were invited, in part, to plan press facilities for the coverage of the Allies expected invasion of France.

On a muggy day in 1974, Walters chewed a cigar inside the screened porch of his Frankfort home and talked about that London trip. It was another rare occasion when he chose to devote more than five minutes to yesterday. "Knight and I spent our evenings visiting London newspapers, studying the four- and six-page newspapers," he began. "The London editors were doing a tremendous job of covering the news in a very limited amount of space. They did great things with very few words."

The London editors knew about Walters. They had seen what he and George Gallup accomplished in Des Moines. Cecil King of the *Daily Mirror* had visited Des Moines and returned home to begin applying what he learned. Arthur Christiansen, Lord Beaverbrook's great editor, subscribed to the Des Moines and Minneapolis papers.

Walters and Knight spent time with King, Christiansen, and others, discussing ideas for revitalizing the *Chicago Daily News*. Never mind that Walters was still thoroughly employed by the Cowleses, and Knight's ownership of the *Daily News* was merely a dream.

As Knight's dream got stronger, he decided to see if he could make it come true. Before Walters left London, Knight asked him if he would join the *Daily News* if Colonel Frank Knox would sell out to Knight Newspapers. Walters, who had unsuccessfully tried to persuade the Cowleses to buy the *Daily News,* said yes. He was anxious to apply the Gallup formula again.

Knight's interest in the *Daily News* grew after a group of Chicago businessmen

. . . persuaded me to consider the purchase. . . . They were interested in preserving the newspaper's traditions as originally practiced by the late Victor Lawson. When Frank Knox died (in April 1944), I was approached by Smith Davis, a newspaper broker, and that led to my further conferences with Chicago civic leaders.

Knight's interest heightened to the point that he became involved in what he later described as a "mild bidding contest with a group of *Daily News* employees headed by Adlai Stevenson (later to be defeated twice for the presidency by General Dwight D. Eisenhower) and a number of other individuals who were interested in the purchase."

Despite not having the highest bid, Knight won the bidding war. The trustees of Knox's estate, following the colonel's wishes, chose Knight because they felt he would best preserve the paper's character and tradition. So on October 18, 1944, Knight possessed a fourth major newspaper, one which was slipping in circulation and required fresh ideas to save it from its deathbed. He had agreed to pay $2,151,537 in cash and assume an indebtedness of $12 million.

Before accepting his London war appointment, Knight had employed Professor Robert Gunning to apply his new readability test to his weekly "Editor's Notebook" column. Gunning earlier used his formula, based mainly on sentence count and three-syllable words, on various newspapers. In testing stories for comprehension and clarity, he found the *Wall Street Journal* to be the most readable newspaper in America. Next came the *Des Moines Register and Tribune* and the Minneapolis papers. Although not associated, Gunning and Gallup/Walters had much in common.

Gunning's test impressed Knight. Aware of the professor's newspaper rankings, he took greater interest in Minneapolis's Walters. In London, Knight found more to like about him. Before returning to America, he knew that in Walters he could hire "an outgoing individual with an insatiable curiosity about people and events . . . [an editor] with some distinct ideas about newspaper readability which I found most useful."

In 1977, at the age of eighty-three, Knight, when asked what he thought were Walters's greatest strengths as an editor, replied in a letter:

> His ability to discern what people liked to read, and the fact that he was a first-rate newsman and often directed the copy desk himself. He was not an "office-bound" editor, but circulated freely throughout the building, and he knew at all times what was transpiring in the community.
>
> He had a great news sense and was a shrewd and accurate judge of public opinion. He knew what he liked to read and he regarded himself as a typical reader, and not as a remote and unavailable editor.
>
> Stuffy was a warm and intelligent individual who was interested in everything that was transpiring about him—including the world. His personal involvement in the direction of the newsroom established a fine rapport with his

staff. He was a good judge of what people were talking about and what they thought about the events of the day.

I would say that his intense curiosity about men and events provided the genius with which he was able to produce highly interesting and readable newspapers.

Knight knew, or sensed, all of that in 1944—and he wanted Walters immediately, with or without the *Chicago Daily News*. Thus, once again, Walters did not actively seek a job; Knight asked him to join his small group. Although Knight was still negotiating for the *Daily News* with no assurance he would acquire it, Walters said yes.

Knight sent him to Detroit as executive editor of the *Free Press*. Walters took along his now-famous good-luck piece—a large chromo picture of a crouching lion—to hang behind his desk. It had been behind every one of his desks since joining the Cowleses sixteen years before in Des Moines. It didn't let him down.

Reporting Walters's change of jobs in its May 15, 1944, edition, *Newsweek* wrote, "Of late, Walters's jobs have entailed too much public relations and not enough newspapering, his only true love. 'Knight is the man I'm betting on . . . to get (me) back,' he said."

Knight was generous with Walters's salary. Basil and Rhea were able to rent a lovely home in the exclusive Grosse Pointe Farms area. They were forty-eight years old, with a daughter away at Pine Manor School in Boston and two growing boys at home.

One day Rhea returned home with the boys from Bloomfield Hills, where they had been playing football, and found a note from her husband. He'd gone to Chicago. Knight's dream was now reality.

For Basil Walters, it meant another session of "shuttle journalism." His newspaper medicine was needed on the *Daily News* immediately. So Walters began taking a 7 A.M. flight from Detroit. He gained an hour going west, arriving in Chicago at 7 A.M. He lived in Chicago for four days—Monday through Thursday—and doctored the *Free Press* the next three.

After nine months, Walters had played a major role in revitalizing the *Free Press*'s sickly Sunday edition. While watching streetcar riders skip the front page and turn directly inside to pages filled with offbeat, non-conventional subjects, Walters hatched a Sunday formula. He and others, particularly a sub-editor named Bill Coughlin, felt the key was to determine people's major interests and then make sure a newsy story or two appealing to those interests appeared each Sunday.

As the 1980s approached, a new crop of editors talked about producing newspapers that appealed to the interests of the "Me Generation." The editors pointed to research that showed people wanted newspapers to be useful, to help them cope with the increasing complexity of life, and to report the news in a succinct, meaningful fashion.

Walters and a few others in the mid-1940s already knew that— "Me Generation" or not. In Detroit, they built a Sunday formula that began with a classification termed "Survival," which covered a multitude of areas: (1) health (from curing typists' hangnails to dealing with high or low blood pressure), (2) earning a living (how to get and keep a job or the personality of the typical boss as seen by psychiatrists), (3) fire peril in autumn, (4) ice storms in winter, (5) dangerous swimming practices in summer, (6) home safety the year around, (7) how-to-reduce (enough stories which, if weighed together, would have probably outweighed any five members of the staff), and (8) sex (which proved to be the toughest assignment for a family newspaper).

Other major classifications included: (1) "Gregariousness" (where a fellow could conveniently gather with the gang), (2) "Mingle" (profiles of interesting neighbors and occupations), (3) "Supernatural" (everything from the most respectable forms of formal religion to any kind of speculation on the "fearful unknown"), (4) "A Day in the Life Of . . ." (which dealt with a priest, a policeman, a teacher, a telephone operator), and (5) "Hope" (stories of people whose pessimistic futures turned into bright tomorrows).

As the ten-month lease on the Grosse Pointe Farms house neared expiration, Walters decided to move permanently to Chicago. Basil and Rhea chose temporary residency in Evanston, north of Chicago, before settling for good in Kenilworth, another northern suburb. It would be the last career move and, like the others, one that would result in great accomplishments and rich rewards.

Joining Illustrious Company

When Walters went to the *Daily News* in 1944, he joined an illustrious company of men who had served as the paper's leaders.

The *Daily News* published its first edition December 23, 1875. It was a one-cent, four-page product produced in a windowless room on the fourth floor of a narrow building at 15 North Wells. Melville E. Stone, who had knocked about on various newspapers, was the founding publisher. He was determined not to answer to anyone and produce a newspaper free of bias in the briefest possible form. Stone eventually played the major role in establishing the Associated Press, a concept that grew out of his earlier idea to be the first newspaper with a worldwide network of correspondents.

Stone's *Daily News,* begun with a borrowed $5,000 from a British newspaperman, almost didn't make it even though circulation grew from nothing to 6,000. By July 24, 1876, it appeared the paper would die within a week if it didn't receive a financial transfusion.

Victor Fremont Lawson provided it. He and Stone were friends at Chicago High School. His father, Ivar, had acquired the building at 15 North Wells after migrating from Norway in 1837. A print shop, Anderson & (Victor) Lawson, operated in the basement, and printed, among other things, a daily Norwegian language newspaper called *Skandinäven.*

Ivar, who had prospered in Chicago real estate, died in 1872, leaving Victor the building. Three years later, high school chum Stone sought space. Less than eight months later, Lawson watched the *Daily News* gasp for breath. Friendship aside, he felt the infant publication should be saved. On August 1, 1876, he assumed the paper's debts—the type was still not paid for—and kept Stone as editor.

Lawson knew Stone possessed editorial brilliance. The two men made a deal. Stone, then twenty-seven years old, agreed to a salary of $25 a week and a third interest in future profits. Lawson became sole owner in 1888, remaining at the helm until 1925. By then, he had taken Stone's worldwide correspondents idea and developed it into the Daily News Foreign Service. And by then, he had become an outstanding editor himself.

When Lawson died, his heirs sought someone with his ideals, character, and integrity. They chose Walter A. Strong, Lawson's business manager, who made the purchase with the help of other investors. Strong served as publisher from 1925 to 1931, when Colonel Frank Knox came along. The publisher of a New Hampshire newspaper, Knox had risen from beat reporting to general manager of the Hearst chain along the way. His past was colorful: follower of Teddy Roosevelt up San Juan Hill, vice-presidential candidate in the disastrous 1936 Alf Landon campaign, Secretary of the Navy in World War II. Knox served as publisher until his death in April 1944.

Charles Dennis finished his editorship under Knox as publisher. He had joined the paper in 1882, going through the chairs of associate editor, chief editorial writer, and managing editor before succeeding Lawson as editor in 1925. He retired in 1934 to become editor emeritus. The editor's job was vacant for two years.

Paul Scott Mowrer became editor in 1936. He had achieved fame as a foreign correspondent, winning the Pulitzer Prize in 1928. He had hopped from war to war across Europe and Africa and written novels on the side.

Aside from these leaders, other men who achieved greatness worked in the *Daily News*'s ranks: Carl Sandburg, of Lincoln fame, wrote movie reviews and sometimes strummed his guitar, barefoot, in the city room; Ben Hecht, who punched out a local column that dug into Chicago's soul, when not writing brilliant plays and books; Robert J. Casey, considered by some people to be the greatest war correspondent in history; Eugene Field, the noted children's poet ("Wynken, Blynken and Nod"), who became the country's first daily columnist while on the *Daily News.*

In its first eighty-five years, the *Daily News* had only three editors, aside from the publishers who also held the title. Walters was the third. He would not be far from the last.

The Battle for Chicago

T HE competitive fight in Minneapolis in 1937 shaped up as a city-wide brawl when Basil Walters first arrived to direct the *Star,* a dying third, against two solidly entrenched foes. It was different in Chicago in 1944. Walters found a newspaper war zone of much greater depth and intensity.

Foremost among the competitors was Colonel Robert R. McCormick, a "press lord" who insisted he was always right and almost everyone else was wrong. His *Tribune,* which dubbed itself the "World's Greatest Newspaper," had long been the monarch of Chicago journalism. It far outdistanced the field in circulation, but it was losing ground while the others were making gains.

Richard Finnegan, described by contemporaries as a low-keyed man who surprised people with bursts of dynamic action, was quietly building his *Daily Times* in the afternoon field. It was the city's only tabloid. Over at the *Sun,* Marshall Field was receiving high marks as his paper grew, cutting into the *Tribune*'s morning lead.

And then there was Louis Ruppel. An ex-marine captain, Ruppel was executive editor of William Randolph Hearst's afternoon *Herald-American.* He arrived a few weeks after Knight and Walters assumed command at the *Daily News* and immediately let the troops know that a lot of marine remained in him. He told his people, "What I want around here is a lot of sock! And if I don't get it I'm going to shake you guys up!"

The Chicago newspaper scene was painted in the June 30, 1945, issue of *Collier* magazine. An article entitled "Battle in Printer's Ink," by Herbert Asbury, said, in part:

> Briefly, the editors and publishers of the Windy
> City are rarin' to go, but because of the newsprint

shortage, there is little they can do now except make occasional raids upon rival personnel and plan post-war projects, all of which seem aimed at putting the other fellow out of business. But once wartime restrictions are removed, things should begin to happen.

Almost every newspaperman in Chicago looks for an outbreak of the exciting journalism for which the city has always been famous. Specifically, they expect a circulation war which may bring nostalgic memories of the bloody battles of more than thirty years ago.

Walters and Knight found Chicago journalism circles bubbling with rumors. Field was going to merge his *Sun* with the *Times,* it was said. He eventually did. Another report said that Hearst, America's number one "press lord," was going to re-enter the morning field. He had earlier closed down his *Examiner.* Others insisted that The Colonel, the number two "press lord" in America, was studying the afternoon field.

McCormick had long fought with his foes, and he wasn't about to back down as World War II came to a close. Early in 1945, the *Tribune* had slipped below a million in circulation for the first time in years, deeply angering the Colonel. And, as Asbury reported, Field had stunned McCormick by stealing Milton Caniff from the Colonel's Tribune-New York News syndicate. Caniff had established himself as one of the country's best comic-strip artists, drawing "Terry and the Pirates," which was being sold to 220 papers at that time. Caniff, however, had to wait until October 1946 to join Field, because he didn't own "Terry"—the Tribune-News syndicate did. It meant he would have to create a new strip. He did. A native of Dayton, where the Wright brothers gave birth to aviation, Caniff came up with air force hero Steve Canyon, which went on to outdo "Terry."

Knight and Walters did not let the rumors, the jockeying for position, the theft of key personnel, and the overall atmosphere distract them from their mission. They were determined to revive the *Daily News* by creating a lively, heavily-local product that featured crisp writing. They wanted to abandon a stodgy, foreign service-dominated product that featured heavy intellectual writing.

That change in direction led to Paul S. Mowrer's resignation as editor three days after Knight took over. It meant the end of a long,

"Stuffy's" parents,
Frederick and Nancy
Walters.

Indiana University debate
team, 1916. Walters, *second
row, left;* Wendell Wilkie,
front row, fourth from left.

Walters, U.S. Army Am-
bulance Corps, World War I.

Editor Walters, speaking in Minneapolis. Earl Gammon, Minneapolis radio executive, and Rhea Walters listening attentively.

Friendly competitors: T. J. Dillon, managing editor, *Minneapolis Tribune* and Walters, *Minneapolis Star*.

Minneapolis Star newsroom, late 1930s. *Left:* Walters; *right:* Dave Silverman, managing editor.

Walters, *far right,* and top newspeople meet with President Harry S. Truman, 1945.

Walters, *center,* executive editor of the *Chicago Daily News;* Robert P. O'Banion, *left,* of *Corydon* (Ind.) *Democrat;* and Franklin D. Schurz, *right,* business manager of the *South Bend Tribune,* at the annual convention of the Hoosier State Press Association, 1951.

President Dwight D.
Eisenhower addresses April
1953 convention of the
American Society of Newspaper
Editors. ASNE President
Walters looks on.

Walters and John Knight,
1953.

Walters, 1970, addresses
"Editor's Day" meeting of the
Southern Short Course in Press
Photography, University of
North Carolina.

dedicated relationship with the *Daily News* that had spanned some forty years.

Mowrer said Knight's editing of the *Daily News* gave him a feeling of desecration. Asbury wrote in *Collier's,* "Most of the changes in which Mowrer objected were the brain children of Basil (Stuffy) Walters. . . . Walters is a newspaperman of the dynamic, high-powered school; he believes in flash, a generous use of blackface type, likes an abundance of short, striking human interest stories on page one."

Knight and Walters took the high road to avoid any kind of nastiness with McCormick, Ruppel, or others. When Colonel Knox owned the *Daily News,* the paper responded to McCormick's editorial attacks against it with a series of cartoons portraying McCormick as Colonel McCosmic, a pompous gung-ho, General George Patton-type. Knight ordered the cartoon caricature be dropped. He would win the circulation battle the way he had won others—with unbiased news and staking out the political middle ground between the New Deal-leaning *Times* and *Sun* and the arch-conservative *Tribune* and right-leaning *Herald-American.*

Inside the newsroom, Walters spread praise generously and established a "ping pong" process in which ideas were batted back and forth from Knight to Walters to key editors. Walters encouraged managing editor Everett Norlander, city editor Clem Lane, foreign editor Hal O'Flaherty, and news editor Ed Akers to bounce ideas off each other and himself.

Meanwhile, Walters had been putting together a confidential notebook of improvements he wanted to introduce one week at a time. He didn't want to do everything at once, "so as not to disturb the solid, though diminishing, core of loyal readers."

Even before arriving in Chicago he knew the paper's news philosophy had to change from an emphasis on foreign service dispatches to much more local news. He felt he was inheriting a good local staff. But he found many reporters were so busy writing books and lecturing, they didn't have enough time to always do a good job for the people who paid them. When he asked a reporter one day why he had not written a good story, the reporter said it was too good for the *Daily News* and that he was saving it for his book.

The foreign staff's dominance discouraged local initiative. One day shortly before Knight's purchase was official, Walters counted only three local stories in the paper. Ed Lahey, who became one of

America's great reporters, told Walters jokingly—but bitterly—that the only way to get a local story into the paper was to cable it to Paris and have it cabled back under a Paris dateline.

Less than a month after the purchase, Walters decided to unveil his little strategy notebook to Arthur E. Hall, the *Daily News'* circulation manager.

Hall, told to keep what he saw and heard in the room, bubbled over the planned reforms. He insisted they all be introduced immediately. The situation was so desperate, he argued, the paper couldn't wait for the week-by-week treatment. He revealed that the tabloid *Times* would pass the *Daily News* any day, leaving the *Daily News* fourth in a five-paper field. Said Hall, "The *Times* is cheering every funeral procession by saying, 'There goes another *Daily News* reader.'"

Hall was so convincing, Walters decided to go full throttle and emphasize the new *Daily News* by completely changing it typographically. Histories of the *Daily News* that appeared in the seventies described the changes with mixed views. In the June 1971 edition of the now-deceased *Chicago Journalism Review,* a story appeared entitled "Betraying the Past at the News." It said, in part, "It was under Knight that Executive Editor Basil (Stuffy) Walters reshaped the News, eliminating its gray image and giving it a spicier 'bobby-sox' look. But even in bobby-sox, the News was still wearing football shoes to tromp on people who were stealing or oppressing the public." In the March 4, 1978, issue of *Editor and Publisher,* a former Chicago newsman named Budd Gore wrote, in "A Brief History of the Chicago Daily News," that Walters, "to the horror of the oldtimers, 'jazzed up' the paper, made it typographically exciting, gained new readers steadily."

What Walters actually did was simple: he made the *Daily News* more readable. He went from an all upper case Gothic typeface to headlines with caps and lower case. As in Minneapolis, he pumped in more white space, in part by fluctuating type styles in the same story. Asterisks were used to separate paragraphs in key parts of a story. (Once, when someone in Minneapolis who had lost track of Walters asked about him, the other person replied, "He's growing asterisks on a farm in Chicago.")

After Walters retired and became the first appointment to a new journalism chair at Syracuse University in 1972, he described the typographical changes in his second seminar before students and faculty members:

> The type and makeup we used were adaptations of those developed at Des Moines and Minneapolis after the Gallup survey and further refined during the planning Knight and I did at the *Detroit Free Press* during the summer preceding the purchase of the *News.* We had even printed a mockup, under the pretense we were planning it for the *Free Press,* and so we had a pattern ready for use by staff members. The resulting product won the *Daily News* the Inland Daily Press award year after year.

The initial changes in the *Daily News* weren't all cosmetic. Walters knew that content and clarity would have to change quickly, too.

Budd Gore, in his sparse *Editor and Publisher* history of the *Daily News,* wrote, "The quality of writing may have suffered, but business improved [after Knight and Walters assumed command]."

Indeed, from an intellectual standpoint, the writing quality may have suffered. But from a newspaper standpoint, where the average reading level was far below that of a high school graduate, the writing improved. Walters pushed the principles Gunning outlined in his book, *The Techniques of Clear Writing.* Editors push the same principles today: write to express, not impress; tie in with your readers' experience; use terms your readers can picture; use action verbs; avoid unnecessary words; prefer the familiar word; keep sentences short; prefer the simple to the complex.

Knight and Walters posted a note on the bulletin board: "Short leads and short sentences. No lead is to be more than three typewritten lines, two if possible." Knight set an example in his weekly "Editor's Notebook." He used punchy, snappy short sentences. (His column won the Pulitzer Prize for editorial writing in 1968.)

Foreign service correspondents disagreed with Walters's and Knight's writing ideas. After Walters sent a memo on clear writing, one correspondent answered that he was writing for the University of Chicago and Northwestern professors. Goaded by this remark, Walters went to a University of Chicago faculty meeting with a batch of foreign service copy. He found that even the professors did not readily understand some of the pretentious prose.

Walters and Knight went beyond that test to demonstrate that their ideas were correct. Studies at the time showed that the average adult's reading speed was comparatively slow. They sent Howard Vincent O'Brien, a *Daily News* columnist, to the University of Chicago to take a reading test. O'Brien was a Yale graduate and one of the best read men on the *Daily News* staff. But the test, given by the Adult Reading Clinic under the auspices of the School of Education, showed that O'Brien had ninth grade reading ability.

"I had long suspected that I was a slow reader, but I was hardly prepared for what the movie of my eye movements revealed," O'Brien told *Editor and Publisher* in April, 1946. "Instead of proceeding from one group of words to another, as normal eyes should, mine hesitate, jump from word to word . . . and then jump back to start the process over again. I am long on 'fixations,' short on number of words fixed. . . ."

O'Brien scored seventy percent on central thought, that is, understanding about three-fourths of what he read. But he slipped to fifty percent when tested on details. He scored eighty percent on interpretation, but dropped when tested on integration of ideas to only forty-two percent.

Walters said such research studies "are bringing a new thought into editorial circles generally. The thought is that there is not neccessarily a relationship between intelligence and ability to read. Also, there are indications that the use of type, or rather the misuse of type, is involved in the failure to attract and hold readers."

The *Editor and Publisher* article gave an example of how more "eye appeal" was being achieved with shorter leads. The lead of a story written in August 1945 on the War Manpower Commission appeared this way:

> A crew of 20 specially trained men to assist in interregional recruiting of 96,000 workers needed in the next two months for the lagging munitions programs will be dispatched from Washington to areas including Illinois, the War Manpower Commission (WMC) revealed today.

Editor and Publisher reported that this is the way the *Daily News* jumps into a WMC story today:

> Some 20,000 workers were needed December 1 for critical jobs in Chicago. Today the requirement has been reduced to 16,200.

Managing editor Norlander told the magazine, "We are trying to publish a paper that is interesting, authoritative, fair and honest. We recognize that newspapers are not always written at a readability level for the average person, so we are trying to make the Daily News easier to read and easier to understand.''

The local staff supported Knight and Walters for the most part, especially after editors were told that the foreign staff must compete for space with all other news available, whether it be from the wire services, the Washington bureau, or locally produced. With the exception of a powerful few who were foreign service oriented, the local editors were delighted. Thus local staffers, whose copy was no longer being written for the wastepaper basket, rallied behind the new program. The once-powerful few left.

It was a foreign story, however, that produced Walters's first big splash in Chicago.

Despite his tremendous patriotism, Walters generally refused to cooperate when the Central Intelligence Agency asked him to be more permissive in allowing the agency to use *Daily News* correspondents. He felt strongly about compromising the paper's integrity by getting involved with government intelligence activities. But one exception led to a famous exclusive on the Ciano Diaries.

Raleigh Warner, a *Daily News* company director, came to Knight's office shortly after Knight's purchase and said the Office of Strategic Services (OSS) was trying to get the diaries of Count Ciano, Italian Prime Minister Benito Mussolini's son-in-law. Ciano had been executed by the Fascists after going over to the Allied side. Absolute secrecy must be preserved, Warner cautioned.

Allied and German intelligence officials were searching madly for the diaries, which contained strategic details of the plans Germany and Italy had developed to defeat the Allies. Only the Count's widow, Edda, knew the diaries were buried in a garden in northern Italy. The count had revealed that shortly before his execution in January 1944. He also told her about John Whittaker, who represented the *Daily News* in Rome. Whittaker, before being killed as a soldier in the war, had told Ciano that if he decided to publish the diaries, he should offer them to the *Daily News*.

After her husband's death, Edda found the diaries. When she crossed the Swiss border for asylum in a Swiss monastery, she carried the diaries strapped to her body under her clothing, which made her look pregnant.

Edda would talk only to representatives of the *Daily News,* the OSS learned. Knight assigned Walters to the project. Without legal advice, Walters drew up an offer for world publishing rights and advanced $10,000 to be delivered by the OSS in Geneva to Paul Ghali, a *Daily News* correspondent, for payment to Edda. A substantial additional payment was to be made later.

The OSS was to handle the transmission of the diaries to the United States and deliver either the diaries or copies and translation to Walters, with the understanding that the OSS participation remain secret for several years.

Walters was advised to visit Washington. He asked if he could include foreign editor Hal O'Flaherty in the secret. He could. In Washington, the two men were led into a windowless room and given a large volume of typewritten sheets. There was no desk in the room. The two men had to hold the book between them and read simultaneously, frequently changing sides to relieve tired arms.

It was all revealed before their eyes—the eyewitness story of the Hitler-Mussolini alliance by a man who was present at their meetings and who frequently was an envoy.

Walters and O'Flaherty were told they could pick up a translation and copy of the microfilm in a week. A week later they went back to Washington and found resistence at the OSS reception desk. There was no explanation. Walters worried. The European war was drawing to a close; the diaries' value would be greatly diminished if there should be a long delay in securing them. He and O'Flaherty returned to Chicago.

Ten days passed. The *Daily News*'s business office asked Walters to account for the $10,000. Knight fronted for his editor. On the eleventh day after Walters's and O'Flaherty's second tirp to Washington, Walters found two small tin cans containing microfilm on his desk. He had returned to it after being away for only a few minutes to visit the news room. He never learned how the microfilm got there.

Walters called Northwestern University and arranged for translators. He contacted his old pals at the Register and Tribune Syndicate in Des Moines. They undertook the sale to other newspapers for publication to start the next week.

The *Daily News* simply announced that the diaries had been obtained by Ghali from Edda Ciano. Walters and O'Flaherty vouched for their authenticity. The worldwide sale exhausted all potentials within the week. Fascinating details of Hitler's and Mussolini's war and political strategies were soon pouring across the globe.

Walters was not through, however. There was the additional payment to Edda—and it proved difficult to complete. Restrictions on the transfer of money abroad were in effect. Technically, Edda was an alien enemy. If the *Daily News* made too much fuss, the money would be seized. But the paper was determined to live up to the agreement John Whittaker had made with her years before. An agent finally reached her with the additional cash.

That kind of scoop was needed. The *Times* had topped the *Daily News*—for one month, October 1944, the month Knight took over.

The slide was quickly halted. Within one year, the *Daily News* fought its way to second place, trailing only McCormick's *Tribune*, which had built a substantial lead over the entire field. In a year, starting September 30, 1944, the *Daily News* grew from a circulation of 421,418 to 461,602. This was a tremendously successful twelve months under Knight. In a front-page signed editorial, "After One Year," Knight noted that for September 1945, the daily net average was 479,840, an increase of 44,892 over September 1944.

Knight took that opportunity to reiterate the aims he had announced when he assumed control: (1) to keep the *Daily News* politically independent; (2) to insist that the newspaper's first responsibility is to the general public—uncontrolled by any group, faction, party, or special interest; (3) to fight for those principles the *Daily News* believes to be right and resist any encroachment upon the liberties and inalienable rights of people; and (4) to serve as an impartial portrayer of the news, a fearless interpreter of the moving events of our times, and a faithful, sincere, and honest servant of the people.

Meanwhile, Hearst watched his *Herald-American* fall from second place. The *Daily News* had chewed away a lead of about 60,000. Impressed, Hearst approached Walters and offered him a job in his vast publishing empire. Starting yearly salary: $150,000. Walters said no, telling the press czar, as tactfully as he could, that he didn't want to be part of Hearst's sensationalism.

"Besides," Walters recalled in retirement, "I was having too much fun with the *Daily News*. Jack Knight was one of the swellest guys you could work for."

Knight's foreign correspondents didn't think Walters was so swell. He was reshaping the service Victor Lawson had put together after Melville Stone first hatched the idea because of the lack of accurate reports on the Spanish-American War.

For years, the *Daily News*'s service was not only the first, but the finest. By the time Walters and Knight arrived, however, it had slipped. Some bright lights were still around, but, to a large degree, the service was riding on its reputation.

Walters and Knight saw beyond the reputation. As Nixon Smiley wrote in his book on the history of the *Miami Herald* (*Knights of the Fourth Estate*), Knight

looked upon the News' (foreign) coverage as merely voluminous and dull. He wanted a newspaper that would be read. This meant brighter, succinct writing and the discouragement of long, ponderous articles. In Walters he had selected an editor who could make changes, and gradually they were made.

Foreign correspondents weren't the only people who complained about the changes. Carl Sandburg was so angered he refused to enter the *News* building. While he and Walters remained friends, they would often argue over the changes.

Some readers squawked, too. Smiley wrote in his book, "When a foreign policy dilettante demanded to know why Knight no longer attempted to produce the kind of paper that Frank Knox had published, Knight snapped: 'If this paper had continued to be edited as it was, there wouldn't be any Daily News.'"

Some observers wondered whether Walters actually wanted to dismantle the foreign service or reshape it. They noted that Walters was dedicated to rebuilding local coverage. But Walters proved that killing the foreign service had never entered his mind. He merely wanted to apply the successful ideas of George Gallup and Robert Gunning to the foreign dispatches, enabling readers to relate to stories whether they came from Boston or Bombay.

Walters even got involved in the sales efforts, resulting in new clients. By 1957, twelve years after concentrated effort, *Newsweek* wrote in a story about Walters:

> The once-ill CDN service . . . is getting healthy. Currently it has 57 subscribers, more than ever before. Moreover, there are those who contend that the New York Times' recent effort to brighten its overseas copy was a result of grudging appreciation for the Knight-Walters system.
>
> Characteristically, Walters is not satisfied. "I'd like to make it a hundred clients before I retire in

> five years," he says, and unstuffy Stuffy may do it.
> "Edit everything that needs it," he once instructed a
> Daily News department head. "And that goes for
> everybody's copy—even John S. Knight's."

Walters fell short of getting 100 clients, but made significant progress. When Knight bought the *Daily News,* there were thirty-eight clients. When Walters retired in 1962, the foreign service had sixty-two clients and, at times, the figure approached seventy.

The growth was accomplished by not only improving the service's quality, but also with strong promotion. The *Daily News* published a large promotional advertisement November 29, 1955, that also appeared later on the cover of *Editor and Publisher.* Walters was the focus. Outlined by a map of different foreign countries patched together, Walters—cigar in mouth, glasses firmly in place, phone to left ear, usual smile of delight on his face—sat in his overstuffed office chair. That same photo appeared much smaller in the middle of the map, with lines running from the smaller photo to the larger photo. That was the top half of the ad.

A headline separating the photo from the text below said, "Dig for the Significant." The copy began:

"He is as modern as TV and contemporary architecture. . . . He can smell propaganda right through 3,000 miles of ocean cable." In this way, recently, Publisher John S. Knight described the executive editor of the *Chicago Daily News* and the director of its famed Foreign Service . . . Basil L. (Stuffy) Walters.

Later in the copy, a paragraph proclaimed:

Stuffy does not crush his correspondents with fatuous rules. "Dig for the significant . . . tell it interestingly" is his key instruction. And all on his staff are aware that their aim is not so much to tell WHAT happened—since the news agencies do this—but to tell HOW and WHY it happened and what it MEANS.

The ad proclaimed that the foreign service had "the largest assignment desk in the world. . . ."

The *Daily News* Foreign Service Walters directs—America's oldest—is bought and published by more than 50 big-newspaper editors across the nation . . . all linked to Stuffy by 6,593 miles of leased wire. It was strictly a

Walters idea to accept "hunches" for timely stories from these distinguished editors along his wire. Result: His assignment desk has become literally the largest in existence—a clearing point for story suggestions sparked by America's top editors from coast to coast.

Walters always looked for a "spectacular attention getter" for the service—even as late as 1959, after Marshall Field, Jr. bought the *Daily News* from Knight. Walters, who had agreed to remain with Field, wrote him a memo on April 7, giving him details on a foreign service "spectacular" so the new publisher "will have the background of the methods we have employed in building a solid list of wire clients."

Walters told Field the service planned to send reporter John Smith to Australia with a farmer named Yankus to show how agricultural controls there compare with those in the United States. Walters wrote in his memo:

We haven't had a man in Australia for some time. We try to have people in every important part of the world two or three times a year and time the visits to fit in the coverage with some event which creates public interest in the area. This type of thing seems to have worked out as quite a suitable program for a supplemental foreign service. We have felt for some time that we need at this stage some sort of rather spectacular attention getter to the foreign service. This seems to be the best bet now available.

The memo's last four paragraphs illustrate Walters's selling techniques and his understanding of editors and egos. He wrote to Field:

I used the prospective Yankus trip as an excuse to discuss our foreign service with Gene Pulliam last night. It is not available to his Indianapolis papers because his competition has it, but it is available in Arizona (where Pulliam owned papers).

Gene said his foreign editor, Michael Padev, had told him frequently that the CDN service is tops of all the supplemental services.

The problems of selling a top man is the danger of offending the managing editor. If a managing editor feels there has been an end-run to the boss, the sale usually doesn't last beyond the original contract period.

I'll call my friend, Harry Montgomery, assistant to the publisher at Phoenix, at the right time, and offer him the Yankus trip stories for free and then later I'm sure we will have an excellent chance of getting the wire into Phoenix.

The *Daily News* sought new foreign service clients by periodically sending promotional material to editors. A four-page letter, single-spaced and making ample use of Walters's beloved asterisks, was sent January 5, 1956, under Walters's signature. The letter reads like an "advance" story newspapers write before a major event or meeting. The letter lays out the world scene as 1956 opens, working in the views of foreign service correspondents, such as the famed Keyes Beech. Midway through the letter, Walters writes, "We are watching the Middle East particularly this year. Russia is fishing in troubled waters there. Oil is of course the great prize, but the Asiatic countries are showing signs of interest in industrialization and modernization."

The fear that some had over the foreign service's future eventually faded. Walters wanted more local news, but he had never ignored the international scene and wasn't about to in Chicago. In fact, the truly major stories in Walters's first few years came from overseas. On May 8, 1945, eight months after arriving in Chicago, Walters watched his staff put together a front page reporting the Nazi surrender and the seizing of top German leaders Hermann Goering and Heinrich Himmler. A short dispatch from Paris, by the foreign service's Helen Kirkpatrick, led off the page, reporting how Admiral Doenitz seized control of the German government before it finally fell.

On August 7, 1945, the *Daily News* devoted most of its front page to the atomic bomb being dropped on Hiroshima. And a week later, the *News* dragged out three-inch headline type for "War Ends."

Again, most of the front page was related to Japan's surrender, including a small United Press story out of San Francisco. It ran at the bottom of the page. The headline: "V-J Fun Has Everything/—Even 2 Nude Beauties." Two nude women had stepped from a taxi near the civic center servicemen's dormitory and plunged into the center's lily pond. The servicemen applauded as the women briefly cavorted. Then they emerged, gratefully accepted towels, re-entered the taxi and were seen no more. It was the kind of story Walters loved, the kind that had "Page One" written all over it.

A year later, August 6, 1946, a local story with tremendous impact broke. William Heirens, a seventeen-year-old University of Chicago student, confessed before State's Attorney William J. Tuohy that he had murdered six-year-old Suzanne Degnan, ex-Wave Frances Brown, and Mrs. Josephine Ross, a widow.

Reporter Alfred Prowitt's opinion was allowed to creep into the main news story. He wrote:

> Calmly, without hesitation, he gave full details of his shocking crimes before a circle of police officials in Tuohy's office.
>
> But at times his glance fell to the floor as if he were ashamed of the brutal acts he had committed.

Prowitt quoted Heirens as saying he "strangled her (Suzanne) as she lay in her bed." Then, using short, staccato paragraphs—the Walters style—Prowitt described, with some sensationalism, how Heirens killed the young girl. Here's a touch of his story:

> "How long did you keep your hands on her neck, would you say?"
> "About two minutes."
> "You squeezed as hard as you could?"
> "Until everything went limp."

The Photographer's Friend

Based on his earlier successes with news photography in Des Moines and Minneapolis, Basil Walters continued to stress the importance of pictures. He was a graphics pacemaker as the *Daily News* galloped toward greatness in the latter half of the forties.

Walters' leadership in news photography was illustrated in the September 1947 issue of *Journalism Quarterly*. His byline appears over an article entitled, "Pictures vs. Type Display in Reporting the News."

Walters opened the piece by recalling that shortly after the advent of wirephotos on January 1, 1935, editors at the Associated Press Managing Editors' convention were startled by a suggestion that at least half of the 1936 convention be devoted to newspaper photography. Some widely known editors felt that would be putting undue emphasis on the illustrative side of newspapers. Walters wrote, "Pictures, they reasoned, should not be permitted to encroach upon the written word in newspapers."

But Kent Cooper, a fellow Hoosier who headed the Associated Press, supported the picture advocates. Half of the next convention was devoted to pictures. "This gave birth to a new consciousness of the value and the necessity of pictures in American newspapers," Walters wrote. He noted:

Men of my generation who now are in control of the newsrooms have been brought up in the TYPE school. When we were breaking into the game, pictures, quite often made from syndicated mats, were used largely as decorative material or to fill up space in early editions. It was common practice to throw out pictures, regardless of reader interest, for type of limited significance.

Even then, in 1947, pictures were handled "as nuisance jobs by city editors, news editors or managing editors," Walters wrote. He asserted that "these busy men" do not study photo cropping and reproduction the way they study the written word, adding, "A badly cropped picture or a picture which does not reproduce well is as severe an indictment of a newsroom executive as is a sloppily prepared type story."

He was correct. He was on target, too, when he wrote that caption writing is "a neglected art. This r 'igence must be corrected before newspapers will be doing a real job in pictorial journalism."

As Walters neared the close of his article, he touched on newspaper graphics in general, reiterating their importance. Thirty years later, graphics became a question of prime importance and consideration among editors. Television—not television news by itself, but television overall—continued to introduce innovations in the visual arts that almost hypnotized some people into automatically turning on their sets and ignoring the visually dull newspapers. Walters wrote:

The whole excuse for the printed page is to serve as a medium for the conveyance of a thought from one mind to another. If that thought can best be conveyed by the written word, type should be used. If it can best be conveyed by a photograph, then a photograph should be used. If it can best be conveyed by an artist's sketch, then an artist's sketch should be used. Frequently all three methods must be combined.

Again, looking ahead, Walters wrote that the "great shift in appreciation of pictorial reporting in newspapers may come with more general use of offset printing."

A few years later, the smaller newspapers took the lead as offset printing developed. Pictures gained considerably in reproduction quality. Editors started to adopt the phrase, "If it's a good shot, play it one column larger."

Fighting for Freedom

O FFSET PRINTING, already being tested by some small newspapers, came to Chicago's six dailies sooner than Basil Walters and other publishing executives wanted. It came out of absolute necessity.

On November 24, 1947, as the newspapers' advertising staffs were primed for the Christmas crush, printers of the Chicago Newspaper Publishers Association struck. Members of Local 16 of the International Typographers Union walked off their jobs after the publishers rejected their demands for wage increases of $14.50 to $15 a week.

The publishers insisted that they had repeatedly agreed to negotiate for a retroactive wage increase within the framework of a contract. They rejected a union demand for an immediate pay increase that would give day workers $100 a week, night employees $106. The publishers stated, "We have at all times been ready to negotiate a wage increase, if the union would agree to put the wage scale and other terms of employment in a lawful contract of reasonable duration."

The printers met in Plumbers' Hall for a strike vote. Although the six dailies, including the *Journal of Commerce,* employed only 1,493 printers in their composing rooms, all 5,200 members of the Local were allowed to vote. The result: 2,330 to strike, 61 to stay on the job.

The newspapers were determined to publish without the printers, and they did. They reproduced typewritten stories through photoengraving. The newspapers used Varitypers—electric typewriters that could self-justify themselves, allowing typewritten lines to be set evenly to fit column width. Headlines were made by using tab letters. The newspapers hired batteries of experienced typists to work on the Varitypers around the clock.

The tabloid *Times* reported the story tersely in a headline across page one of its first post-strike edition: **"Printers Out—Times Is, Too."** The *Daily News* made the strike its second most prominent story in its November 25 edition. It chose to lead with a Wisconsin prison rebellion. Huge headline type—two inches in size—reported:

CONVICTS GIVE UP
IN WISCONSIN PRISON

The *Daily News*'s front page, which *Editor and Publisher* reproduced in its November 29 edition, was four columns wide. The columns were double the normal one-column size. In the left-hand column, a three-line headline, in type about a fourth of the size used on the Wisconsin prison story, read:

A Statement
To Our Readers
on the Strike

Signed by Knight, the statement reported on the labor situation.

The strike spread from Chicago. By mid-December, during the peak Christmas advertising season, fifteen dailies were struck, including papers in Allentown, Pennsylvania; Jamestown, New York; Bartlesville, Oklahoma; and Norristown, Pennsylvania.

By the third week, Chicago's dailies began to find a production rhythm. Using the Varitypers, IBM electric typewriters, Electromatic typewriters—even regular typewriters in some cases—the newspapers began typing each story twice. First, the copy was typed with a notation at the end of each line telling how many spaces were used in the line. Then the copy moved to the Varitype operators, who adjusted their machines according to the notations, allowing for quick newspaper-column justification. Finished and original copy went to proofreaders—mostly news department people pressed into service—and then back to the typists who retyped lines and pasted them onto the copy. The stories moved to the art department, where they were pasted up into page form. Meanwhile, the art department produced headlines by pasting strips of individual tab letters together with Scotch tape. Nancy Walters, who exhibited artistic ability, helped paste up *Daily News* pages.

George Brandenburg, the Chicago correspondent for *Editor and Publisher,* wrote a few weeks later:

> CHICAGO—Regardless of what printers or publishers may do, the photo-engraved newspaper is here to stay.
>
> This was the prediction of Basil L. Walters, executive editor of Knight Newspapers, made before more than 400 members of the Inland Daily Press Association at their mid-winter meeting here this week. Walters was one of a panel of speakers who spoke on the "cold type" method now used by Chicago dailies and the Hammond (Ind.) Times, whose printers have been on strike for 11 weeks.

Walters warned the Inland members, the vast majority of whom represented small newspapers, that the photo-engraved method is particularly adaptable to the small-town field. "Many of you will have competition of one kind or another from photo-engraved papers within the next five years," he said.

Walters, as so often in the past, was right. By the mid-1970s, newspapers of all sizes began experiencing the competition Walters mentioned. Shopper publications, with free and allegedly total market circulation, produced type and pages with relatively inexpensive equipment. They jobbed out their press work—some to the newspapers from which they had begun to siphon off vital advertising dollars.

Despite the long strike—it ended September 14, 1949, after twenty-two months—the *Daily News* made its greatest circulation gains. Knight later concluded that the larger type produced by the Varitypers helped the increase. (As late as 1980, Knight was trying to persuade editors to increase type size, saying that the Chicago strike "should have taught us something.")

Walters, in 1970, talked about the strike in a long, taped discussion with Copley Newspapers executives. The discussion was printed in the September issue of *Seminar,* Copley's quarterly review for newspapermen. "Now, in Chicago we proved that a newspaper can be published without the use of hot type," Walters said. "Actually, during the strike, we made more money on the Daily News than we did before or after the strike was settled. It was before the day of offset, and the engraving process was slow because after we pasted up the

cold type, we had to engrave it and then had to run it through stereo-
type. The only people who walked out during that strike were the
printers. Everybody else stayed in . . . it was the most amazing situation that you can imagine.''

When Walters wasn't directing his striked-hampered troops he
was giving attention to freedom of the press. Such attention was
nothing new. In fact, it was quite old. He had read and re-read John
Stuart Mill's essay, ''On Liberty,'' and recommended his children do
so. Youngest son Jim read the famed essay for the first time in the
seventh grade.

Walters's concern for press freedom was so strong that some people thought he went overboard. The issue of journalism school accreditation resulted in an exchange of opposing views between Walters
and Kenneth E. Olson, dean of Northwestern's noted Medill School
of Journalism.

The debate broke into the open in 1947. Walters said he feared
that a program of accrediting journalism schools might be a step
toward the licensing of newspapermen. He made his views known
before the American Society of Journalism Administrators in Chicago
on June 28.

His speech was reported in the July 5 issue of *Editor and
Publisher*. The second paragraph of reporter Dwight Bentel's story
reads:

> Walters charged the accrediting program,
> recently inaugurated by the American Council on
> Education for Journalism, with containing poten-
> tialities for becoming a ''bureaucratic monopoly . . .
> effectively putting the stamp of approval on the man
> or woman who wants to write.''

Walters told the journalism administrators that, as a former
director of the American Society of Newspaper Editors, he assisted in
creating the accrediting committee by voting financial aid. But in the
back of his mind, he ''always had a fear'' about the accrediting committee. He explained:

> If the committee will carefully confine itself and its work, I still think it
> may do a service. But if it should lend itself to becoming part of the
> bureaucracy of educators who may become more concerned with the ''how''
> than they are with actually turning out well-trained students, this committee
> could become a factor in what I fear is a growing danger to freedom of ex-
> pression in this country. . . .

The reason I fear the trend which I think is developing toward trying to establish writing as a licensed profession is that I think the very future of this nation is tied up with man's . . . right to write and publish and distribute as he pleases. . . .

Obviously, some can be licensed. But to attempt to license thought and expression is to strike at the very fundamental liberty and freedom of man. . . .

The danger of freedom of the press lies in compromise and acceptance in an easy path that might permit drifting into a swift current which would sweep us all to destruction. . . .

Dean Olson and the others fired back a week later in *Editor and Publisher.* Dwight Marvin, editor of the *Troy* (N.Y.) *Record* and president of the American Council on Education for Journalism, responded,

Isn't Mr. Walters seein' things at night? It is incredible that he, a working newspaperman, can be scared by such a synthetic ghost. . . . [Accreditation] is not half so dangerous as multiple newspaper ownership—the growing number of networks of chain organizations—in which Mr. Walters himself has been a willing participant. If newspapers cannot remain free from bureaucratic monopoly in spite of chains and accreditations, the whole business is a puling infant.

The magazine gave Olson's views the greatest amplification:

I am afraid my good friend Basil Walters has scared up bogeymen with his fears that a program of accrediting journalism schools might be a step toward licensing of newspapermen.

Nothing is further from the thoughts of the newspapermen and educators who have been working on this program since 1939. From the beginning, we have taken a stand against such licensing. . . .

No one contemplates that graduates of schools of journalism will be asked to take a state examination for admission to work on newspapers. Nor are newspapers compelled to hire journalism graduates. They may employ anyone they wish.

But the increasing number of newspapers who are employing journalism graduates have the right to know that these graduates . . . have been taught by men with practical experience in journalism. . . .

For one of the few times over the years, Walters's view proved to be wrong. The call for the licensing of journalists came forth periodically, but the accreditation of journalism schools was not involved.

Walters, however, was not wrong in seeing other dangers to a free press. He gave no thought to his military experience and strong feelings toward patriotism in defending *Daily News* correspondent Keyes

Beech when the reporter was accused of "sensation mongering" by
Major General Hugh J. Casey.

In a July 1948 dispatch from Tokyo, Beech wrote:

> A large part of MacArthur's Headquarters doesn't want the American
> people to know what is going on in Japan, in this correspondent's opinion.
>   Time and again in recent weeks, officials of the Supreme Command for
> the Allied Powers have flatly refused to answer legitimate inquires. They have
> imposed rigid censorship on subordinates or deliberately stalled in hopes that
> correspondents would lose interest.
>   Not only have MacArthur's men refused to answer inquiries, but they
> have tried to shut off correspondents from Japanese sources. . . .
>   Three weeks ago I approached Maj. Gen. H. J. Casey, Gen. MacAr-
> thur's chief engineer, on Army construction and occupation costs in Japan, a
> subject which nobody at GHQ appears willing to discuss. Casey suggested
> that "The People of Chicago are not interested in details of such a story."
> Pressed, he asked for a written list of questions. A list was promptly sub-
> mitted, but is now buried somewhere. . . .

Beech attached a note to the story that said, "Fully aware implications today's story. Prepared stand back of it."

Casey answered these accusations in a letter to Paul Smith, *San
Francisco Chronicle* editor. Casey took issue with a *Chronicle* editorial criticizing general headquarters' censorship of news, based on
one of Beech's dispatches. Questioning Beech's motives in asking
about occupation costs and construction, Casey wrote:

> It would appear that, in reality, he hoped to uncover some sensational
> story by reviewing the exact costs in dollars and yen of multitudinous projects
> and subfeatures of the program including the exact amount of U.S. materials
> expended on each feature, specific items and value of Japanese war stocks
> returned to the Japanese and miscellaneous related detailed information.

Beech responded, "Casey put it well. That's exactly what I
wanted and still want."

Walters wrote, in a letter to Casey, "This is in line with the policy
of the Knight Newspapers of keeping an eternal spotlight on all public
employees. Our foreign correspondents are instructed to serve as the
eyes of the American people abroad. The people of the United States,
we feel, are entitled to information about how their funds are ex-
pended. . . . I want to assure you, General, that this is in no way to be
taken as lack of appreciation for the work of the military."

Thus Walters had become personally involved in a domestic censorship case that originated on foreign soil. At the time of the Beech-

General Casey hassle, Walters was serving as the first chairman of the American Society of Newspaper Editors' (ASNE) Committee on World Freedom of Information.

Alice Fox Pitts, in her book on ASNEs first fifty years, reported that the organization's drive for press freedom began in 1923. ASNE President Casper S. Yost, of the *St. Louis Globe-Democrat,* suggested then that the organization "defend the rights of the profession when attacked or threatened by legislative or administrative powers."

In 1945, Pitts noted, ASNE sent a three-man committee around the world to promote the free flow of news across national borders. Later the committee "tried to prod the United Nations into guaranteeing all peoples free access to information." They were game efforts, but both failed.

Walters, as committee chairman, discovered that barriers to information not only existed overseas but within the United States, too. Pitts wrote, in her book, ". . . Basil L. Walters . . . pointed out this fundamental fact in a statement that has since become a classic:

Our responsibility lies in the domestic field as well as in the international field.

There is a growing tendency of some officials in some of the smallest governmental units, as well as the largest, to forget they are the stewards of the people and to act instead as though the taxpayers were their servants.

Our duty as newspapermen is to act always as the eyes of the American public and to keep the eternal spotlight of publicity on all servants of the people, including the military.

The (World Freedom of Information) Committee "fired from the hip" whenever anything resembling intrusion on freedom of information came into range. We didn't wait to see any white of the eyes.

Also we were quite brave in telling editors, "You fight 'em."

In many cases this worked.

Walters, himself, did more than just tell editors, "You fight 'em." In a case that drew national attention, he got deeply involved. It centered around James F. Etzell, the crusading editor of a weekly, the *Star-Gazette,* at Moose Lake, Minnesota.

Etzell was twenty-eight years old when he bought the paper in the summer of 1947 from people who had owned it for more than forty years. A native Minnesotan, Etzell saw Moose Lake, a quiet little town of 2,000 people, as a good place to practice the highest principles of journalism. The only problem with this was that Jim Etzell didn't pick his editorial fights very carefully. Not long after taking over the paper, he began editorializing on a wide range of subjects. He spoke out on changing the site of the city dump. He argued that the Women's Christian Temperance Union should not be allowed to furnish an instructor to teach temperance in the schools. He asserted that the Gideons should not be allowed to bring the King James version of the Bible into the schools.

The issue that propelled Etzell into the national spotlight occurred in the late spring of 1949, when he became embroiled with county clerk Joseph Poirier. Etzell demanded complete access to all vital statistics and criminal records. Poirier refused to release information that he felt reflected on people's personal lives.

Etzell criticized Poirier's action in an editorial that also attacked the county board, which supported the clerk. The board sued Etzell for libel. Walters offered to help with the legal costs but Etzell, though grateful, declined. Etzell won the suit when it was shown that state laws allowed public access to the records Poirier sought to conceal.

But while Etzell won the fight, he lost the war. Advertisers began to desert him. He said it was a boycott. Anti-Etzell forces denied his claim, arguing that as Etzell angered more people with his editorials, merchants dropped their advertising.

In the *Star-Gazette*'s May 4, 1950, issue, a banner headline read: **THE SQUEEZE IS ON!** An editorial referred to the *Moose Lake Magnet,* a shopper-type tabloid, which was scheduled to publish its first edition the next day. Etzell wrote that twenty-nine of thirty-one usual advertisers he solicited that week turned him down. He wrote in part:

> Several times during the past 2½ years people in this community have accused The Star-Gazette editor of selfish interests in the fights this newspaper has been involved in. They have said that we have "crusaded" in order to gain wide circulation and thereby make money.
> The present economic boycott against this newspaper should dispel that accusation.
> Rather than grab for material wealth, The Star-Gazette editor and his wife have fought for the ideals of a democratic America. We made a decision months ago that we stick with.

Some Minnesota editors came to Etzell's defense, including Gideon Seymour at the *Minneapolis Star.* But it was Walters, a former Minnesotan, who backed Etzell's press freedom ideals the strongest. The *Daily News* of May 31, 1950, called attention to Etzell's plight.

Walters sent a copy to Leslie H. Blacklock, a Moose Lake attorney who was in the forefront of the anti-Etzell forces. Blacklock responded with a tough letter to Walters, writing in part:

> From your experience in the newspaper field, as well as the human field, you should know that there are two sides to every question . . . why have you not checked both sides of the question.

Along with his letter, Blacklock sent a copy of the *Moose Lake Magnet*'s fifth issue. The entire front page was devoted to "An Answer to the Star-Gazette's Criticisms of the Village of Moose Lake and Its Citizens." The lone headline under this wording read:

Report on the Local
Newspaper Controversy

Seven columns of unbroken gray type followed and the article jumped to page four, the back page of the publication. There the last twelve inches of the article ran, surrounded entirely by ads.

The Minnesota Editorial Association (MEA) was drawn into the controversy after Etzell, in late June of 1950, was presented the freedom of information award made each year by Sigma Delta Chi, the national journalism fraternity. The award was presented in Chicago. In reporting on the award in its July 1 issue, *Editor and Publisher* quoted parts of Etzell's acceptance speech. The story prompted Bill Sweetland of the Gazette Publishing Company in Wheaton to write to Pi Johnson, MEA president.

Sweetland said the "story seems to be one of a mounting number that imply that Mr. Etzell's Minnesota newspaper colleagues have walked off and left him to the wolves. And that is what makes my Irish blood rise."

Later, Sweetland wrote, ". . . I am inclined to believe that Mr. Etzell led with his chin and is now hollering for colleagues to cover up for him. I hope I am wrong. I hope that all the fuss he has raised is not the wolf-cry of a self-righteous zealot."

A copy of Sweetland's letter made its way to Walters via Etzell. Walters wrote to Sweetland, "I have quite a file on this whole case, which probably will be used in a national foundation study of Moose Lake, small town newspapers, etc. This boy, judging from dealings with him over a couple of years and from his speech here, is no 'self-righteous zealot.' He may have on occasion 'led with his chin' but what good newspaperman hasn't?''

The Sigma Delta Chi award was sweet for Etzell and Walters, but Etzell's financial condition was sour. The loss of advertising had almost flattened him. Walters, while visiting with Etzell after the Sigma Delta Chi award, offered financial help to keep him going. Again, Etzell declined.

By now, Etzell had developed a bleeding ulcer. His wife, Elizabeth, was ill, too. The strain had overtaken them; they knew they had to sell. Walters advised them to get some rest after completing the sale. Etzell did before moving on to Helena, Montana, where he worked on publications for that state's public health agency. He stayed in Montana for only nine months.

In 1952, Etzell returned to Minnesota. He lived in Bertha and worked out of St. Paul for state highway department publications. Bertha to St. Paul meant a 165-mile trip one way. Etzell came home on weekends—with newspapering still in his blood.

In 1954, he moved to Long Prairie, thirteen miles from where his brother owned a printing business in Clarissa. They planned on either starting a paper or acquiring one. He and his brother did well in job printing, but they were never able to acquire a newspaper.

On April 16, 1960, Jim Etzell, still hoping to raise enough capital to buy another paper, suffered a heart attack in his home. He was dead at the age of forty-one.

"He was an idealist and perfectionist," his wife recalled. "I think he was right. If he were alive today it would be hard for him to watch people compromising freedom more and more. . . . Mr. Walters was great to us. . . .''

Long after Jim Etzell was gone, Walters kept a vigil over press freedom. When I. A. Elliot, president of Montana Radio Stations, Inc., wrote to Walters that he was interested in organizing a freedom of information group in that state, a delighted Walters replied, "We have to be constantly careful in America lest our liberties slip away by default. Unless we are constantly on guard, we by carelessness establish habits that would make it very easy for somebody to take over in time of crisis. . . .''

More mail involving press freedom arrived at Walters's desk. In 1955, Larry Shaffel, a University of Illinois student, sought Walters's help in a research project. Schaffel asked Walters to define freedom of information. Walters replied, in part, "We now know that we cannot safely delegate important decisions—we must all share in those decisions. The collective judgment of all the people, if fully informed, is better than the judgment of any one man or small group."

In his long, taped discussion with Copley editors in 1970, Walters said:

> Press freedom means just what it says . . . freedom to expand the voice and the speech . . . to try to inform and to persuade your fellowmen.
>
> The posters we see on the picket line are all part of the free press. Duplicated letters are part of the free press. The misnamed "underground" newspapers in the U.S. are part of the free press.
>
> All of these contribute to the debate in a free society out of which an intelligent public opinion gradually emerges.
>
> Any attempt to regiment all these divergent opinions is dangerous indeed. . . .
>
> We must never attempt to license either the tongue or the press. . . .

Winning the Zenger

In August 1735, in a warm, packed courtroom in New York City, John Peter Zenger went on trial. Arrested in the fall of 1734, he was charged with criminal libel for having printed criticisms of the governor. Never mind that the criticisms were true.

Zenger was fortunate. In Andrew Hamilton he had one of the finest lawyers in America. Hamilton made a powerful case before the jury, arguing that much more was at stake than the fate of one man. Zenger, he said, was fighting for the right to speak and write the truth. He was fighting for liberty—a liberty that everyone would acquire if the jury found him not guilty. Hamilton's oratory resulted in victory. Zenger walked out of the courtroom a free man. The principle of a free press in America had been established before an independent nation was born.

In 1954, the University of Arizona established the John Peter Zenger Award. Douglas D. Martin, a Pulitzer Prize-winning former editor of the *Detroit Free Press,* gave birth to the idea. He headed the University of Arizona journalism department at the time. The first award, given to the *Denver Post*'s Palmer Hoyt, coincided with the 250th anniversary of the founding in 1704 of the *Boston News Letter,* the first successful newspaper in the United States.

Thirty outstanding newpaper editors from coast to coast were asked to vote on the 1955 recipient. A nine-member nominating committee of prominent newspaper executives proposed two candidates: Basil Walters and Russ Wiggins. Twenty-nine responded. Walters was chosen. Two years later, Wiggins won the honor. Sandwiched between Walters and Wiggins was James Pope. Thus, the Zenger Award went quickly to the three men most prominent in the American Society of Newspaper Editors' freedom of information efforts of the late 1940s and early 1950s.

The choices could not be more fitting. In a 1958 Nieman Fellowship lecture, Mark Ethridge spoke on "The Dynamics of Journalism." Ethridge, then publisher of the Louisville newspapers, talked about truth:

> Basic to any understanding of the truth is knowing the truth. As a nation we do not know it. I am not talking about freedom of the press; I am talking about its handmaiden, freedom of information, without which freedom of the press is a mockery anyway. . . . Even so recently as 1950 when Basil Walters, Russell Wiggins and James Pope began to pull the bell rope of warning that there was a growing suppression of information, I had a supercilious attitude of amused tolerance. I did not realize that the bell was tolling for me, too. It tolls for all of us.

Douglas Martin, in presenting the award to Walters, said he won the award on the basis of his policy that "the people must know." Martin continued, "(Walters) was the toughest, the crusadingest, the fairest newspaperman I've ever known. And on top of that, he was one of the sweetest, most kind hearted men."

The *Arizona Alumnus* magazine, in reporting that Walters won the 1955 award, began its story this way:

> The only shirt-sleeved in-the-slot executive who can handle a pencil, a piece of copy, a hamburger, a cup of coffee and a conversation at the same time—and improve the copy—is Basil L. Walters.

This is the way one of his contemporaries has described the winner of the 1955 John Peter Zenger Freedom of the Press Award.

On January 15, 1956, Walters acknowledged the award at a luncheon meeting of the Arizona Newspapers Association in Phoenix. He told the gathering:

I have erroneously been credited with being the (ASNE) chairman of the first freedom of information committee.

The first "chairman," of course, was John Peter Zenger. . . . we are now in a new type of war that calls for different tactics. We must not permit ourselves to be paralyzed into inactivity by the stultifying fear that the overall problem is so vast that we as individuals cannot make a contribution to its solutions.

The first great contribution to revival of American newspaper interest in the right to the people to know how their business is conducted and how to participate in important decisions was made by a weekly newspaper editor in Moose Lake, Minnesota. The county clerk wanted to write out for him the news from the records of his office that the clerk thought good for the citizens and to omit that which he judged was none of the public's business. . . .

The dramatic fight that resulted drew national attention and was the "Plymouth Rock" out of which has grown our whole modern day freedom of information crusade.

Walters told the gathering that of all his work in journalism, he was proudest of the fact that he had a part "in arousing my fellow newspapermen to the necessity for these freedom of information committees."

As he did so often, Walters ended his speech with journalistic food for thought:

There should be more editorial criticism between newspapers, there should be more debate about them, but it is better . . . to preserve freedom of speech and press than to tamper with the First Amendment or to endanger it—for if the First Amendment perishes, so does America.

Success Piles Up

T HE *Chicago Daily News* was rolling. And as the summer of 1950 dawned, the *News*'s public relations department wasn't bashful about letting fellow newspaper folk know about the paper's success.

A series of ads in *Editor and Publisher*, which had become the dominant trade magazine, told the *Daily News*'s success story. In a large ad on June 24, 1950, the *News* trumpeted that its circulation had reached its highest month's average in history—553,791, an average net paid May 1950 that was up 33,978 over the previous May. "22 Records in 22 Months!" the ad proclaimed, reporting that starting in August 1948 and continuing through the next twenty-one months, the *News*'s circulation reached an all-time high for each of those months.

A Pulitzer Prize awarded in 1947 to cartoonist Vaughn Shoemaker helped the *News*'s image and circulation. Shoemaker's winning work, entitled "Still Racing His Shadow," was about workers and their battle with inflation.

Another Pulitzer came along in 1950. It went to George Thiem, who shared the prize with Roy J. Harris of the *St. Louis Post-Dispatch*. They won the Public Service Award after exposing newspapermen who were on the Illinois state payroll.

The story broke April 14, 1949, simultaneously under Thiem's and Harris's by-lines. They reported that editors and publishers of at least thirty-two Illinois newspapers were on the state payroll during Governor Dwight H. Green's administration.

Later, the two reporters revealed that fifty-one newsmen had collected more than $480,000. A few of the "payrollers" actually worked regularly at the statehouse, Thiem and Harris reported. But the chief function of many others "was to print canned editorials and news stories lauding accomplishments of the Republican state administration." The combined circulation of the affected dailies and weeklies was 350,000.

The *Daily News* and *Post-Dispatch* attacked their fellow journalists with editorials and cartoons. Some of the guilty immediately resigned. The rest were removed when Adlai E. Stevenson—the man who had once competed with John Knight for the purchase of the *Daily News*—became governor.

Walters's men made it back-to-back Pulitzers in 1951, when Fred Sparks and Keyes Beech won the 1950 award for international reporting, chiefly for their Korean War stories. Sparks, a brilliant reporter and writer, free-lanced all of his life except for one short period when his good friend Walters talked him into signing on with the *Daily News*. Beech, meanwhile, had become a mainstay of the foreign service.

The *Daily News* used *Editor and Publisher* again to publicize its triumph. The ad copy read in part:

> Twenty million Americans in 50 cities glimpsed this in Beech's words at the Korea kickoff: "I have a feeling that I have just witnessed the beginning of World War III." They saw it in Sparks' warning 20 days before Mac-Arthur's "Home for Christmas" announcement: "If China enters the war we'll be back clinging to the Pusan beachhead in a few weeks." They followed the twisting Korean campaign through many a Beech exclusive. They walked close to death with Sparks through the hidden jungle war. . . .

Pulitzers are nice but they don't pay the bills. Only cash will do— and the *Daily News* was raking in its share. The February 13, 1950, issue of *Time* magazine made note of such. The magazine reported that soon after Knight bought the *Daily News,* he stood in the plaza in front of the *News* building with Walters and eyed the bubbling fountain in the center. Walters told Knight, "When we pay off the mortgage, I'll take a bath in that fountain." Knight responded, "You'll have whiskers down to here."

Less than six years later, *Time* continued, Walters had reason to hope that he could jump into the pool with no beard at all. The *News* had paid off nearly $8,700,000 of its $12,000,000 mortgage, taken a commanding advertising lead over Hearst's *Hearald-American,* and hoped to pass that paper, again, in circulation to lead the afternoon field. *Time* commented:

> Privately, Hearstlings thought they knew why the News was gaining on them. In the Herald-American, Chicagoans were still getting the Hearstian

formula of sex, sensation, antivivisection and MacArthur-for-President.
Herald-American staffers were sure that they could do better by dropping the
canned crusades in favor of more local news. That was just what Knight's
News was giving Chicago: fresh, warm-hearted, local-angle stories, sometimes crusading, almost always lively. With the playing down of its foreign
coverage and the jazzing up of its typography, the paper lost some of its
prestige among old News readers, but it was more saleable than ever.

The *Time* article reported the *News*'s exposé of newsmen on the
Illinois state payroll. And the magazine noted that the *News* had "successfully plumped for reform Mayor Martin Kennelly and started a
cleanup of the shocking Skid Row conditions."

Five months after the *Time* article appeared, Walters developed a
Journalism Week speech at the University of Missouri into an article
for the July 1950 issue of the *Quill*. The headline read: **"Newspapers
Face Lively Ten Years."**

Walters expounded on new ways and new ideas he foresaw. Much
proved to be on target.

Pointing to the Chicago printers' strike, he said it showed that
newspapers could be produced "in one of the great publishing centers
of the world without movable type." Equipment being developed, he
said:

will be operated much as a secretary now operates an electric typewriter. By
merely shifting levers and pushing buttons, the operator will have at her or his
fingertips a great variety of type faces and type sizes to select from. Electronic
processes will justify lines and finally deliver film, galleys of phototype ready
for make-up. . . . There (will) be no linotypes, no typecases, just a desk with a
glass top make-up table standing nearby. . . .

The number of large newspapers in America will constantly decrease . . .
a natural development. . . . The great papers that survive . . . will have to keep
flexible in order to fit themselves into constantly changing conditions. . . .

The greatest weakness in the American press generally today lies in its
failure to pay adequate attention to the local scene. This is where the so-called
community papers will fit into the scene. . . .

The new processes of production will be primarily in the suburban field
. . . competition there will be in the form of once-a-week or twice-a-week publications. . . . The old established paper will be forced to improve or perish. If
I had a county seat daily today I would be improving my staff and local
editorials. . . .

Saturday has now become a day of leisure. Therefore, isn't it logical that
there should be developed in this country in some of the larger cities a great
weekend paper?

Walters answered his own question. The result: one of his most
successful Chicago moves occurred in the spring of 1951. The *Daily*

News did not have a Sunday paper, so Walters turned the Saturday edition into a "Sunday paper."

He and circulation director Arthur Hall doubled the Monday through Friday price to 10 cents. The result: 1,000 more subscribers on Saturday a year after the beefed up "Saturday Triple Streak" was introduced.

Advertisers loved it. They got weekend advertising at daily rates. One Chicago department store sold $20,000 worth of dresses after using a Saturday roto section ad. It prompted the store to buy eight pages in the roto section a few Saturdays later.

Added advertising revenue aside, the *Daily News* gained more than $500,000 in circulation revenue each week. The increase in the Saturday paper meant a boost in home delivery price of 30 to 35 cents.

Editor and Publisher reported in its May 3, 1952, edition, "The *Daily News'* experience is all the more remarkable in comparison with what has happened to other evening newspapers in the 10 largest cities. These papers show average Saturday drop-offs of more than 20 percent. The *Daily News'* Triple Streak for weekend reading has gone from a 7 percent drop-off last summer to an actual gain."

The readers probably got the best deal of all. Included in the Triple Streak were sixteen pages of tabloid color comics, the tabloid rotogravure section and a regular news section. "This Week," the popular, slick, colorful tabloid that appeared in hundreds of Sunday papers, had been a *Daily News* Saturday bonus for years. It remained in the new Triple Streak. A new magazine-type back page replaced the regular picture page. Inside the main news section was a fly page containing the following week's television program listings.

The redesigned regular news section included two "front pages"—a Walters innovation later copied by many newspapers, large and small, across the nation. Page three became the second "front page." Free of ads, it provided editors with greater flexibility to display news and feature material.

Several months after the Triple Streak proved successful, Knight received a letter from a friend that carried this postscript, "I think the Saturday Daily News has been greatly improved. I don't know how much you ended up paying for the property, but Stuffy Walters is worth a good percentage of it. It's such a shame the Internal Revenue boys won't let you depreciate him the way they do the physical assets."

The second "front page" contributed greatly to the much improved Saturday edition. It was simply another good idea in a long line of typography/packaging innovations Walters began pouring forth starting in Minneapolis. His typography ideas became so widely recognized and accepted that in 1952 the *Daily News* accomplished a rarity—it won the Inland Daily Press Association's annual typography contest for the third straight year, taking permanent possession for the trophy in its class (newspapers for 75,000 circulation and above). After the third straight first place award was announced, Walters said he worried that perhaps his newspaper's typography was stressing horizontal makeup too much. But in the years that followed, horizontal makeup became even more popular with newspapers across the country.

Walters's weekly television page, which cut deeply into magazines that highlighted television listings, also caught on. But not with everyone. Some editors argued that television was a major threat to newspapers and that by providing readers with convenient television listings, newspapers were hurting themselves. Walters was no fan of television—in his last years he criticized it heavily, arguing it slanted the news—but he thought television was not a menacing competitor. He believed it was something that could help newspapers.

In an April 6, 1951, speech before the Hoosier State Press Association in Indianapolis, Walters said, . . . "television will stimulate interest in newspapers, but newspapers must revise their approach to news presentation."

Citing the crime hearings that were recently conducted by Tennessee Senator Estes Kefauver, Walters said that television, rather than detracting from reader interest in the hearings, increased it tremendously.

In asserting that editors must revise their treatment of news, Walters continued:

I came up in the deadpan era of factual reporting. That no longer will pass. We must get into the interpretive phase. The (Kefauver hearings) gave the television watcher a real sense of participation in his government. The watcher became his own reporter. And television alerted the reader interested in the newspaper which is doing good reporting.

Walters told the Indianapolis gathering that "straight reporting no longer will satisfy the readers. We can't just throw a lot of wire copy into the paper and expect to get by. We must interpret. . . . We must have good editorial writers."

Walters expressed the same theme two years later, on June 18,

1953, in a speech before 500 circulation specialists at the International Circulation Managers' Association. "The principal potential value of television to newspapers lies in the news interest telecasts create," he said. "Television has the ability to create greater interest than it can satisfy. People are now quite familiar, through watching telecasts, with great personalities and events of our times. They want to read about them."

Walters told the circulation managers that newspapers must modernize their reporting and editing techniques. "We have a great new interest to satisfy," he said. "Most effective television news coverage is limited to the spectacular and to one event at a time. If it holds on for the routine and for too long a period, it loses its viewers. People rely on news reporters to sift the wheat from the chaff and to fill in the details, the background and the explanation that the television camera cannot encompass."

Walters talked about better reporting and editing when he and noted *New York Times* columnist James B. "Scotty" Reston addressed the American Society of Newspaper Editors' convention in the spring of 1952. "There is nothing wrong with our political coverage that a great deal more brain work and leg work and less guess work will not cure," he said. He was alluding to the 1948 election campaign, in which the press reported that New York's Thomas Dewey had the presidency locked up.

"In 1948 newspapers may have relied too much on polls and columnists," Walters continued. He asserted:

They may have their place, and I think they do in political coverage, but let's be sure that we keep them in the proper perspective this year.

It is the line of least resistance to use as sources the campaign manager, the union official, the farm lobbyist and so forth, for a pulse. But do they actually control solid blocks of votes, and does their thinking actually reflect the thinking of voters?

The newspaper business did not doubt enough in 1948. We were too blamed cocksure. We did not bother to go out and put our hands on the voters before we reported with a tone of finality who the next President was going to be.

Maybe we should reappraise and revalue some of our thinking about objective reporting. I fear we may in reality find that it is really deadpan reporting, or even lazy reporting.

A month later, John Knight, in an Editor's Notebook column about the *News*'s foreign service, made it clear that Walters practiced what he preached. He wrote:

"Stuffy" Walters is the type of newspaperman who views all government handouts with suspicion and he can smell propaganda right through 3,000 miles of ocean cable.

. . . like the editors of an earlier day, he wants to know where the body is buried.

"Stuffy's" firm adherence to "investigating everything" and "auditing government" has won him national renown as an editor who doesn't think that merely printing the news ends a newspaper's responsibility to its readers.

That kind of accolade came often. It resulted in more recognition. As 1953 drew to a close, Walters received one of journalism's finest honors—selection as a Fellow by Sigma Delta Chi.

Also chosen was Hodding Carter, editor and publisher of the *Greenville* (Miss.) *Delta Democrat-Times,* who had won the Pulitzer Prize in 1946 for editorial writing. (His son, Hodding III, later received nationwide praise as the chief spokesman for the State Department in Jimmy Carter's administration.) The third Fellow chosen was William H. (Bill) Henry, who had a long, distinguished career with the *Los Angeles Times,* CBS, and NBC, reporting for many years from Washington after serving as a war correspondent.

John Cowles, Walters's former boss in Minneapolis, was also honored when he was named honorary president of Sigma Delta Chi.

Bits and Pieces

When it came to government malfeasance, Walters was especially suspicious of welfare departments. He constantly pushed for records to be opened to the press and the public.

At the spring meeting of the Hoosier State Press Association in April 1951, Walters told its members that the *Indianapolis Star* deserved much praise in leading the campaign to strip away secrecy from the Indiana welfare law.

Walters had special praise for *Star* publisher Eugene C. Pulliam, a founder of Sigma Delta Chi, which stresses press freedom. Walters said that in 1950, more than $4,600,000 in federal, state, and local tax-raised money was "paid out confidentially last year for welfare."

He said he was particularly proud of the Indiana legislature, because the lawmakers "insisted on opening the relief rolls to the public, even at the risk of losing $15,000,000 (estimates on this amount run as high as $22,000,000) in federal grants.''

* * *

Walters was asked by a University of California journalism instructor to outline his hiring policy for young people seeking newspaper work.

Editor and Publisher printed Walters's answer in its April 7, 1951, edition:

1. I want integrity.
2. I want people who want to learn all through their lives—not those who think a diploma ends education.
3. I want people who are not afraid to work—people who really love the newspaper business.
4. I want people who are more interested in achievement and risking new things than in so-called security.
5. I want people who have a sound understanding of America, her traditions, the blessings it affords the individual—whose background in economics, history, politics, etc., will enable them to be something more than ''stenographic'' and ''deadpan'' reporters.
6. I want experts who can audit government, who can examine records intelligently, who can write with intelligence about science, business, labor, etc.
7. I want people who can spell.
8. I want people who can think well, who can observe with accuracy, and who can write fluently in simple language.
9. I prefer those who have had some journalistic training, but who have not confined their college courses. For this reason I do not confine hiring to graduates of accredited schools.

* * *

The duffle bag days of the late 1930s, when Basil Walters commuted between Des Moines and Minneapolis each week carrying a compressed ''wardrobe'' that included a clean suit of B.V.D.s, were only a taste of the travel to come.

Fortified by his boundless energy, Walters usually had a suitcase packed—ready to see things for himself, ready to accept speaking invitations halfway across the country, ready to attend important meetings, ready to move fast when needed in John Knight's growing news-paper empire.

In the spring of 1952, for example, Walters took a lengthy tour of Europe for a combination of reasons: to trade notes with *Daily News* foreign service correspondents, to attend a meeting of the International Press Association, to explore—mostly by auto on back roads —European life through his "down-home" eyes, and write a series of stories on what he absorbed.

Practicing what he preached, Walters wrote stories that were devoid of the stilted prose and deep think that once monopolized foreign dispatches. Often resorting to the first-person, Walters wrote in a touristy tone that mixed just enough fact with fluff to keep the average reader going beyond the first three paragraphs.

In two separate London dispatches, readers learned that "colorful flowering trees have been planted along many of the London roadsides" and, in the country-side, "there is no litter anywhere. Village streets appear freshly scrubbed."

In another story from England, Walters reported, "We were able to get lodging—for $5.25 a person—at a converted 'stately home' . . . located two miles from Stratford-upon-Avon. David Lawrence, the columnist and magazine editor, is registered there for next week-end. I left a note for him saying 'Stuffy' slept here."

Nary a word was said about Stratford-upon-Avon being the birthplace and burial place of one of history's greatest playwrights, William Shakespeare.

And in a story from Paris, readers learned that the Folies-Bergere show "lived up to all the billings. The naughtiness is there, but has been overemphasized."

Readers loved it. And they learned something, too —because after the first few stories, Walters's pieces got meatier as he mixed in more interpretation, thought, and background. From Bonn, he wrote:

One thing I am dead certain. We want and must have these industrious and skilled people of Germany on our side and as our friends.

They are going to be hard competitors for world trade. But with the world so direly in need of the products they can produce, perhaps here lies the key to a peace built on a better general living standard for everybody.

Upon returning to the States, Walters spent a short time in New York, where he wrote two wrap-up pieces that were even harder in tone. He had gradually shifted the diet from cotton candy at the start of his voyage to meat and potatoes at the end.

A *Daily News* story on June 17, 1952, with a United Nations dateline, was put in the *Congressional Record* by Illinois Repesentative Marguerite Stitt Church. The main headline read: "**U.S. Officials Help Stalin Bankrupt Us.**"

An all-cap kicker over that head read: "**AN AMATEUR LOOKS AT EUROPE.**" And a drop head below the main head read: "**Hysteria, Russ Secret Weapon, Blamed for Big Spending.**"

Walters's opening three paragraphs still had meaning in 1980 as the United States boycotted the Moscow Olympic Games in protest of Russia invading Afghanistan. He wrote:

> UNITED NATIONS, N.Y.—Several Europeans told me that American hysteria is Stalin's greatest weapon.
>
> Stalin is reported to have told his associates some years ago that the great advantage he held was due to the fact America feared war more than he did.
>
> Exploitation of this fear therefore got first priority in the Russian cold-war strategy.

Walters said the Europeans told him that Stalin's moves prompted Washington to pour monstrous sums abroad to help in rebuilding Europe's war-torn economy. Walters wrote, "Too many department heads raise their own private hysteria in order to frighten Congress into voting billions blindly."

Walters believed that if America protects its sound economic position and maintains "a sensible but less lavish interest" in world affairs, Europeans are hopeful that their countries will escape the fate of Czechoslovakia, which was crushed when it tried to fight Soviet rule. But, Walters continued, if America "bankrupts itself through squandering, they (the Europeans) reason that an American isolationist reaction will be as extreme as they now regard the lavish American expenditures."

Agreeing with the Europeans he spoke with, Walters said the American program had done "great good to date,'' but that the United States should start shifting the program of rebuilding post-war Europe back to the various nations.

A day later, Walters wrote another piece from the United Nations, again centering on financial waste. His lead paragraph read:

> I came away from Europe with the feeling that the greatest weakness of our foreign program is the result of too lavish spending of American tax money.

Walters asserted that while many overseas American government workers spend tax money conscientiously, "they are often better paid than Americans at home doing similar jobs in private business. They can enjoy better housing and cheap servants. If there are difficulties, there are 'hardship allowances.' In some cases, the U.S. taxpayer builds them new homes.''

The result, Walters wrote, is that the United States is "developing a new 'vested interest' class—people who contribute nothing to American production. Through taxes required to support them they add substantially to the American cost of living. . . . They are in effect parasites.''

Cutting even deeper, Walters said, "It is natural that these Americans with high incomes, hardship allowances, large cars, nursemaids and servants should become country club in their attitude. They mingle only with themselves or with a few of the upper crust of Europe's social and governmental life.''

This story was not inserted in the *Congressional Record,* but its contents received a great deal of attention. Some newspapers wrote editorials and John Knight wrote a column deriding "Our International Boondoggling'' and "Waste of Our Dollars''.

*   *   *

Walters achieved something rare in 1953. He was elected president of the American Society of Newspaper Editors—a major honor in itself—and thus became one of a handful of editors to serve as president of both

ASNE and the Associated Press Managing Editors association during their careers.

One of Walters's final acts as ASNE president, in 1954, was introducing the convention's main speaker, President Dwight D. Eisenhower.

Ike, a well-known golf fanatic, had just returned to Washington from the famed Masters Tournament in Augusta, Georgia, and he wasn't feeling well.

Reah Walters laughed as she told what happened when the president of the United States and the president of the country's top press group met backstage shortly before the chief executive was to speak.

Stuffy told me later, "You know, Eisenhower asked me to feel his forehead, to see if he had a fever."

And Stuffy did. I don't know what he said to Eisenhower. I suppose it was somethig like, "You feel okay, Mr. President."

What I remember the most about that occasion was Eisenhower's talk, because he gripped the podium so stiffly, so tightly, because he was so uncomfortable.

* * *

Walters's honors over the years went beyond journalism.

In September 1954, for example, Walters was one of five Hoosier newsmen to receive an honorary doctor of law degree from Indiana University. The degrees were awarded as part of dedication ceremonies for the new journalism-publication building, Ernie Pyle Hall.

Also honored were A. A. Hargarve, ninety-eight, editor and publisher of the *Rockville Republican* and dean of the state's weekly editors; Frederick A. Miller, eighty-six, president and publisher of the *South Bend Tribune* and dean of Indiana's daily newspapers; Roy W. Howard, chairman of the executive committee of the Scripps-Howard newspapers, who began his career in Indianapolis; and Eugene C. Pulliam.

Walters's longtime friend, J. Russell Wiggins, then managing editor of the *Washington Post* and chairman of ASNEs committee on freedom of information, gave the dedicatory address.

In later years, Walters, who didn't stay around Indiana University long enough to earn a bachelor's degree, joked with friends by saying, "Just call me Doctor Walters."

* * *

Go to work for Uncle Sam?

Walters faced that question as 1955 opened. He received a letter in January from John Knight, saying that Defense Secretary Charles Wilson wanted Walters to serve as assistant secretary of Defense in charge of public and congressional relations.

Knight and Walters had previously talked about the possibility and Knight made it clear in his letter that his view had not changed—it would be a mistake for Walters to accept the assignment. There were problems, Knight said, which would make it impossible for "any man to emerge from the job with an enhanced reputation."

Knight also made it clear that he was looking out for himself. He wrote:

However, the important thing is this: I need not tell you anything about the hotly competitive situation we are and always will be facing in Chicago.

You are the man I need on the Chicago job. Who else would have had the vision to prepare for the Asian situation as you have done with our foreign correspondents? Who else could get out the type of newspaper that is proving so successful in Chicago?

Walters felt honored to be sought after, but kept right on newspapering. And John Knight breathed a sigh of relief.

* * *

Several years after retiring, Walters got a telephone call one afternoon from the young editor of the *Frankfort Times*. Could he visit and kick around an idea? Walters, who never tired of visitors to his farmhouse, told him to come right out.

"I'd like your opinion of starting a second front page," the editor asked, not knowing Walters had created it. "I know the idea is not new. I've heard a few other papers are trying it, but they're large newspapers. Do you think a small county-seat daily like the *Times* can do it?"

Walters looked over the mock-up before him. "I think it's an excellent idea," he said. "I think it can work on a small paper like the *Times.*"

The young editor, Raymond Moscowitz, drove back into the city pleased. The great editor had liked what he, Moscowitz, had come up with.

Two years later, Moscowitz was reading *Functional Newspaper Design,* published in 1956. It was written by Edmund C. Arnold, considered by many editors to be the foremost expert in newspaper typography. In a discussion on section pages, Arnold had written:

An interesting technique is one that Basil Walters, executive editor for the Knight newspapers, developed for that chain: *The second front page,* on page three, is left entirely free of ads and is another page one which includes a full-size flag. Its typographic treatment is the same as the front page. State and local news get the big play. This makes possible localized editions for various metropolitan communities with a minimum of replating; page one need not be changed and yet the second front page will carry the kind of specific area news that builds circulation.

Unfortunately, only the largest newspapers can afford all this wide-open space. But the thinking that created this innovation is to be applauded. We ought to explore constantly new ways to do newspaper jobs better.

Moscowitz smiled and put down Arnold's book. He thought back to his meeting with Walters—a meeting in which Walters had said absolutely nothing about being the creator of the second front page.

*   *   *

Most advertising and editorial departments on newspapers tolerate each other, at best. There are frequent debates over what's news and what's advertising puffery.

Walters was one editor who seldom had a problem with advertising executives. He understood advertising much better than the average editor or reporter. The correspondence course in advertising that he took while in the service had been valuable to him.

In appearing before the Hoosier State Press Association in 1951 and discussing, primarily, the impact of television, Walters also mentioned advertising. "Many newspapermen do not even understand the function of advertising," he said. "It is more than a source of livelihood for a newspaper. Advertising makes it possible to achieve a higher standard of living. Schools of journalism should revise their courses. Many of them have done that already, but many more are sticking too close to the technical side of newspaper production."

It was another occasion when Walters was on target.

CHAPTER THIRTEEN

The Hodge Scandal

B ASIL WALTERS'S Saturday routine: hole up in his tiny office over-
looking the Chicago River, catch up on his mail, have a leisurely
lunch with business friends, clean up some office odds and ends,
return to his suburban Kenilworth home.

That routine was snapped May 12, 1956. Walters was interrupted
by a visitor. He was given a tip: Orville Hodge, the Illinois state
auditor, was stealing state funds. Thousands of dollars.

Later, the name of the visitor would be revealed publicly: Michael
J. Howlett, the Democratic nominee for Illinois state auditor. Howlett
knew Walters's Saturday routine, knew he would be alone in his office.

Walters had a problem. Hodge's opponent was making serious
charges. Like every editor, he did not want to waste any of his staff's
time sifting out gossip and malice and wind up chasing bogeymen. On
the other hand, Howlett was a solid guy. He had managed Paul H.
Douglas's first campaign for the U.S. Senate when Douglas was a
Chicago alderman. And, as regional administrator for the former Office of Price Administration, Howlett had tipped off newspapermen
to the illegal sale of ground horsemeat as beef. The subsequent investigation revealed that food inspectors under Governor Adlai Stevenson
accepted bribes from slaughterers to approve horsemeat for human
consumption. Stevenson's own investigation followed, resulting in the
governor firing the guilty employees.

After Howlett left Walters's office, the editor thought about Carl
Sandburg, his Kenilworth neighbor. Sandburg had given Walters an
autographed copy of his book, *Remembrance Rock,* which noted the
sacrifices made by the country's pioneers. The book had prompted a
Walters speech before the American Society of Newspaper Editors, in
which he said he feared the American people were letting their liberties

slip by default. "The whole theory of the American dream is that officials are servants of the people," he told his fellow editors.

Before that Saturday was over, Walters also thought about the lesson he learned as a cub reporter: when an official hides his records from the public, something not in the public interest is probably taking place.

Walters told managing editor Ev Norlander and city editor Clem Lane about the tip. Check it out, he said.

On Monday morning, May 14, George Thiem was in the Statehouse pressroom. A one-time farm editor who had shifted to politics, Thiem had recommended to Walters that the *Daily News* become the first paper to open a full-time bureau in Springfield. Walters agreed, and the bureau was opened in January 1949, shortly after Stevenson was elected governor in November 1948.

Now, as another work week was about to begin, Thiem received a call from Chicago. It was Ev Norlander. Thiem wrote about the conversation in his book, *The Hodge Scandal:*

"George, there will be a gentleman down to see you tomorrow morning," he said.
"He'll call at your home. Wait for him there. Listen to what he has to say, and do it."
He identified the caller as Michael Howlett . . .
I knew Mike Howlett slightly and had a good opinion of him. . . .

Thiem knew Hodge even better. He had served three terms as a member of the legislature from Granite City before being elected auditor. Like many people, Thiem knew Hodge as a genial, handsome, well-liked politican who was a top vote-getter. Like others, too, Thiem assumed Hodge was a wealthy real estate and insurance man. That assumption was based on Hodge's extravagant lifestyle—expensive suits and ties, monogrammed shirts, a suite of rooms he maintained at the Abraham Lincoln Hotel in Springfield, regular visits to Springfield nightclubs in the company of fellow politicians and attractive women, a remodeled summer bungalow on Lake Springfield. There was much more, such as two airplanes that he kept at Springfields's Capital Airport and used for duck-hunting trips to Arkansas and visits to the Florida motel he operated.

Thiem wrote in his book:

It was reasonable to believe that a politician wouldn't make such a display of his wealth if he were siphoning it off from public funds. . . .

Yet, if Orville was diverting some of the extra money he got from the legislature for his personal use, there was only one way to play it. Take it easy. Get into the office and scoop up as much information as possible before alarming anyone.

The auditor's office was like a second home to Thiem. He had spent considerable time there in 1947, when he and Roy J. Harris of the *St. Louis Post-Dispatch* began checking vouchers in the payroll padding case involving Illinois newsmen.

Within a week of getting his tip on Tuesday, May 15, Thiem told Walters, "This thing is going to reveal a million dollar steal if I can nail it down."

It wasn't easy. From the start, Hodge tried to block the reporter. Office employees were told not to talk to Thiem. Certain records could not be found. Others were obtained only after persistent demands.

Persistence paid off. When Thiem asked Hodge if Anna Mae Harris, a Granite City legislator's wife, was on the auditor's payroll, Hodge said no. Thiem, however, learned that the state treasurer kept a monthly ledger record of payroll warrants. When he checked them, the name of Anna Mae Harris of Granite City jumped out at him.

Thiem confronted Hodge with the facts: "Orville, you lied to me about Anna Mae Harris, and I don't like to be lied to. I've been looking at your payroll in the treasurer's office. Somebody tampered with the payroll records in the county books. A lot of names are missing that ought to be there."

Hodge agreed to provide his latest payroll to Thiem. When he got it, lines had been drawn through several names, with the word "terminated" next to them. Thiem learned that some of those people, some of whom were Hodge relatives, had been "fired." Thiem wrote a front-page story that appeared June 4, 1956:

State Auditor Fires 15
After Query on Payroll

SPRINGFIELD, ILL.—State Auditor Orville E. Hodge has fired 15 persons after the Daily News had started an investigation of reported payroll padding and other irregularities in the office.

The story was practically lost in the later editions. The big item that day was another revelation—that of a secret speech by Russian leader Nikita S. Khrushchev which savagely attacked his predecessor, Joseph Stalin, as a ruthless tyrant.

A day later, Thiem reported that all but $33,000 of the auditor's contractual services fund of $1.4 million had been spent in just the first eleven months of the 1955–57 biennium.

The June 4 and 5 stories prompted a *Daily News* editorial.

Audit The Auditor

> One of the needs in Illinois is a state controller, some official with more authority than mere auditor, to inquire into the propriety of official expenditures, as well as checking the books. State law does not give the present auditor, Orville E. Hodge, the power that we describe.
>
> One of the reasons this state needs such an office is the condition of Mr. Hodge's own office, as disclosed in Daily News dispatches from Springfield. It turns out to have been a haven for relatives and friends and politicians and friends of friends, relatives and politicians.

Hodge was now thoroughly on the defensive. He barred reporters from the auditor's office. The action brought him embarrassing nationwide publicity—and a stern rebuke in another *Daily News* editorial written by associate editor A. T. Burch.

Hodge's secretiveness prompted Walters to write to V. M. Newton, Jr., managing editor of the *Tampa Tribune,* who was Sigma Delta Chi's national Freedom of Information Committee chairman. Newton, in turn, wrote to Hodge, "(wishing) to lodge a most vigorous protest against your action in barring reporters . . . from the records of the state auditor's office."

Hodge's troubles were only beginning. Thiem asked State Treasurer Warren E. Wright for access to his warrant reconciliation card file, which shows the face of each check issued by the state auditor. Wright wanted to cooperate with the reporter, but to protect his position, he asked Attorney General Latham Castle for an opinion on the legality of opening his files to the press. Castle immediately replied that public records are just that—public—and should be open to news people.

Thiem's digging in the treasurer's office resulted in a June 15 story revealing how Hodge's contractual fund had been spent and disclosing the names of persons to whom checks had been issued.

Thomas H. Fitzgerald, a Chicago attorney, was listed as receiving a check for $9,000 from the contractual fund. Fitzgerald, who had worked for several state auditors for nineteen years, returned from a Canada vacation and called Lane. "I never saw such a check," an angry Fitzgerald said. "I never had any money coming."

Thiem wondered about who endorsed the Fitzgerald warrant. Who cashed it? Who got the money?

Thiem remembered being told that the treasurer's office micro-filmed state warrants until January 1, 1956, when Hodge took over the job. On Friday, June 29, Thiem asked if he could check the micro-film. He could.

The Fitzgerald warrant came up on the screen, showing both the front and back. Thiem was impressed by the typewritten endorsement. The type face was from a late model typewriter. The endorsement read: "For the Deposit and Credit of Thomas H. Fitzgerald."

The stamp of the Chicago Federal Reserve Bank was visible, but it was not clear which corresponding bank had cashed it. Thiem suspected it was the Southmoor Bank & Trust Company, which had approved a large loan to Hodge at low rates for his Florida motel.

The Fitzgerald warrant was among fifteen that totaled $180,000, all apparent forgeries, all endorsed with the same typewriter, all cashed the same day. Thiem learned it was not unusual for checks presented for deposit to the payee's account to be endorsed with a typewriter.

Thiem had his big break.

Meanwhile, Lane ordered every person on the list of people for whom apparently forged checks had been written, which was published June 15, to be interviewed. He assigned three tough reporters to the task: William Mooney, Robert Schultz, and Robert Gruenberg. They learned that of the other fourteen on the list there were thirteen like Fitzgerald, who had never received checks and were not due them.

As July turned the corner, the *Daily News* had its biggest story in hand, but was afraid to print it. The paper's attorneys worried about a libel suit. They wanted documentary evidence—photostats of the forged checks.

Wright refused to let Thiem take the microfilm to Chicago for copying. But Wright, who had received anonymous threats for open-ing his files, decided he would take the microfilm to St. Louis for copying.

Wright brought back the photostats on July 3. They were of poor quality, not good enough as evidence. Nothing could be accomplished

on July 4. Tension built so high that day that Lane suffered a heart attack and was taken to a hospital. On July 5, a second set of prints was
made. They were much better—and usable.

The *Daily News* was ready to publish. On July 6 it backed into the
story:

> On June 15, the Daily News published a partial
> list of payments made by State Auditor Orville E.
> Hodge showing how in 11 months he spent all except
> $8.33 of a two-year contractual service fund of
> $197,832.
>   Included in the list was a $9,000 payment to
> Thomas H. Fitzgerald. . . .

Walters asked Thiem to take a copy of the July 6 *Daily News* to
Governor William G. Stratton. Then Walters and Burch called Stratton, suggesting that a guard be placed over all state records. Hodge,
the State of Illinois, the *Daily News,* and the governor, himself, would
be protected by such a move. Stratton moved immediately.

A two-line banner headline, in all caps, was splashed across page
one of the Saturday, July 7, issue: **"GUARD STATE AUDITOR'S
RECORDS: FOUR-WAY INQUIRY IS UNDER WAY."**

Initially, the other Chicago newspapers didn't follow up the *Daily
News*'s leads. They were, in part, hesitant to think that Hodge—
popular, likable, generous with a buck, outgoing with a smile—would
do such illegal things. Even as more details came forth, some people
defended Hodge, asserting he was underpaid and that a little forgery
wouldn't hurt the Illinois taxpayers much.

When it was all over, the investigation revealed that "a little
forgery" had resulted in a $2.5 million theft from the Illinois tax-
payers.

After initially trying to dodge guilt, Hodge pleaded guilty to stealing state funds totalling about $1.5 million. He was sentenced to
twelve to fifteen years imprisonment. Two of his associates in the illegal checks scheme also pleaded guilty and were sentenced to lesser
terms. They were Edward A. Hintz, who was president of the Southmoor Bank & Trust Company, where more than $600,000 worth of
the phony state checks were cashed, and Edward A. Epping, Hodge's
first assistant.

For George Thiem, another Pulitzer Prize was on the way.

A Guarding of Confidences

A gang of curious lawyers awaited Basil Walters's speech before The Law Club of Chicago on October 5, 1956. Walters knew they were curious.

Four days earlier, the *Daily News* had published an Associated Press story out of Decatur with this headline: **"'I Gave Tip on Hodge': Howlett."**

The story reported that Michael J. Howlett said he furnished the *Daily News* with the initial Hodge tip. The story went on to say that while Walters declined to confirm that Howlett was the informant, Thiem confirmed it was Howlett.

The AP story quoted Thiem as saying, "Howlett came to Basil Walters, executive editor of The News, with the information after getting it from another source. I assume he got his information from somebody in the auditor's office."

Walters told the lawyers, "I hope this properly confuses you at the start."

Walters told the lawyers that when he issued a "no comment" to the Associated Press, he did "one of the smartest things" he had ever done. Explained Walters,

I have not been released from confidence by many of the people who provided us with valuable information in the Hodge investigation. I must respect those confidences. If I start confirming or denying all reports about who supplied us with information, your temporarily parked disciplined minds would confirm my fear that I would soon become a runaway witness and that through elimination and deductions smart guys would force me to break confidences.

Walters then gave a brief narrative on the Hodge case before concluding with these words:

Some folks have asked me if I thought the Hodge sentence was severe enough. My answer is yes. I do not believe in vengeance. I believe in reform.

Hodge is serving a sentence for a crime of carelessness, selfishness and thoughtlessness of which all of us are guilty.

I don't like the role of reformer. I like to publish cheerful news.

I'd like to turn the job of law enforcement back where it belongs, to the lawyers.

Much was written about the case. On July 26, 1956, Forrest Allen, commenting on Hodge's downfall in the *Cleveland Press,* wrote, "Despite his imposing titles of executive editor of the Daily News and executive editor of the John S. Knight Newspapers, Stuffy Walters is just a reporter with a bigger desk and an efficient secretary. A reporter, also, with 'sources.' "

Hodge would be Walters's last great investigative story as an editor. And, fittingly, it would easily be his best.

Clark Mollenhoff, an outstanding investigative reporter for several years for Walters's former employers, Cowles Publications, recognized that fact. In an October 1956 letter to Walters, Mollenhoff wrote, "As more than a casual observer of investigations, I feel that it [the Hodge scandal] is probably the finest investigative job that has ever been done by a newspaper. It is even more to your credit that there was so little enthusiasm from some other papers as it started."

Although Hodge would be Walters's last great investigative story, it would not be his last exclusive story in the five years that remained before retirement beckoned in 1961.

CHAPTER FOURTEEN

Exclusives from the Middle East

IVE years after first visiting his European correspondents, Basil
Walters winged across the seas again in the spring of 1957. At
mid-trip, *Newsweek* magazine devoted almost an entire page in its
June 4, 1957, issue to Walters's career and style, headlining the article:
"ONE EDITOR'S WORLD."

At one point, the *Newsweek* piece told readers, "Unlike most of
his staff, Walters is no hot-shot reporter." True. As Walters's fellow
newspapermen knew by then, Walters was actually a hot-shot editor
who knew what to do with hot-shot reporters.

Newsweek opined that Walters's interview with Lord William
Beveridge in London produced "only the news that the father of Britain's 'cradle-to-grave' security system was having trouble living on the
inflated pounds being paid him by British social security." (Beveridge,
a liberal economist, had proposed in 1941 Great Britain's program of
comprehensive social insurance.)

Time had earlier viewed Walters's Beveridge piece in a more
favorable light. In its May 20 issue, in an article that centered on John
Knight, the magazine wrote, "In a dispatch from London . . . Editor
Walters, on tour, was busily exposing Lord Beveridge and Britain's
womb-to-tomb social-security system."

The *Newsweek* article was positive in its criticism. It said the
Beveridge story was "like Walters's later stories from France, Belgium
and the Netherlands . . . brief and readable. That, Walters has made
clear, is what he wants."

In noting that Walters is a "bug on short stories," *Newsweek*
quoted him as saying, "What I like is the whole situation wrapped in
one beautiful package of 600 words." The magazine reported what
was commonly known in the profession—that Walters's critics con-

tended that there are more than a few stories that cannot be told in a 600-word package, no matter how beautiful the wrapping.

Walters's critics had less to argue about when it came to deciding what the foreign service should cover. By then, the foreign service had only seven full-time people. Walters exhibited an uncanny feel for shifting them to where a major story would break. *Newsweek* commented:

> Ed Lahey, the Knight newspapers' gifted Washington bureau chief, offers a good case in point of Stuffy's intuitive feel for news. In 1954, on a "routine" assignment from Walters, Lahey just "happened" to be in Egypt when the British suddenly withdrew from the Sudan. Later that year, Lahey was back in Washington covering the Army-McCarthy hearings when the Supreme Court handed down its desegregation decree. Walters sent him hurrying south, but called him off that assignment with a quick and apparently inexplicable order to proceed to Guatemala. Lahey arrived in time to cover Guatemala's anti-Communist revolution in June.

Walters had a special fondness for Lahey. He told a group of Copley Newspapers executives in 1970:

> I don't know how far (Lahey) got along in school. He wasn't a high school graduate . . . he was a checker of freight cars out of the yards in Chicago, counting the cars and getting the numbers down, and he saw reporters out there one day. And he said, "I'd like to be reporter." He got a job. And he was one of the great reporters of our times.

As the *Newsweek* story noted, Walters's 1957 trip concluded in the Middle East. One suspects that he especially looked forward to this part of the trip. By then, he had taken a deep interest in the Middle East conflict, having frequently discussed the situation at lunch with Jewish business friends and exchanged correspondence with Arab and Jewish leaders in the public and private sectors.

Walters's Middle East visit produced a journalistic coup—exclusive interviews with three major leaders: Egypt's President Nasser, Israeli Prime Minister Ben-Gurion, and young Jordanian King Hussein.

Perhaps many Zionists, particularly those in Chicago, felt that Walters was anti-Semitic. But non-Zionist Jews, many in leadership positions within the Chicago Jewish community, knew Walters was not anti-Jew. They knew that when Walters debated a point that favored the Arabs he was debating from a position of honest belief, not prejudice.

Walters saw himself as a healer in the Arab-Israeli dispute, which grabbed center stage on November 29, 1947, when the United Nations General Assembly voted 33-13 (ten abstentions) to partition Palestine into separate, independent Israeli and Arab states effective October 1, 1948.

On October 20, 1955, Walters received a letter from a Jewish reader that began, "I'm getting a craw full reading your sour-pussed, dispeptic correspondent, George Weller, he of the ill-concealed anti-Semitism." Later, the reader wrote, "Like the man with the monkey on his back, we will have to pay the piper for these violent backward peoples who will parlay our emotional fear of Russia into economic bankruptcy."

Before publishing the reader's letter, Walters wrote to the man, saying,

> It is the obligation of a newspaper to report to its readers all views, the minority as well as the majority. . . . I have been disturbed by the loose way in which "anti-Semitism" is used in describing anyone who runs counter to the hopes of the state of Israel. That, I believe you will agree, on reflection, is not in keeping with the American spirit of tolerance for those who do not exactly agree in all respects with their own thinking. . . . I wonder if on reflection you would want to see in print the reference to the Arabs as "violent backward people." Some of them are, but a great many are cultured. All are human beings.

Eight months later, Walters wrote an editorial that rebuked the Syrian ambassador to the United States, Farid Zeinddine. In a speech at Illinois State University in Normal, Illinois, Zeinddine compared Zionism with Naziism, claiming that Zionism is anti-Semitic and has a chosen people just as Naziism had its super race.

"The American Jew is not an American emotionally or even ultimately," the Syrian envoy said. "A Zionist cannot have real allegiance to the country in which he lives."

Walters's editorial began with this headline: **"Vicious Falsehood."** He wrote, "For a sample of the kind of reasoning that blocks a peace between Israel and the Arab nations we give you the remarks of Farid Zeinddine."

After quoting the ambassador's remarks about an American Jew not being committed to America as a nation, Walters wrote:

> The effrontery of this attempt to pass on the qualifications of American citizens is matched only by the bitter prejudice that it reveals. It is interesting to note that a substantial number of American Jews are opposed to Zionism,

giving as one reason that it would invite this false allegation. But it is equally a falsehood when applied to the great numbers of Jews who support Israel.

Walters charged that Zeinddine's remarks were "totally out of place in the language of an accredited diplomat from another country."

But despite the tough tone of that editorial, the Syrian envoy and Walters apparently harbored no bitterness toward one another. After Walters returned from his 1957 trip, he wrote the ambassador in Washington saying he had tried in vain to find a lariat tie for a Captain Saleem Ibrahim, who was attracted to it.

Walters had offered the lariat tie to the young officer, but Ibrahim had refused, because he knew Walters had received it as a gift from his wife, Rhea. When Walters couldn't find the same kind of tie after returning home, he bought eight similar ties as souvenirs for the Syrian army officers he met.

In his letter to Zeiddine, Walters asked the ambassador to explain the circumstances and requested that the ties be forwarded to Ibrahim and five other officers listed by name. The two extra ties were in case he missed anyone.

By the time Walters wrote that letter and sent the ties, his Middle East stories had appeared in the *Daily News* and the foreign service's clients' newspapers. The combined circulation came to 25,000,000.

The interviews Walters conducted with the leading Middle East leaders on his trip produced stories that, while mixed in quality, undoubtedly scored heavily with readers. Again, they were written in a conversational tone to which Joe Chicago or Jane Boston could easily relate. In fact, what Walters wrote were conversations, not interviews. He did not take notes, leaving that chore to his youngest son, Jim, a Navy lieutenant based in London on leave.

The *Daily News* bought the July 13, 1957, cover of *Editor and Publisher* to advertise that Walters had become the only man to exclusively interview all heads of the leading Middle East nations.

The exclusivity didn't produce any information to excite Middle East watchers, but the stories contained interesting, relevant, significant insights into the troubled region. And the stories, after all, were not intended for Middle East experts, but for the guy down the block. The "hot-shot" reporting exhibited by his correspondents—as *Newsweek* earlier noted—was missing. But "unstuffy Stuffy's" instincts for news that would grab the average reader were as sharp as ever.

Walters was quite good at making the material relevant—so relevant that as 1982 dawned, twenty-five years later, it still applied to the dynamics of the Middle East situation. After his "Big Three" interviews appeared, Walters wrote a piece that appeared June 24, 1957. Datelined Jerusalem, Jordan, the article carried the headline: **"What Can Be Done With, for Refugees?"** Above that sixty-point headline was a twenty-four-point kicker headline: **"No. 1 Mideast Problem:"** The opening paragraphs are especially relevant today.

> Some day, somehow, the politicians of the world will have to sit down and solve the problems of the Arab refugees from Palestine.
> This remains, after nine long years, the No. 1 humanitarian and political problem of the Middle East.
> The longer the problem remains unsolved, the more dangerous the consequences will be, Henry Labouisse, director of the U.N. Relief and Works Agency for Palestine Refugees, recently warned the U.N. special political committee. . . .
> Nothing short of the return of the refugees to their old homes will suffice, I was told repeatedly.

The world would be given similar advice over and over again in the twenty-five years to follow. It is clear now, to many observers, that the Arab-Israeli dispute will not be solved until a Palestinian state is established on the West Bank of the Jordan River, which Israel wrested from Jordan in the brief 1967 Arab-Israeli war.

The *Daily News* gave Walters's interview with Egyptian President Gamal Abdel Nasser extraordinary front-page display on June 17. The sixty-point, two-column headline read: **"Our Editor Has a Talk With Nasser."**

Toting one's horn? Yes. But why not in fiercely competitive Chicago journalism? Actually, Walters's long piece probably deserved the headline treatment it received. It was among the best he wrote during his six-week journey.

Typical of not overwhelming the reader with political substance, Walters's Nasser story concentrated on general impressions. The piece displayed the humanness Walters always sought. The reader did not have difficulty identifying with the prose. It had a "common man" tone that made one feel as if he were sitting in on the conversation.

The timing of Walters's long chat with Nasser could hardly have been better. The interview took place in Nasser's home less than a year after the 1956 Suez Canal crisis dominated the world's front pages.

Before the crisis, Walters knew that Nasser had been miffed by what he felt was western interference in key Middle East affairs. Nasser had responded by recognizing Communist China and ordering armaments from Czechoslovakia. In turn, the United States on July 19, 1956, withdrew its offer to help finance Egypt's crucial Aswan Dam project. An angry Nasser countered a week later by nationalizing the Suez Canal and imposing martial law along the 102-mile waterway. Nasser ordered all canal income funnelled into the dam's building costs. By September 14, Egypt had control of one of the world's most strategic shipping routes.

When diplomatic efforts to place the canal under international control failed, aerial warfare broke out between Egypt and Israel on October 30. After Nasser warned the British and French that he would fight to keep the canal, they responded with an ultimatum: their troops would be sent to the Suez if Israeli and Egyptian troops didn't withdraw ten miles from the canal and cease fighting by a designated time. By nightfall that day, Egypt reported British and French planes were bombing Egyptian cities in an attempt to force Egyptian evacuation of the Suez.

A day later, Israel accepted the British-French ultimatum, providing Egypt also accepted. Nasser answered on November 1—by breaking off diplomatic relations with Britain and France and seizing their property in Egypt. Jordan entered the fight by severing her ties with France and telling Britain she would no longer be allowed to use ground or air bases in Jordan. On November 2, the city of Gaza, in that finger-like stretch of land in northern Egypt, fell to Israeli forces. The second major Middle East war in less than ten years was in full swing.

British, French, and Israeli forces scored a quick victory and by December 26, 1956, clearance of sunken vessels and mines in the Suez Canal began. But the hostilities and diplomatic rhetoric continued to glow like a gigantic fire that refused to die.

With those events fixed in his mind, Walters sat in Nasser's Heliopolis (a Cairo suburb) home and fired off some blunt questions, including, "Are you a dictator?" Walters wrote: "'Dictator or liberator, it's how you look at it,' Egypt's tall, stalwart President replied with a chuckle.

"Lincoln used to tell the fable of a shepherd who prevented a wolf from eating his sheep. To the sheep he was a liberator. But to the world he was a dictator."

Those two paragraphs launched the Nasser story. But a political discussion did not follow. Instead, Walters followed up by putting the reader on the grounds and inside the house with some excellent descriptive prose.

About Nasser's residence:

> It is the same broad, two-storied house, slightly enlarged and enclosed by a high wall, where as a lieutenant colonel he forged the 1952 revolution ousting portly King Farouk and the Parliament.
>
> Conspicuous in the courtyard, guarded outside by white-clad sentries, was a child's hobby horse.
> . . .
> His office in the left-handed wing is plain, with simple green leather furniture and a long, flat desk piled with dossiers. He is boss on this side.
>
> But in the right-hand wing it is obvious that Mrs. Nasser rules. Gray wall-to-wall carpeting is the base for the classical heavy lounge chairs and divan in bright oriental motifs.
>
> Lined on the marble mantel were six silver-framed photographs of Nehru, Chou En-lai, Sukarno, Tito, President Kuwatly of Syria and India's President Rajendra Prasad.

Turning to Nasser's rise to power, Walters wrote:

> Looking backward for my benefit, Nasser methodically retraced the revolution ousting the "corrupt" parliament, as he called it.
>
> "After the revolution, we were without a program, and so we took as our program the broken promises of a generation of corrupt premiers.
>
> "From my boyhood on I always heard politicians promising electrification of the Aswan Dam, more schools, social centers, steel mills and distribution of land to poor farmers. Nothing was accomplished because the leaders were corrupt."

Later, the story traced Egypt's siding with Russia. Nasser talked of the Soviet Union selling Egypt wheat after the United States refused, of Russia buying Egyptian cotton after European nations refused.

Further down—perhaps too far in the story that filled almost a half-page of type—Walters got into the Israeli question by writing:

> Heatedly, Nasser denied any intention to annihilate Israel. "I have never said that I would drive Israel into the sea, even though American editorial writers are always making me say so," he said gravely.
>
> "I have never dreamed that I could overrun Israel. Why not? Simply because today the whole world is closely bound together. Nobody wants war. Anybody can begin a war. But nobody can foretell —as Ben-Gurion now realizes—how world opinion will turn against him."

Walters's long interview with Nasser wasn't the only piece out of Egypt. He wrote a lengthy story on Egyptian life and its people. His lead: "From my hotel balcony I counted nine moderate-sized skyscrapers in various stages of completion. The Nile Hilton and the New Shepherd's hotels are almost ready for guests." What followed was a travel editor's copy—in a time when few travel editors were sent by newspapers to Cairo, Egypt.

Ever the editor, Walters got a story out of son, Jim, who had graduated from the University of Michigan with a degree of engineering. He would eventually become a bank executive in Kalamazoo, Michigan. But, judging from the story he wrote about a new Egyptian steel mill, he could easily have followed in his father's footsteps.

Walters's visit in Egypt came after Lebanon, where his Middle East trek began, and stops in Syria and Jordan. In Hashemite Jordan, twenty-one-year-old King Hussein Ibn Talal was in the early stages of his long rule.

Walters portrayed Hussein as "Jordan's gallant young David (who) said that the United States should offer him enough slingshots to discourage Israel from taking more lands of the Bible."

Those words in the story's lead are again followed by scene-setting material that makes no attempt to weave in the political, military, and philosophical discussions that eventually follow. Walters, true to his belief in simplicity, demonstrated that the small details needed to give a long story color and foundation cannot be integrated with descriptions of complicated issues.

The third, fourth, and fifth paragraphs illustrate Walters's long-held ability to edit stories into concise, detailed, easily understood word packages:

> Wearing a plain business suit, Hussein received me in an austere office in his single-story hilltop palace. His doors were guarded outside by elderly Circassians, fur-capped, black-clad refugees from southern Russia who wore bandoliers across their chests and daggers at their waists.
>
> The 21-year-old King astonished me by the candor, coolness, precision and maturity with which he answered questions. His manner was quick and direct.
>
> A buffer state without natural resources, Hussein's parliamentary kingdom has 1,600,000 people —slightly less than Israel. One third of them are Palestinian refugees living in an almost waterless desert under intense anti-Western propaganda, both nationalist and Communist.

That setting aside, Walters's next paragraph consists of a simple question that cuts to the core of the interview: " 'What does Jordan need most?' I asked the king."

Hussein, who had become king on his eighteenth birthday, May 2, 1953, gave an answer that was as simple as the question. His nation needed a chance to "make a living peacefully without the constant insecurity imposed by its more powerful neighbor, Israel."

Hussein's grandfather, King Abdullah, had been assassinated by a Palestinian extremist July 20, 1951. Abdullah's son, Talal, had become king on September 5, 1951, but his reign lasted less than a year. The Jordanian Parliament, citing mental disorders, removed Talal in August 1952, and young Hussein, still not 18, assumed power under a regency until he became 18. The young monarch was deeply concerned about the unifying of his nation, which had suffered through this period of instability.

"We can unify Jordan only if we are free of fear," Hussein told Walters. "Only through obtaining somewhere adequate arms to pacify our people's fears of Israel can Jordan gain internal peace."

More than twenty years later, Hussein had his arms, acquired in large part from the United States. But his desire to free his people from fear continued to elude him.

Israel was Walters's final stop, but passage into that nation was not possible from an Arab country. Walters thus flew from Cairo to neutral Greece, then on to Tel Aviv. There he interviewed the father of Israel, David Ben-Gurion, only two days after talking with Nasser.

The interview appeared on page one June 19 with this two-column, three-line, bold-face headline: **"100-Yr. Peace Envisioned by Ben-Gurion."**

Describing Ben-Gurion as "bushy-haired" and "fiery," Walters led by reporting that the Israeli leader was prepared to make a 100-year peace pact with his Arab neighbors.

That revelation came after Walters remarked that Ben-Gurion's Arab neighbors feared Israel planned to expand its borders by force.

"We would keep the status quo, both of us. Would that be enough for them?" Ben-Gurion responded. He asserted that all Israel needed to do was build up herself as a nation "and continue what we already have done in turning a desert into a flourishing home for happy people."

Saying he felt Israel will be a force for bringing back the former prosperity of the Middle East, Ben-Gurion told Walters, "If there will be peace between us, we will be able to help give (the Arabs) the use of our experience and knowledge."

Ben-Gurion was upbeat—condescending, too, some would say—in the opening of the interview:

> We will help our neighbors make their homes really what they should be—remove poverty, ignorance and disease. The Arabs are our distant cousins. Sometimes two brothers quarrel more than foreigners.
>
> But certainly Hebrew is close to Arabic. Yesterday I read a fine sentence in a British paper: "The most easy second language for us English is the American language."
>
> I cannot say that Arabic is as close to Hebrew as American is to English, but there is an affinity. The main thing for us both is peace.

Ben-Gurion's initial softness soon turned into toughness. When Walters told Ben-Gurion that Nasser felt the only way to save the Middle East from communism was by helping nationalism, Ben-Gurion became angry. Walters wrote:

> "I am sorry to say that that fellow is a liar," snapped back Ben-Gurion. "I would not have said

that four years ago. I had then certain hopes on him and more on Naguib (Maj. Gen. Mohammad Naguib, who Nasser succeeded). Nasser brought communism into the Middle East. What he said to you he would not say to a Russian. He knew you were an American.''

Ben-Gurion then charged that Nasser brought the Communists into Syria. The Israeli leader had become fiery by now. Walters quoted him:

''I will tell you in a few words what is the trouble with the Arab world. They don't know the meaning of nationalism. There is no constructive element in their nationalism, and I have known their movement for at least 50 years.

''They have done nothing to spread literature, education, to properly cultivate their land, to lift up the fellah (peasant) or do away with poverty and disease.''

Later, when Walters told Ben-Gurion that great emphasis was placed by the Arab world on a solution of the refugee problem as a preliminary to a settlement, Ben-Gurion replied with determination, ''The clock cannot be turned back.''

Ben-Gurion blamed Arab leadership for having persuaded the Arabs to leave Israel, arguing that the country they left no longer exists—points still used today by Israelis in the war of words over who has the right to the land Israel now occupies.

Walters wrote that Ben-Gurion at seventy-one was the peppiest man he had met on his Middle East journeys.

Walters met a peppy woman in Israel, too, when he interviewed Golda Meir as part of a summing-up article. The lead ran seven paragraphs. It provided the foundation for his talk with Mrs. Meir, who was then Israel's foreign minister. She later became prime minister, carving a major niche in world history.

Personalizing his writing immediately, Walters began:

I have now traveled both sides of the armistice line that separates Israel from its Arab neighbors.

I have traveled by foot, jeep, plane and auto along that line on the Arab side from Lebanon

> through Syria and Jordan along the Dead Sea and
> over Aqaba Gulf to Egypt. . . .
>   I have talked with potentates and with peasants.
> Without exception they dream of peace. Yet there is
> no peace. Christ had his crown of thorns. The Holy
> Land of three great religions, Christian, Jewish and
> Moslem, today has its crown of rusty barbed wire.
>   Two weeks ago near Jerusalem, Jordan, I
> walked along the Arab side of a village street
> separated in the middle by the ever-present barbed
> wired.
>   Today I walked down the Israel side of the same
> street.
>   A few miles away is ancient Jericho. The walls
> of Jericho were collapsed, the Bible tells, by
> trumpets.

At this point, Walters made his transition to Mrs. Meir, working the "nut graph" into his story: "Mrs. Meir thinks the time is ripe for the trumpets of world opinion to lift the crown of barbed wire from the brow of the Holy Land."

The article is one of Walters's shortest—more along the lines he advocated in earlier days with George Gallup and Robert Gunning. The last three paragraphs are simple, but they make a powerful statement. They are Mrs. Meir's words:

> The big powers should come to the United Na-
> tions and make no recriminations, no preconditions.
> They should merely say:
>   1. Israel is here to stay.
>   2. Let's sit down and make peace.

Walters saw water as a key to Middle East peace. He wrote:

> Israel has done the best job in utilizing what
> water it has. It is indeed today a land of milk and
> honey and happy people. The mountains are being
> reforested.
>   New cities and villages have been built. The
> country is tied together in a vast network of irriga-
> tion pipes that have turned the desert into citrus
> groves, vegetable gardens, dairies and farmland."

Shortly after returning home, Walters told George Brandenburg of *Editor and Publisher* that American newsmen ought to report more of the achievements made by Arab countries and Israel, rather than just wait for sensational—usually negative—news to develop.

He told Brandenburg he was convinced that Israel is here to stay, Arab unity will come sooner than many people think, and most of the tensions will ease, including the Arab refugee problem, because there is a sincere desire for peace in all Middle Eastern countries.

Walters's predictions would rate about a B–. He was on target when he said Israel was here to stay. He was partially correct, at best, in saying Arab unity would come sooner than later. Arab unity has occurred to some degree since 1957, but, overall, it has not solidified to a point that would clearly threaten Israel's existence or accept Israel as being a reality. He was partially correct, too, in saying that tensions will ease, including the refugee problem. In the spring of 1981, Israel was at peace with Egypt, but relations between the two nations were shaky because of the refugee problem. It still was the crux of the Middle East conflict. Egypt insisted that the Palestinians must be given an independent homeland on the West Bank; Israel resisted, asserting that the West Bank was an integral part of Israel's history and must never be relinquished.

Walters also told Brandenburg that the Arabs "have a right to complain they have not had good coverage in the American press. This is their own fault to some extent, of course. Israel has been much wiser in this respect and has invited American coverage." If Walters was less than accurate on his predictions, he was perfect in his view of press coverage for the two antagonists.

He warned American newsmen going into the Middle East to avoid "labels" and to approach the people with a friendly attitude.

"I was looking for the good, instead of the sensational," he explained to Brandenburg. "Citizens talking to citizens can pave the way for a better understanding between our country and the Middle East."

Those views alarmed some of Chicago's Jewish community, a part of which was already leery of Walters. They had never heard such pro-Arab talk before. Never mind that he praised Israel. Never mind that he said Israel was here to stay. Never mind that he, one of the most influential editors in the country, had urged his fellow journalists to be more positive in their reporting.

Walters's thick skin, though—the thick skin every journalist needs to survive—easily repelled the attacks. And his Jewish friends, while not agreeing entirely with his views, admitted that for the most part he was correct.

Coffee, Tea, or an International Incident

While visiting with King Hussein, Basil Walters crated an "international incident" involving a cup of Jordanian coffee.

George Weller, the *Daily News* Middle East correspondent who accompanied Walters, wrote about it in a front-page article that allowed Chicagoans to have a good laugh on their portly little editor.

The "incident" began as Walters and his party awaited an audience with King Hussein. "A tall, skinny Arab in ankle-length gown served the short, plump Walters . . . with slugs of a mysterious dark brown liquid, poured from the huge brass kettle strapped to the shoulder of a Bedouin server," Weller wrote.

"Say, this is wonderful," Walters bubbled. "How do you get this aromatic flavor? Spices or something?"

No, he was told, a small, very special bean grown in Jordan is put into the boiling liquid.

Walters bit into the bean zestfully. It tasted "something like a camphorated clothes closet and tasted bitter," Weller told Chicagoans.

Walters nevertheless had praise: "Boy! What aroma! This is the kind of tea we just can't get back home."

Son Jim leaned over and whispered softly, "Coffee, Dad."

"What you say?" Walters responded in a challenging tone. "What coffee?"

It's coffee we are drinking," his son replied "Just their kind of coffee."

Walters was not convinced. "Say, is that right?" he asked. "Honest? This wonderful tea of yours is really coffee?"

A bit uncomfortable, no one dared to respond immediately. But then Hussein's secretary bowed very gently, said, "Coffee, Mr. Walters."

The cosmopolitan editor who had come up from a country farm in Indiana wasn't through. "But you do drink tea here, don't you?" he asked.

The secretary sent out for tea, which was served very sweet in small silvery glasses and was not aromatic at all.

"Mighty fine tea, this," Walters commented carefully.

Returning to wife Reah, who had stayed behind at their hotel, Walters produced some beans. He learned from her that his precious discovery was known to her as cardamon. She had a canful in her pantry at home.

We are going to try them in both tea and coffee," Walters said.

"We are not," said Mrs. Walters, shuddering—and with a smile on her face.

Harold Macmillan's Unusual Question

On the afternoon of his arrival in London to start his 1957 tour, Basil Walters was surprised to hear that Prime Minister Harold Macmillan had extended an invitation to meet him.

As Walters walked into the prime minister's office, Macmillan pulled up a chair for him next to his large desk, filled a pipe and borrowed a match.

Macmillan had recently succeeded Anthony Eden, whose party was voted out of power after Britain's poor handling of the Suez Canal crisis. Walters figured that perhaps the new prime minister wanted an American viewpoint on the current state of Middle East affairs.

But no.

"What is a Hoosier?" Macmillan began.

Although he did not expect such an opening question, Walters was not taken aback. He knew Macmillan's mother was born in Indiana and he figured, since he was the son of Hoosier parents, that made him and Macmillan Hoosier brothers. (Macmillan's mother was Helen Artie "Nellie" Belles, born in 1856 at Spencer, in southern Indiana. At nineteen, she married a musician, but he died six months later. In 1876 she went to Paris to study sculpture and voice. She met Maurice Crawford Macmillan of Scottish heritage and married him.)

Walters told the prime minister that one explanation is that city folks in pioneer days used to call farmers "Hoosiers." Because Indiana was developed by farmers, all residents of the state became known as "Hoosiers."

Walters sensed that definition didn't satisfy Macmillan, so, upon returning to Chicago six weeks later, he asked Ed Akers, news editor of the *Daily News,* and Don Maxwell, editor of the rival *Chicago Tribune,* to rally up answers. Akers and Maxwell, like Walters, were native Hoosiers.

Walters's request resulted in a well-researched piece in the *Tribune* by Alfred Ames that gave Macmillan— and Walters—plenty of answers. Ames listed more than a dozen explanations of what a Hooiser is. For example:

Husher. A term applied to strong men who were able to hush any opponent with a single blow.

Hoosa. An Indian word for corn.

Hoosier. The family name of one of the contractors for the Louisiana and Portland canal, being built from 1826 to 1831. Most of Hoosier's employees were from Indiana.

Who's yere? Long ago when riders approached a house in Indiana, the inhabitants shouted out: "Who's yere?"

Whose yere (ear)? Attributed to the great Indiana poet, James Whitcomb Riley, who kidded that the early settlers in Indiana were vicious fighters, given to biting off noses and ears. On the morning after, anyone sauntering into a barroom might see an ear on the floor and say, "Whose yere?"

Ames's column was a winner, the kind Walters loved and knew his readers enjoyed. Only this time, *Daily News* readers had to read it in a competing newspaper.

CHAPTER FIFTEEN

Hooking up with Field

As 1957 expired, another major award came to the *Daily News,* but there was little time for Basil Walters and other *Daily News* executives to celebrate. They faced more rounds in a continuing battle with a group of newsroom employees who sought a guild shop.

In October 1957, the newspaper received the Distinguished Community Service award at the Inland Daily Press Association's fall meeting. It is given by the University of Missouri's journalism school, recognized by many media people as the nation's best. Dr. Earl English, then dean, said The *Daily News* was chosen for, among other things:

—study and presentation of the problems of juvenile delinquency, and sponsorship of an annual youth rally;
—revelations concerning conditions in Illinois mental hospitals;
—windfall profits made by some state legislators in race track stock; and
—the Orville Hodge exposé.

The Missouri honor was later listed in a *Daily News* promotion pamphlet that said the newspaper had won twenty-seven "important awards in 1957 . . . a tremendous accolade for a great newspaper."

It could be argued that some of the awards weren't so important—the Mark Twain Travel Writing Award, for example—but the pamphlet was a winner, an impressive sales tool for advertisers and talented would-be staffers.

But Walters and other top *Daily News* executives had to forget about the awards as a new year opened. For years, a group of editorial employees fought for a union shop, in which new staffers would be required to join the American Newspaper Guild after thirty days' employment. A Guild contract existed in Chicago, requiring such things as a forty-hour week. But while some people were members and paid dues for such benefits, many oldtimers were not members and got a "free ride" under the Guild contract.

The *Daily News* management successfully thwarted the guild shop in the late 1940s and early 1950s, forcing those who sought it to reduce their demand to a modified union shop. Under this arrangement, not every new employee would have to join the Guild, only a percentage of all employees.

Among those in the pro-union forefront was reporter Bob Gruenberg, who had helped in the Hodge investigation and had built a good reputation as a tough city hall reporter before eventually leaving Chicago and news reporting. "We knew we couldn't get a Guild Shop, so we tried for the modified shop," Gruenberg recalled. "News people are independent people. We knew we couldn't get everyone to be a member."

Walters led management opposition to any kind of union arrangement. In a March 12, 1956, "Dear Ev" memo to managing editor Everett Norlander, Walters wrote:

I hope The Daily News staffers will think through and debate among themselves the full implications of the proposal for the Guild Shop. . . .

All of us as American citizens have a lot at stake in the preservation of a press that is not regimented. . . .

This sounds corny, I know. But The American Dream is in world conflict with Communism. The American Dream is based on individualism. The Communist depends on collectivism. . . .

The American press has a mighty obligation in the period just ahead. . . .

That press must be kept free of central authority either governmental or private. There must be no licensing of newspaper people. . . .

Guild proponents may have scoffed at that reasoning, arguing that Walters's fear of licensing obscured the real issues. Perhaps his fear did. But Walters was being sincere. The licensing fear had troubled him for a long time, back before he worried what accreditation might mean for journalism schools. As he got older, his opposition hardened against anything that might restrict the press in any way.

Freedom for Walters, of course, went far beyond a free press. The ideal of freedom was tatooed on his heart and strongly implanted in his mind. He wrote to Norlander in his memo, "It is proper for those newspapermen and women who so desire to join The Guild and to remain members so long as their conscience so dictates. But I feel strongly it is an error for a great newspaper such as The Daily News to compel its staff members to join or not to join. . . . We have protected the right of an employee to belong if he so desires but we must also protect the conscience of an employee who prefers not to belong and to employ anyone we please without requiring him to join.''

Walters warned Norlander about the arbitration issue. He said *Daily News* management cannot risk important decisions affecting the conduct of its news or editorials to either the American Newspaper Guild ''or to an outsider who knows nothing about the newspaper business.''

Walters repeated those views on April 4, 1958, when he rejected the Guild's proposal for a modified guild shop. He added this point, ''To (accept the proposal) would deprive us of shopping competitively in the market place for talent. Talent is not confined to one political party, one religion or one labor union.''

The *Daily News*'s tough stance prevailed. A modified guild shop was denied. Those editorial employees who fought for it weren't in a strong enough position to achieve their goal. If they walked off the job, there would still be non-Guild staffers on hand—mostly old-timers—to get out the newspaper.

But shortly after John Knight sold the *Daily News* to Marshall Field, Jr., in January 1959, a modified guild shop was implemented at the *Daily News*. Field, who owned the *Sun-Times*, had no choice when he went into the first session of new contract talks with his new employees. The *Sun-Times* had a modified guild shop; Field could hardly deny the same provision to the *Sun-Times*'s new sister.

Field assumed ownership of the *Daily News* a short time after a tragedy of sickening, searing proportions struck Chicago, forcing Walters's troops to quickly mobilize and stay on the job for extended hours.

The first day of December 1958 was cold and clear, thanks to a typical brisk Chicago wind. It blew dead leaves of autumn through streets and alleys. Soon, there would be human dead.

Our Lady of Angels Church was a focal point of a northwest Chicago neighborhood, towering over the church's grade school and modest homes and apartment buildings. The school, at 3808 Iowa, was shaped in a ''U''—two rectangular buildings connected by an annex.

Just before school was dismissed, an explosion rocked the building. Chicago firemen soon confronted a major blaze—and uncontrollable panic, as students began leaping from upper-story windows.

Among the 1,400 students who managed to escape, but not before suffering severe burns, was thirteen-year old Michele McBride. In her 1979 book, *The Fire That Will Not Die,* she wrote about how she jumped out of a window through the thick smoke to the cement below. The temperature in her classroom had reached an estimated 1,000 degrees, a heat so intense that her skin and extremities burned, but not her clothes.

The *Daily News*'s final edition that December 1 carried this bold, black headline across six of eight columns: "**35 Known Dead in School Fire.**"

Mrs. Anna Kroot of 920 North Hamlin told a *Daily News* reporter "every window in the top floor was in flames . . . children passed out in the alley, and alongside the school. . . ."

A short sidebar reported the horror witnessed by Mrs. Joseph Mio, 938 North Hamlin:

> "The children were jumping from windows. There were just thuds, and they lay there.
> "Oh, it was terrible, just terrible.
> "The kids were at every window . . . they were all screaming. They started jumping.
> "The firemen came and shouted . . . 'Don't jump! Don't jump!' But the kids kept jumping and screaming and breaking their legs."

The thirty-five figure almost tripled. Ninety-five people died—ninety-two children and three nuns.

The school fire was the last significant local story for Walters. A final, major Chicago story followed. It did not have the significance and sadness of the school fire; it was a story of momentary euphoria and joy: the White Sox winning the 1959 American League pennant.

The baseball championship almost set off panic of it own. A banner headline in the September 23 issue read: "**SORRY ABOUT SIRENS: DALEY.**" The story began:

> Mayor Daley apologized Wednesday for any panic or alarm caused by air raid sirens that marked the White Sox pennant victory.

The White Sox triumph, achieved under colorful owner Bill Veeck, gobbled up most of the front page that day. In all, there were four stories and one large picture that showed jubilant fans greeting the team at Midway Airport.

Basil Walters, a man who had never been deeply interested in

sports but who had acquired his famous nickname from a sports
figure, knew the importance of the White Sox triumph. One front-
page story, in the upper left corner of the page, carried this headline:
"Here's How Sox Won Flag: Speed, Daring."

When the reader's eye moved diagonally to the lower right corner
of the page, he saw this headline: **"God Helped America, Nikita Tells
Farmer."**

The story out of Coon Rapids, Iowa, told how Prime Minister
Nikita Khrushchev "of atheistic Soviet Russia" and Bob Garst, a
wealthy American farmer, "looked at the abundance of Iowa's crop
and talked about God Wednesday."

It was the kind of short story Walters gloried in. A copy editor
had taken the wire dispatches and made one story. After the lead, the
rest of the article read:

> "I must admit you are intelligent people,"
> Khrushchev said, "but God has helped you."
> "You are right," Garst replied. "God is on our
> side."
> "God is on our side, too," said Khrushchev.
> "But we are growing faster than you are."
> "God helps those who help themselves," said
> Garst. "This is an American saying."
> "God helps intelligent people," Khrushchev
> said as he closed the exchange.

By the time the Sox had won the pennant—the last one for more
than twenty years—and the exchange between Khrushchev and farmer
Garst was held and widely publicized—the *Daily News* was under new
ownership.

On Monday, January 5, 1959, a banner headline read: **"Field
Buys the Daily News."** Control of the *Daily News* shifted that day
from John Knight to Field Enterprises. In buying Knight's majority
interest—75 percent—Field agreed to pay $50.00 a share. No an-
nouncement was made on how many shares changed hands, but inside
sources said about 360,000 were involved—meaning $18,000,000 cash
for Knight. Industry analysts recalled that Knight had paid $2,000,000
in cash and assumed $6,600,000 of outstanding debt when he bought
the *Daily News* almost fifteen years earlier. Of course, whereas the
Daily News in 1944 was a candidate for the intensive care ward, the
1959 *Daily News* was in the pink. Under Knight and Walters it had

built its circulation to 547,796 and turned an average annual net profit of $1,250,000.

To raise the bulk of his $18,000,000, Field sold *Parade,* the slick Sunday supplement, for an estimated $12,000,000. The buyer was John Hay Whitney, who was then U.S. Ambassador to the Court of St. James and owned controlling interest in the then-great, now-dead *New York Herald Tribune.*

The *Daily News*'s sale price at the time was the largest ever for an individual newspaper in the United States. Four years earlier, press baron S. I. Newhouse spent $18,700,000 to buy the Birmingham News Company, which included the *Huntsville Times* and broadcasting companies. And in 1958, the *Toronto Star* was sold for $25,555,000, but the purchase included a variety of other assets.

Field, in making the acquisition, had known for months that he would eventually acquire a sister for his *Sun-Times,* which a year earlier had moved into a new $21,000,000 edifice on the Chicago River. New presses worth $5,000,000 were installed for the *Sun-Times*'s run of 534,000 copies. The run took only 3½ hours, meaning the expensive equipment was idle too many hours to adequately pay for itself.

On the other hand, Knight's mechanical plant was obsolescent. He knew he could not continue to compete with the dominant *Tribune,* which, in October 1957, had outbid Field and Knight for Hearst's *American* and was getting ready to print it, too.

The January 5 *Daily News* carried joint announcements by Knight and Field on page one. Knight wrote:

> My reasons for selling the *Chicago Daily News* at the time of its greatest progress are entirely personal. Quite frankly, they arise from a desire to curtail my administrative responsibilities after nearly forty years in the field of journalism.

Time magazine, in its January 19 issue, wrote: "(Knight) has had a heavy heart since his youngest son, Frank, who was being groomed to take over the empire, died at 30 last spring of a brain tumor. After 40 years of answering the midnight bell, Jack Knight wanted to 'relax a little.'" (Some six months after Knight bought the *Daily News* in 1944, his oldest son, John S. Knight, Jr., was killed in Germany as Allied troops stalked the retreating Nazi army.)

Field, in his announcement, told why he bought the *Daily News* and thus became its sixth publisher. He wrote:

> I have today assumed responsibility for publishing the Chicago Daily News. I do so with a sense of dedication and humility. It is a sobering challenge to continue its great tradition of service to Chicago and the Middle West.

A week later, Field announced what he and Knight had approved during the negotiations: that Walters would be the editor of the *Daily News* and resign as executive editor of Knight Newspapers. Walters's relationship with Knight, however, would not be completely severed. Field granted Knight's request that Walters remain as a member of the Knight board of directors. At the same time, Milburn P. Akers, executive editor of the *Sun-Times,* became editor "to assure complete editorial independence of the Sun-Times," Field said. Lawrence S. Fanning, assistant executive editor, became executive editor.

There was never any doubt that Walters could remain with the *Daily News* if he wished. He was one of very few men who knew sale negotiations were taking place between Knight and Field—in fact, he played a key role in advising Knight, making quick trips between Chicago and Miami that winter.

Walters, who had already begun his own consulting business, offered to resign and retire early from daily newspapering at age sixty-two. After all, he had been half serious on more than one occasion, in his early Minneapolis days, when he talked of retiring at forty and returning to his farm.

But Field wanted Walters for at least two years—he'd seen what Walters had done as a competitor for almost fifteen years. Now he wanted him on his side.

In making the announcement about Walters, Field said, "For nearly fifteen years, Mr. Walters has had a great part in building the *Daily News*'s great tradition and in bringing to the *News* more circulation and higher prestige than it had ever achieved before. For its notable readability, enterprise and vigor, he deserves much personal credit. . . .

"Mr. Walters has edited several great newspapers with outstanding success. He has won many of the highest honors in journalism. . . .

"He has my complete professional confidence, and my warm personal affection."

Said Knight about Walters's appointment, "The appointment of Basil Walters as editor of the *Chicago Daily News* has my hearty endorsement. . . .

"I feel the appointment is in his best interest and he carries my affection and best wishes."

Aside from the page one announcement story, the *Daily News* published three other articles on Walters, including a biographical sketch headlined: **"Hoosier Success Story: 'Stuffy' Walters, Editor."** Another story told of the famous men Walters joined as editor, and a shorter piece explained how Walters got his nickname.

Not much changed under Field. Norlander continued as managing editor and A. T. Burch remained associate editor in charge of the editorial page. Walters continued to direct the Daily News Foreign Service and maintained his office half way between the editorial offices and the newsroom.

Field was the fourth of a distinguished family line of merchants, publishers, and philanthropists. His great-grandfather, Marshall Field, I, founded Marshall Field and Company department store.

After graduating from Harvard magna cum laude, Field received a law degree from Virginia Law School in 1941, where he was president of his class. On October 1, 1950, he succeeded his father as editor and publisher of the *Sun-Times*. And in November 1955, he led ground-breaking ceremonies for the $21,000,000 plant. Now, at forty-two, he warmly greeted the sixty-two-year-old Walters and looked forward to the battle ahead: his *Sun-Times* and *Daily News* opposing the *Chicago Tribune* and the *Chicago American*. There had once been nine newspapers in Chicago. Now there were four—owned by two companies. Walters's last two years of daily newspapering, under Field, were no different than the forty previous years. They were years of innovation, years of speaking out about newspapers and freedom, years of honors from inside and outside the profession.

Invited to speak at the ninety-third convention of the Minnesota Editorial Association on February 19, 1959, Walters urged editors to write "thought-provoking editorials . . . to sharpen up their editorials to create debate and make their readers more active, responsible and participating. . . ."

Walters asserted that the country was relying too much "on the glib writers of the radio and TV commentators or the national syndicated writers." He said some of the clearest thinking "I have ever read has been contained in locally written editorials on small-town newspapers.''

There it was again—the grassroots strain that never left him, no matter all the sophistication he had acquired over the years in New York, Chicago, Cairo, London, Paris, Rome, Minneapolis, Milwaukee, Detroit . . . or in drinking Jordanian coffee.

Two months after helping hand out awards at the Minnesota convention, Walters received another of his own. He was named the Indianapolis Press Club's Indiana Newspaperman of the Year.

A few months later, as the sixties dawned, Walters was involved in his last major project, the *Weekend Chicago Daily News.* It made its debut on Saturday, March 5, 1960, as a six-section newspaper selling for fifteen cents. The first issue sold an additional 30,000 copies.

The new weekend paper was an extension of the Triple Streak that Walters had pioneered earlier. The emphasis continued to be on leisure activities, but Field said he hoped the newspaper could become ''an important forum for Midwest thinking and debate.''

Typographically, the weekend paper closely resembled the daily product—and for good reason. The *Daily News* was still one of the easiest newspapers in the country to read. That was proven, again, at the spring meeting of the Inland Daily Press Association, when the *Daily News* took first place in the association's annual contest. Since first entering the competition in 1948, the *Daily News* had won the award in 1948, 1950 through 1954, and in 1957—making 1959 the eighth time in eleven years. (One year Walters deliberately did not enter the contest.) The second place winner in 1959: the *Minneapolis Star.*

The Inland honor, perhaps the most prestigious given for typography, was fitting. It came a year before Walters, who had broken new ground in the use of type and design, announced he would retire from daily journalism. Fitting, yes, but for Walters a bit ''ho-hum.'' Not that he wasn't pleased—awards of this nature gave him the kind of recognition he loved. But by the time Field had assumed command, the *Daily News* had won 124 awards since 1944 for editorial excellence.

Before departing, Walters received another noteworthy honor: he was chosen as the first recipient of 660 civic service citations to be presented by the Chicago Convention Bureau to business executives who had played key roles in the city's vitality and growth.

Walters, too, watched as the *Daily News* moved into its new home, cozying up with the *Sun-Times* under the same roof. It was clear, however, that what was once a war was now a sibling rivalry. In fact, the *Daily News* opened its own Washington bureau; the *Sun-Times* already had one. Walters named Irvin Peter (Pete) Lisagor to head the *Daily News* bureau, moving him off the foreign service staff. Ed Lahey, who had headed the Knight Newspapers' Washington bureau since 1957, remained in that post.

Walters, almost sixty-five years old, resigned effective June 1, 1961. But while he was through with the grind of daily newspapering, he was not through with journalism.

Walters and Hutchins—The Odd Couple

Their views were usually diametrically opposed and their arguments sometimes acerbated, but few men shared a warmer friendship than Basil Walters and the brilliant, controversial Robert Maynard Hutchins.

The friendship began in 1918, when Walters edited the army ambulance newspaper in Italy. Hutchins, three years younger at nineteen, was a staff member who wasn't shy about offering opinions on the publication (and a lot of other things).

After military sevice, Hutchins earned a law degree from Yale while Walters worked in Indianapolis and Milwaukee. Hutchins, however, did not make law a career. In 1929, after four years as a lecturer and professor at the Yale Law School, Hutchins was elected president of the University of Chicago at the age of thirty. He was stamped as the "boy wonder."

Walters's and Hutchins's paths crossed twenty-six years later when Walters went to the *Daily News* in 1944. A year later, Hutchins became chancellor of the university.

By then, Hutchins's ideas had drawn much attention, especially those that advocated academic freedom for professors and students alike. He defended the exploration of ideas. He urged faculty members and students to discover and research freely and without fear.

In his 1956 book, *Freedom, Education and the Fund,* Hutchins wrote, "I still cherish the view that the independent individual is the heart of society, that his independence is his most precious attribute, and that discussion is the essence of democracy. It is hard for me to concern myself with the material prosperity of my country or with that of the individuals who comprise it, because I was brought up to believe that prosperity and power were secondary, perhaps even dangerous."

Hutchins, the civil libertarian, and Walters, the conservative, worshipped freedom in different ways— Hutchins defending left-wing views, Walters arguing that many of those views were communist propaganda that undermined the nation's security.

When Hutchins was asked if he would hire a Communist, he replied, "If he qualified for the job." That was in November 1955, a year after Hutchins became president of the New York-based Fund for the Republic. The Fund had been given an original $15,000,000, no-strings grant from the Ford Foundation. Hutchins had served as the foundation's associate director from 1951 to 1954 after leaving The University of Chicago.

The question of communism was raised at a press conference Hutchins had called to announce that the Fund was giving an additional $150,000 to the Southern Regional Council, which had already received $245,000, to explore race problems in the south. A day before the press conference, the Hearst Newspapers reported that twenty-one directors of the council had past pro-Communist affiliations.

When asked about the report, Hutchins argued that it was "inaccurate and perfidious." He singled out and defended four directors. When reporters said there was iron-clad evidence that four had pro-Communist leanings, Hutchins replied, "A document is a piece of paper. I know these men. I'd bail them out any time."

Those comments prompted a *Chicago Daily News* editorial warning of a Communist conspiracy. It said, in part, "Dr. Hutchins believes that the communists form a political party and as such are entitled to promote their cause by peaceful means."

That statement went beyond the facts, Hutchins responded in a letter to Walters. He wrote:

From the point of view of The Fund for the Republic, it does not make much difference whether you call the Communists a party or a conspiracy. I cannot think of anything that we have done that would have been affected by this distinction. We are interested in freedom. We recognize the importance of security. We are conducting factual scholarly studies to find out what the Communists have done and are doing, and what the results of the loyalty-security programs have actually been. We hope that these studies may suggest how justice, freedom and security can be combined.

A few months before that episode, Walters and Hutchins exchanged conflicting views over whether a group should be formed to appraise the press. Although Hutchins proposed such a group, this idea was not entirely new with him.

In 1947, Hutchins was chairman of the Commission of Freedom of the Press, which, after four years of deliberations, published *A Free and Responsible Press: A General Report of Mass Communication: Newspapers, Radio, Motion Pictures, Magazines, and Books.* The commission made thirteen recommendations it felt would help free the press "from the influences which now prevent it from supplying the communication of news and ideas now needed by the kind of society we have and the kind of society we desire."

One recommendation was the establishment of a new and independent public agency to appraise and report annually upon the performance of the press. The commission said that "some agency which reflects the ambitions of the American people for its press should exist for the purpose of comparing the accomplishments of the press with the aspirations which the people have for it."

Now, eight years later, Hutchins was still promoting such a group when he wrote to John Knight and six other prominent news people.* "The Fund for the Republic is interested in exploring whether an independent agency ought to be established to appraise and report periodically on the performance of the press and other means of mass communications in the United States," Hutchins wrote.

---

* The other six: Joseph Pulitzer, Jr., publisher of the *St. Louis Post-Dispatch;* Philip Graham, publisher of the *Washington Post;* Robert W. Brown, editor of the *Columbus* (Ga.) *Ledger and Enquirer;* Ralph McGill, editor of the *Atlanta Constitution;* Gardner (Mike) Cowles, publisher of *Look* and the *Des Moines Register and Tribune;* and Barry Bingham, editor of the *Louisville Courier-Journal.*

When Knight asked Walters what he thought of Hutchins's proposal, Walters, in a long memo, gave an unqualified no. It's "perfectly within the rights of anyone" to establish such an organization, he said, "but I would not . . . ever want to be responsible for its founding or its findings."

Any study of newspapers should center on individual papers, and they should not be lumped into a mass, Walters argued, adding, "The public votes each day with its dough on the reading matter or the 'listening matter' it prefers."

Walters continued, "You and I are not afraid of any study by any group. We would study the comments with interest, but we would still insist on the right to produce a product conscientiously along the lines we felt best. And we would defend the rights of others to do likewise."

More vintage Walters followed:

> The American way is to permit journalists through debate to arrive individually at their own conclusions. They in turn contribute to the debate by the general public through which intelligent public opinion is formed.
>
> You and I have fought for the preservation of the right of freedom of thought even when individuals involved were in our opinion fools or worse.

Walters said he was surprised that Hutchins, "as great an authority on the philosophy of the freedoms as any American," seemed to have a "blind spot" to the dangers of anybody, no matter how well intentioned, "having general *power* over the press."

Walters passed on his views to Hutchins, who responded with a letter that began:

> I love you like a brother but you are as always crazy as hell. How you make the jump from my proposal, which is criticism, to your conclusions, which is that criticism is an attempt to force on the editors a common behavior pattern, is incomprehensible to me. . . .
>
> I believe that if you were willing to put your mind to it, you could figure out a way of institutionalizing criticism of the press without endangering its independence.

Walters answered with a letter that began, "I just don't like 'institutionalizing.'"

A year later, Hutchins's *Freedom, Education and the Fund* was published. He sent an autographed copy to "Stuffy, for old times' sake." Walters reviewed the book, a series of Hutchins's essays and speeches, for the *Daily News*. "Robert M. Hutchins, one of the most controversial figures of our times, has 'psychologized' himself to find out 'how he got that way'," Walters began.

Later, Walters wrote: "Bob Hutchins is the smartest man I know. But his brilliance, I fear, has made him intolerant of any who lack his brilliance."

Walters said Hutchins's accomplishments would have been even greater if he had paid more attention to what he had been taught as an undergraduate at Oberlin College. That lesson was, in Hutchins's own words, "You were entitled to your own opinion, but only if you were willing to submit it to examination and to change it if you could not survive scrutiny."

Still, Walters found Hutchins's book to be "must reading for all those who want to base their judgment on full information and argument rather than hysteria. In addition to discussing the Fund, the book is an important contribution to American philosophy on freedom."

Hutchins responded to Walters's review with a brief note. "I would like to retain you as my personal advertising agent. I am deeply grateful for your generosity. Now, if you write a book, I will try to do as well for you, though praise from me would probably reduce the sales considerably."

When *Time* reported Walters's retirement six years later, the magazine quoted Hutchins as one complaining, "What can you expect us to do in education when the press is in the hands of men like Stuffy Walters?" The quote indicated that Hutchins was scornful of Walters because he was not a deep thinker and did not advocate the intellectual thrust of education so sacred to Hutchins. The two men knew that the quote, taken out of context, was not fair to either of them.

What *Time* neglected to say was what Walters, Hutchins, their families, and their close associates knew: that the two men, despite their strong philosophical disagreements, enjoyed nothing better than to break bread and engage in spirited debate. Their debating

softened their positions, and they often found themselves in agreement with each other.

After reading a booklet published by the Illinois
State Chamber of Commerce, "Racket Picketing,"
Walters wrote to Hutchins, in April 1957:

> Let me throw out a thought provoker. Is it possible that
> in our anxiety to protect the "fashionable," the so-called left-
> wing dissenter, have we neglected to protect the right of the
> so-called "right winger" to dissent?
>
> There is great need in my thinking for a Labor Depart-
> ment in government. But the Labor Department has fre-
> quently got itself so involved in "big labor" and big labor
> politics that it can't be bothered with the individual little
> laborer who "dissents."
>
> The same is true, I fear, of the Civil Liberties Union. It
> has become an "advocate" on occasion of causes instead of
> the defender of true liberty for the individual as a dissenter.

Hutchins responded in a May letter:

> I happen to share your views. I think that the American
> Civil Liberties Union shares them to a greater extent than you
> think.
>
> Confidentially, we are recommending to our board . . . a
> big inquiry into the operation of labor unions which will
> necessarily involve an investigation of labor racketeering.
> Clark Kerr, the chancellor of the University of California at
> Berkeley, will be in charge.

In December 1957 the Fund published Kerr's
"Unions and Union Leaders of their Own Choosing."
Walters found much agreement in what Kerr wrote,
such as, "It is usually not possible for a union member
just to withdraw in protest, without penalty, if he does
not like the organization, its leaders, or its policy. We
have here, most frequently, a more or less compulsory
organization with substantial impact on the lives of its
members."

Later, when the American Society of Newspaper
Editors (ASNE) grievance committee's question was
raised in a taped interview between Walters and Copley
executives, Walters said, "When Bob Hutchins got up
and gave us hell, maybe we didn't listen as carefully as
we should, and we reacted and yelled, 'endangering the
freedom of the press.'"

Consulting and Corn

S AID Marshall Field, "He is one of the really great editors of our time (which is like saying of all times)."

Said Basil Walters, "Yesterday with me is a canceled check. Tomorrow is a promissory note. I expect to have more fun after 65 than I did before (which would seem impossible to do)."

Those comments were contained in a June 2, 1961, *Time* magazine story reporting Walters's departure from the *Daily News.* He was "headed for his pig farm in Frankfort, Ind.," *Time* reported.

Some of Walters's cosmopolitan friends couldn't understand why he wanted to return to the boondocks—but, as the old bromide goes, you can take the boy out of the country but you can't take the country out of the boy. Walters was coming full circle: from his earliest years on the farm to a small town, then bustling cities, then a metropolis, and finally back to the farm. His new address was Tonaja Farm— named for his children, Tom, Nancy, and James—on Frankfort Rural Route 3, Kelley Road, where only a car would periodically interrupt the solitude.

In planning their return, the Walterses built a new home where the old Walters farmhouse once stood. An office was included for Walters's new venture, Newspaper Research Associates, which quickly signed up three clients: the *Daily News* and *Sun-Times,* the Hearst newspapers, and the *Boston Herald-Traveler.*

When *Newsweek* magazine announced his retirement in its February 20 issue, it gave Walters's new endeavor prominence. "For once I'm going to be president," he quipped to the *Newsweek* reporter. "And I'm going to exploit the skill of every friend I ever had —without paying them anything."

Said *Newsweek*:

Walters is superbly fit for the role of newspaper doctor. He has been one most
of his life. Hired away from the Milwaukee Journal in 1928 to help run the
Cowles chain's Des Moines Register and Tribune, he turned a mediocre property into Iowa's most influential papers. Then, in 1937, Walters moved to the
ailing Minneapolis Star, a Cowles property that was running third in a three-
paper city. He ran the opposition into the ground.

The *Newsweek* piece predicted that, while there would probably
be changes in the future at the *Daily News,* the imprint of Walters's
editorial philosophy would continue. "They tell you in this business
never to follow anyone who could turn into a ghost and haunt you,"
Thomas Collins, Walters's successor, told *Newsweek.* "But we're all
Stuffy's boys. Instead of fighting his ghost, we'll harbor it."

Shortly before Walters's departure, A. T. Burch, one of "Stuffy's boys," volunteered that Walters's new clients "will get their
money's worth, but all these years they have been getting a great deal
from Stuffy at a much lower price. They have been getting the benefit
of Stuffy's example for almost nothing—that is, the trifling price of
buying the papers Stuffy edited."

Field wanted to become Walters's first client. Walters agreed,
with the understanding that he avoid being in the position of looking
over the shoulders of his successors. His principal work was to conduct continuous, detailed studies of the impacts of automobile driving
versus public transportation, shifts to suburban living, and shopping
centers on metropolitan newspaper readers.

Robert Choat, publisher of the *Boston Herald-Traveler,* became
Walters's second client. His retainer called for him to spend one week
a month in the Boston plant, working with *Herald-Traveler* editors.
Walters was to guide a gradual redesign of some of the newspaper's
sections to improve readability.

Ironically, the Hearst papers became the third client. For years,
William Randolph Hearst had tried to hire Walters. It had begun in
Des Moines, when a salesman for King Features Syndicate (owned by
Hearst) told Walters that Hearst was interested in his services. Walters
always demurred.

Walters wasn't interested in Hearst's sensationalism. But he was
intrigued by the offer of Hearst's kin to study the Los Angeles newspaper situation, where the Hearst and Chandler families were bucking
each other.

Thus, almost immediately after leaving the *Daily News,* Walters
and his wife were jetting from coast to coast each month. They still

lived in Kenilworth while their new home was being built in Indiana. "Retirement" meant, typically, leaving Chicago for Los Angeles, returning to Chicago, heading for Boston, making a quick visit to Clinton County, Indiana, to check on home construction, returning to Chicago, flying on to Los Angeles, moving on to Boston, returning to Chicago. Walters's bags, as usual, stayed packed. Reah Walters's, too, because she had become part of Newspaper Research Associates in a variety of ways.

The biggest job was Los Angeles. Hearst, with two papers, and Chandler, with two papers, faced twenty-one community dailies, some two hundred weekly or twice-weeklies, shoppers, and controlled-circulation publications. It was obvious that Los Angeles would be better served if George Hearst, Jr., a grandson of the press lord, and Otis Chandler, a third-generation Chandler, could concentrate on one daily and one Sunday each.

Walters rode on Hearst circulation trucks, visited circulation substations, talked to readers, viewed the sprawling city from helicopters, and got acquainted with everybody from office boy to editor at the two Hearst papers—the morning *Examiner* and the afternoon *Herald.*

Hearst established a "Walters headquarters" in a Los Angeles hotel, where he quietly began planning for a daily and Sunday *Herald-Examiner.* Newspaper people inside and outside the Hearst family thought Walters was employed by the Hearst Journalism Foundation, a highly successful program that worked with young people.

Herb Krauch, of course, knew better. He was the *Herald*'s editor, and each afternoon he would visit Walters's hotel to help design the planned *Herald-Examiner.* Hearst, making money with the *Herald* in the afternoon while losing cash in the morning with the *Examiner,* chose afternoon publication. Meanwhile, Chandler, making money with the morning *Times* while losing with the afternoon *Mirror* (a tabloid), made plans to retain the morning field.

Finally, after weeks of study, including determinations on what staffers to keep in a consolidated operation, the *Herald-Examiner* merger took place. There was only one hitch in the planning—a miscalculation in circulation. Walters and the Hearsts had under-figured by 100,000, creating some initial pressroom problems, the kind every publisher loves to have for awhile.

By 1964, Walters had decided he did not want to work any longer with large newspaper operations. He had initially taken the larger accounts "to prove to myself that just because a guy was sixty-five years old was no sign that he was through." Thus, he resigned his large accounts in June 1964 to give himself time to visit papers that were developing cold type composition. That kind of printing had fascinated him since 1947, when the *Daily News* was forced to experiment with those methods during the printers strike.

Papers of less than 50,000 circulation were leading the way to cold type production—and that fit perfectly into Walters's plans. He wanted to work more with small papers. In a letter he wrote in December, 1965, to former *Daily News* reporter Fred Sparks, Walters asked:

> Why am I so interested in these so-called smaller newspaper operations? I think we need strong voices, and youthful voices, at the grassroots to challenge the giants. Microwave transmission of page proofs to satellite press plants is going to make some of the big papers more powerful. The Wall Street Journal, as you know, has for several years transmitted page proofs by microwave.

Walters, too, saw ahead of his time regarding television. "When there are a few more telstars in the heavens, a few central TV stations will be using them to glance their broadcasts directly into homes everywhere instead of going through regional stations."

Walters, who had worked for Knight, one of the most respected chains in the country, saw a danger

> in this continuous centralization of communications control, unless it is balanced off with strong grassroot newspapers which provide intelligent forums for debate and dissent. There's a danger of national brainwashing in mass communications. . . . We're going to need a lot of independent-thinking "rebels" operating out through provinces to keep these giants in line.

This did not mean he had come to oppose newspaper groups, Walters said later, when asked about his comments to Sparks. He was only saying that a concentration of media outlets in the hands of a few powerful, irresponsible owners could be devastating—a threat to freedom of the press in a different way. Groups, he knew, could be managed responsibly—as witness his years with Knight, in which the newspapers were given great local autonomy and the financial resources needed to produce outstanding products.

Among the small newspapers with which Walters became associated was the *Kenosha News,* acquired by Howard Brown late in

1961. A Chicagoan, Brown was a Princeton graduate with a sharp mind and years of newspapering behind him. He wanted his own paper, but Chicago bankers kept denying him loans—until he talked to Tilden Cummings, a neighbor of Walters in Kenilworth. Cummings said he would talk with Walters. Ironically, Brown had known Walters years before when, as a young man, he worked in the *Daily News* maintenance/supply department.

Walters looked over the Kenosha property and gave the "green light," resulting in an "avuncular relationship," Brown recalled. Walters's view that Kenosha had strong potential was on target. Brown built the paper into an outstanding product, financially and editorially.

Brown had watched Walters closely when he worked at the *Daily News* as a young man. Brown recalled, "He had this tremendous capacity to inspire his subordinates and his associates. This is terribly important. They had confidence in him. The confidence was never violated. They had confidence in him because he knew what he was doing. He knew where to get news, and he would not stand for nonsense."

In becoming more interested in small newspapers, Walters became more interested in talented young people who worked on them. Tom Schumaker, for example, who was working in Bloomington, Indiana. One day Walters called and extended an invitation to Schumaker to visit the farm. Somehow, some way, Walters had become interested in Schumaker, who recalled:

Stuffy talked and Stuffy listened. At the close of the day, he urged me to join Knight Newpapers (now Knight-Ridder). "It's by far the best group in the country and you should always try to work for the best," he said. As a followup, Stuffy wrote a Knight executive and urged them to visit with me. To make a long story short, they did and I joined them.

That was in 1972. In 1982, Shumaker was still with Knight, as publisher of the *Grand Forks* (North Dakota) *Herald*.

"Stuffy kept a close eye on my progress with Knight and Knight-Ridder until his death," Schumaker said. "I always got the strange feeling that Stuffy was almost as excited about me joining Knight as I was."

In searching for small daily clients, Walters hooked up with Copley Newspapers, which, aside from their San Diego paper, owns small papers.

It was while working with Copley that Walters participated in the previously mentioned taped discussion that appeared in the September 1970 issue of Copley's in-house publication, *Seminar*.

When Walters was asked, in that discussion, about Norman Isaacs's proposal that the American Society of Newspaper Editors form an ethics/grievance committee, Walters took his usual nay stance. (Upon taking office as ASNE president in 1953, Walters declared, "There must never be in this country a central press authority, either governmental or private.")

Isaacs, who had built an outstanding reputation as editor of the Louisville newspapers, was the outgoing ASNE president in 1969 and had proposed to his successor, Newbold Noyes of the *Washington Star,* that a grievance committee be established.

Isaacs, in "retirement" as chairman of the National News Council, recalled, "Many of my ideas reflected my own generation of editors, and Stuffy was among a number of 'elder statesmen' who tended to regard me as one of the Young Turks. . . .

"Stuffy, Turner Catledge (*New York Times*) and Ben McKelway (*Washington Star*), in particular, had great influence on . . . Noyes, and he moved to defuse the whole (grievance committee) process when he took over and succeeded in sidetracking it through a special committee."

A few years later, Noyes told the ASNE convention gathering he felt he had made a mistake and wanted to go on record as saying Isaacs was right. And Isaacs eventually got his "grievance committee"—the National News Council.

The news council/grievance committee proposal was not the only subject on which Walters and Isaacs disagreed. But despite their disagreements, Walters and Isaacs respected and liked each other. Their arguments were sometimes tart, but like the vast majority of people who knew Walters, Isaacs found it "impossible not to like Stuffy, even when declaiming how far wrong he was about certain viewpoints."

Asked about his relationship with Walters, Isaacs wrote, in part:

All I can say at this stage (October 1980) is that each of us tried to serve journalism as faithfully as we could. That we differed strongly about our concepts of accountability can be put down, I think, to what happens so often among strong-minded, hard-driving individuals who happen to be "True Believers."

That's one Isaacs viewpoint Walters would strongly support if he were alive.

After ten years of consulting work that took him all over the country, Walters began to reduce his schedule. He said he wanted to start his farming career at seventy-five. And he did.

But he could never leave journalism. And journalism could never leave him. Just a few months before his seventy-fifth birthday, he was invited to speak to journalism students at Kent State University. He told his audience to expect a disjointed speech—and it was. But it contained several good nuggets.

He began by saying he never figured God had put him on earth to solve all the problems. And if anyone present was looking for instant solutions, they could leave. "Devote the time to reading the political columnists and cartoonists or listening to TV commentators," he said. "Some of them will tell you what to think. I won't."

There it was—the long-held disdain for the columnists, the growing negative view of television as a communications medium.

The columnists, cartoonists, and TV commentators have their place, he said, but the most important person in communications is the "see-and-tell" reporter. Then Walters punched activist reporting, which was getting much acclaim at the time.

"We used to call such men 'leg men,'" he said. "They used their legs to get to the sources of facts rather than just sit at their typewriters dreaming up colorful or activist thoughts telling how to save the world from itself, from war, the atomic bomb, the hippies, the poor, the rich, the intellectuals, pollution or other doomsday terrors."

As his speech neared its close, Walters said an underdeveloped field of see-and-tell reporting is news about industry, profits, labor, unions, pension plans, taxes, inflation, shopping, "all of which we might lump together as business news."

Once again, Walters's thinking was ahead of its time—he was saying in 1971 what editors began to discover and say in 1978 and 1979, as they started to beef up their business beats and devote more space to business and industry news.

Walters was correct when he told the Kent State gathering, "I sometimes fear we're a nation of economic illiterates. . . . Maybe we should re-examine some of those saws about 'Easy come, easy go' and 'A fool and his money are soon parted' and 'Waste not, want not.'"

Walters's conservatism then burst through completely. He said that our latest "emotion spree" involves ecology, which is good but must be kept in balance.

"Without chemicals, farmers would be unable to feed the nation," he said. "Without dams, oil, and coal we would have great electrical shortages and our modern living would revert to pioneer hardship. Without profits there would be no taxes to support schools such as this."

One of the great perils of emotion, he continued, is that danger can be "exaggerated to the point that we commit economic suicide. Only the great repoter who keeps his head can explore all angles and maintain proper balance through the airing of all sides."

The Kent State appearance would not be Walters's last on a college campus. In February 1972, as his seventy-fifth birthday approached, Walters was appointed the first M. Lyle Spencer Visiting Professor of Journalism at Syracuse University. The appointment thrilled him—it meant being around young people, and, while he would be a professor delivering periodic lectures over a year's time, he would also be a student, listening to what bright young minds had to say.

A few months after the Syracuse appointment, Walters was chosen, along with seventeen others, for the Indiana Academy. A project of the Associated Colleges of Indiana, the Academy recognizes native Hoosiers for their contributions to the cultural, civic, and social life of the state. Also chosen were Richard Lugar, who would later become a U.S. Senator, and noted industrialist, Eli Lilly.

A year after being honored by the academy, a final major award capped his life—induction into the Indiana Journalism Hall of Fame, sponsored by Sigma Delta Chi. Several people at the awards dinner wondered why Walters hadn't been inducted much sooner. It didn't matter to Walters. As usual, he was thrilled and grateful to receive such recognition.

By then, Walters was doing very little consulting work. "Nobody is interested in my advice anymore," he told friends. His friends knew better. They knew that he simply wasn't interested in "business" anymore.

Walters's home and farm had become his only "business" by the time he celebrated his seventy-ninth birthday on May 3, 1975. On August 28, a typically hot, humid summer's day in Indiana, Walters tended to business, cutting weeds next to his front yard. Later, after dinner, he relaxed until midnight, waiting up for his step-grandson, Paul, due in for a visit from the East.

There would be no visit. About 5:30 the next morning, August 29, Basil Leon Walters suffered a massive heart attack. Four hours later he died at Clinton County Hospital in Frankfort.

His death was given prominence in his hometown newspaper, the *Frankfort Times,* and in the *Indianapolis Star.* But in general, it did not receive the attention some people felt it deserved. Monty Curtis, still a top Knight-Ridder executive at the time, was especially disturbed at the lack of recognition. He wrote in a letter to Reah Walters:

> So Stuffy is gone? Not at all. For me and hundreds of other newspapermen he continues to live through his principles and the skills by which he applied them.
> I am unhappy with the obituaries. They are superficial, surely not the kind of reporting Stuffy practiced.

Later, when Curtis was told a book was being written about Walters and was asked to comment, he responded, "Asking me about Stuffy Walters is akin to dropping a needle on a long-playing record."

While Walters's death didn't receive the attention it deserved—especially in the Chicago and Minneapolis newspapers—his accomplishments certainly got attention during his lifetime. In fact, part of Walters's "obituary" was written while he was still alive—on July 25, 1956.

The *Daily News* had just produced one of the greatest investigative reporting efforts in the history of American journalism—the Hodge Scandal. That prompted the *Minot* (North Dakota) *Daily News* to publish an editorial that began:

Walters—A Great Editor

> When the twentieth century history of American Journalism is put together by some sharp-eyed researcher, the name of Basil "Stuffy" Walters will doubtless stand out in bold relief.
> Newspapermen the world over recognize him as a working editor who has contributed more than any other single individual to the fundamental things that make newspapers a vital factor in proving that if the United States is to remain great that the freedom of the press must be safeguarded to the extent that it is more than an idle expression.

The editorial went on to say that Walters's work proves "better than resolutions by a hundred conventions" of the continuing need to safeguard freedom of the press as guaranteed in the Constitution.

The editorial then repeated its basic themes—praise for Walters and a warning about safeguarding press freedom. It's likely that Walters, the copy editor, would have frowned and crossed out two or three paragraphs. But Walters, the human being, probably smiled widely and puffed happily on his cigarette while he read the piece in print—oblivious, of course, to the ashes cuddled on the front of his shirt.

INDEX

Adams, Cedric, 70, 71, 74, 79
Advertising, 69, 107, 108, 129, 140
Akers, Ed, 99, 164
Akers, Milburn P., 171
Alexander (king of Yugoslavia), 51
Allen, Forrest, 148
Ambulance Service News, 19–20
American Council on Education for Journalism
  accreditation by, 116–17
American Newspaper Guild, 165–67
American Society of Newspaper Editors, 62, 82, 88, 116, 131, 136, 141, 185
  Committee on World Freedom of Information, 119
Ames, Alfred, 164
Arnold, Edmund C., 139
Asbury, Herbert, 97, 99
Associated Press, 29–33, 41, 56, 57, 95
Associated Press Managing Editors Association, 15, 62, 82, 88, 91, 110, 137

Bade, Bill, 67, 68
Barthow, Louis, 51
Beaverbrook, Max Aitkin, Lord, 91
Beech, Keyes, 109, 118, 127
Bell, Wayne, 75
Belles, Helen Artie ("Nellie"), 163
Bender, Robert, 34
Ben-Gurion, David, 150, 158–59
Bentil, Dwight, 116
Berry, Frank, 86
Beveridge, Lord William, 149
Binder, Carroll, 58
Blacklock, Leslie H., 121
Boylan, Rose, 6
Bracken, John, 74
Brandenburg, George, 22, 65, 115, 160
Brandt, Herman, 42
Brown, Howard, 183, 184
Burch, A. T., 144, 146, 172, 181

Cadou, Eugene J., 16
Call, Ambrose, 35
Camp Crane News, 20, 21–22
Caniff, Milton, 98
Carter, Hodding, 132
Casey, Hugh J., 118
Casey, Robert J., 96
Castle, Latham, 144
Catledge, Turner, 185
Chandler, Otis, 182
Chauncey Yellow Robe, 28–29
Chicago Daily News, 55, 60, 82, 94
  circulation growth, 105, 115, 126, 129, 170
  competitors, 97–98
  Distinguished Community Service award, 164
  editorial union and, 165–66
  history, 94–96, 101
  printers' strike, 113–16
  purchase by Field Enterprises, 169–71
  purchase by Knight Newspapers, 91–92
  Saturday Triple Streak, 129, 173
  service, 106–9
  winner of Inland Daily Press Association Annual Award, 173
Choat, Robert, 181
Christiansen, Arthur, 91
Chucker, Harold, 69
Church, Margaret Stitt, 135
Churchill, Winston, 81
Ciano, Count Galeazzo, 103
Ciano, Edda, 103–5
Circulation, 20, 36, 43, 54
Civil War, 11
Clapper, Raymond, 67
Cohn, Angelo, 43, 56, 57, 58, 69, 70, 71, 72, 75, 80, 89
Collins, Thomas, 181
Commission on Freedom of the Press, 176
  A Free and Responsible Press: . . . , 176

Cook, Lewis, 57
Coolidge, Calvin, 25–28
Cooper, Kent, 34, 111
Cortesi, Salvatori, 31
Coughlin, Bill, 93
Cowles, Communication, Inc., 69
Cowles, Gardner, Jr. (Mike), 33, 34, 35, 40, 42
  Jay Darling and, 36–37
Cowles, Gardner, Sr., 33, 34–36, 38, 54, 63, 64
  Harvey Ingham and, 35–36
Cowles, John, 33, 35, 40, 54, 55, 70, 72, 88, 89, 90, 132
Cowles, William Fletcher, 34
Crim, George, 81
Crull, Finton A., 15, 16
Cummings, Tilden, 184
Curtis, J. Montgomery, 43, 58, 66, 188
Custer, George A., 28–29

Daily, Leo C., 46
Daley, Richard, 168
Darling, Jay ("Ding"), 36, 37
Davis, Smith, 91
Dennis, Charles, 96
Des Moines Register and Leader, 36, 52
Des Moines Register and Tribune, 33, 37, 38, 40, 43, 46, 47, 52, 92
Detroit Free Press, 90, 93, 94, 101
Dewey, Thomas, 42, 45, 131
Dillon, T. J., 81
Douglas, Paul H., 141
Duff, Bernard, 83
Dunning, John, 77

Eden, Anthony, 163
Eisenhower, Dwight D., 92, 137
Elliot, I. A., 122
English, Earl, 165
Epping, Edward A., 146
Ethridge, Mark, 124
Etzell, James F., 119–122
Eyerly, Frank, 37, 38

Fanning, Lawrence S., 171
Faries, William W., 19
Farouk (king of Egypt), 153
Fermi, Enrico, 77
Field, Eugene, 96
Field, Marshall, I, 172
Field, Marshall, Jr., 97, 98, 108, 167, 170, 171, 172, 180
Finnegan, Richard, 97
Finney, Nat, 4, 6, 8

Fire That Will Not Die, The (McBride), 167
Fisher, James Shield, 12, 14
Fisher, Nancy Christina, 12
Fisher, Nancy Heaton, 12
Fitzgerald, Thomas H., 145
Franklin, C. P., 20
Fraser, Robert, 4
Freedom, Education and the Fund (Hutchins), 174, 178
Free press, 8, 116–25, 166, 176–79, 183
Fund for the Republic, 175

Gallup, George, 40–42, 43, 44, 59, 62, 91, 106, 160
Gammons, Earl, 70
Garst, Bob, 169
George VI (king of England), 73–74
Ghali, Paul, 104
Goering, Hermann, 109
Good News II, 46, 47
Gore, Budd, 100, 101
Green, Dwight H., 126
Gross, Barbara, 11
Gruenberg, Robert, 145, 166
Gunning, Robert, 92, 101, 106, 160

Hall, Arthur E., 100, 129
Hamilton, Andrew, 123
Hargrave, A. A., 137
Harris, Anna Mae, 143
Harris, Roy J., 126, 143
Harvey Ingham & Gardner Cowles, Sr. (Mills), 35, 50–51
Hearst, George, Jr., 182
Hearst, William Randolph, 97, 98, 105, 181, 182
Hecht, Ben, 96
Heirens, William, 109–10
Henry, William H. (Bill), 132
Herring, Clyde L., 50
Himmler, Heinrich, 109
Hintz, Edward A., 146
History of the United States Army Ambulance Service, 20
Hodge, Orville, 141–48, 165
Hodge Scandal, The (Thiem), 142
Holstrom, Ben, 74
Hoover, J. Edgar, 85, 86
Howard, Roy W., 137
Howlette, Michael J., 141, 142, 147
Hoyt, Palmer, 123
Humphrey, Hubert, 78
Hussein Ibn Talal (king of Jordan), 150, 156–57, 162
Hutchins, Robert Maynard, 23, 174, 175, 176, 177, 178, 179

Illinois Editor and Publisher Highway Traffic Safety Seminar, 87
Indiana Daily Student, 16, 18, 19
Indianapolis Star, 24
Indiana Society of Chicago, 84
Ingham, Harvey, 35, 36, 43, 64
Inland Daily Press Association, 130, 165, 173
International News Service, 57
Isaacs, Norman, 185

Jenstad, Frosty, 59, 68, 69, 70, 71, 77, 78
Johnson, Charlie, 89
Johnson, Pi, 121

Kefauver, Estes, 130
Keller, Leroy, 58, 59
Kennelly, Martin, 128
Kenny, Sister Elizabeth, 80
   Elizabeth Kenny Polio Institute, 80
Kerr, Clark, 177, 179
Khrushchev, Nikita S., 144, 169
King, Cecil, 91
Kirkpatrick, Helen, 109
Kline, Marvin, 84
Knight, Frank, 170
Knight, James, 90
Knight, John S., 82, 88, 90-93, 98-101, 103-7, 114, 115, 127-29, 131, 134, 138, 149, 167, 169, 170-72, 176, 177, 183, 184
Knight, John S., Jr., 170
Knight Newspapers, 55, 87, 118, 148, 184
Knights of the Fourth Estate (Smiley), 106
Knox, Frank, 91, 92, 95, 99, 106
Krauch, Herb, 182
Kreml, Franklin A., 86
Kroot, Anna, 168

Lahey, Ed, 99, 150, 174
Lane, Clem, 99, 142, 145
Latourell, George, 83
Lawrence, David, 134
Lawson, Ivar, 95
Lawson, Victor, 91, 92, 105
Lilly, Eli, 187
Lindbergh, Charles, 49
Lindbergh, kidnapping, 49-50
Lisagor, Irvin Peter (Pete), 174
Look, 39, 57
Loop-the-loop, 48, 67, 72, 73, 80
Lugar, Richard, 187
Lyons, Louis M., 59

MacArthur, Douglas, 118

McBride, Michele, 167
McCarthy, Kevin, 81
McCormick, Robert R., 97, 98, 99, 105
MacDonald, Kenneth, 38, 43, 44, 45, 47, 48, 49
McGill, Ralph, 91
"Machine gun camera," 51-53
McInnis, John Phaelan ("Stuffy"), 15
McKelway, Ben, 185
Macmillan, Harold, 163-64
Macmillan, Maurice Crawford, 163
Martin, Douglas D., 123, 124
Marvin, Dwight, 117
Maxwell, Don, 164
Maytag, F. L., 36
Meifield, Paul, 14
Meir, Golda, 159-60
Menjou, Adolphe, J., 23
Merwin, Davis, 54
Miller, Frederick A., 137
Mills, George, 35-37, 50
Milwaukee Journal, 24
Minneapolis Star, 3-6, 20, 173
   circulation growth, 55, 56, 65, 72
   purchase by Cowleses, 54
Minneapolis Star-Journal, 75
Minneapolis Tribune, 57, 72, 75
   purchase by Cowleses, 81—82
Minnesota Editorial Association, 56, 121, 172
Mio, Mrs. Joseph, 168
Mollenhoff, Clark, 148
Montgomery, Harry, 108
Mooney, William, 145
Morison, Bradley, L., 71, 72, 82
Moscowitz, Raymond, 139
Mowrer, Paul Scott, 96, 98, 99
Murphy, William J., 75
Mussolini, Benito, 103

Naftalin, Arthur, 76, 78
Naguib, Mohammad, 159
Nasser, Gamal Abdel, 150, 153-56
National News Council, 185
New Deal, 50
Newhouse, S. I., 170
Newspaper, readability, 40-42, 92, 102
Newspaper Research Associates, 180
News photos, 47, 51-53, 67-68, 73-75, 110-12
Newton, V. M., Jr., 144
New York Times, 41, 66
Nier, Alfred O. C., 76, 77, 78
Norlander, Everett, 99, 102, 142, 166, 172
Normand, Mabel, 23
Northwest News Bureau (NNB), 57
Not Subject to Change, 10
Noyes, Newbold, 185

O'Brien, Howard Vincent, 102
Office of Strategic Services (OSS), 103, 104
Offset printing, 112–13, 115
O'Flaherty, Hal, 99, 104
Olson, Kenneth E., 116, 117

Padev, Michael, 108
Parade, 170
Parsons, W. D., 65
Pearl Harbor, 81
Peterson, George L., 88
Photo-engraving, 113–15
Photojournalism, 39
Pihl, Harry, 83
Pitts, Alice Fox, 119
Poirer, Joseph, 120
Pope, James, 124
Pope, Vernon, 38, 39
Poundstone, Ramsey, 17
Price, Byron D., 90
Prowitt, Alfred, 110
Pulitzer Prize, 96, 101, 126, 127, 132, 146
Pulliam, Eugene C., 108, 132, 137

Remembrance Rock (Sandburg), 141
Reston, James B. ("Scotty"), 131
Richmond Palladium, 16–18
Riley, James Whitcomb, 164
Roosevelt, Franklin D., 6, 16, 50, 90
Royko, Mike, 70
Ruppel, Louis, 97, 99
Russell, D. A., Jr., 31

Sandburg, Carl, 96, 106, 141
Saturday Triple Streak, 129
Schmitz, Baby Boy, 3–7
Schultz, Robert, 145
Schumaker, Ted, 184
Seymour, Gideon, 88, 89, 120
Shaffel, Larry, 122
Sheldon, William, 10
Shoemaker, Vaughn, 126
Shutts, Frank B., 90
Sidebar, 9
Sigma Delta Chi, 121–22, 132, 144, 187
Silha, Otto, 69
Silverman, Dave, 58, 70, 74
Smiley, Nixon, 106
Smith, John, 108
Smith, Paul, 118
Sparks, Fred, 127, 183
Squalus, 75
Stalin, Joseph, 135, 144
Starling, E. W., 27
Stassen, Harold, 73–75
Stevenson, Adlai E., 92, 127, 141

Stone, Melville E., 95, 105
Stratton, William G., 146
Strong, Walter A., 95
Sullivan, Hassal T., 16
Sunlight on Your Doorstep, 72, 82
Sweetland, Bill, 121
Swensson, Paul, 90

Techniques of Clear Writing (Gunning), 101
Thiem, George, 126, 142, 143, 145
Thomas, Lin, 26
Thomas, Smoky, 25, 26
Thompson, John, 54, 72
Tribble, Hal, 61
Truman, Harry, 42
Tuohy, William J., 109
Typography, 48, 65–70, 78–79, 100–101, 130, 139, 173

United Kingdom, 82–84, 91
United Press International, 57
United States Army Ambulance Corps (USAAC), 19, 20, 23
USAAC Bulletin, 23

Walters, Basil Leon ("Stuffy")
    Cedric Adams and, 70–72
    on Arab-Israeli dispute and Middle East visit, 150–63
    on Calvin Coolidge's visit to South Dakota, 25–28
    carrier pigeons and, 47
    at *Chicago Daily News,* 93–180
    Ciano Diaries and, 103–5
    on columnists, 66–67, 131, 186
    as consultant, 181–86
    on copy editing, 29–32, 48, 67, 131
    Cowles family and, 33–34, 37–38, 54, 88–90
    at *Des Moines Register and Tribune,* 37–39, 40–62
    at *Detroit Free Press,* 93, 94
    early life, 12–16
    on editorial union, 166–67
    education of, 16–19, 22–23
    Marshall Field and, 171–72, 180
    on a free press, 8, 116–25, 166, 176–79, 183
    George Gallup and, 42–43
    and King George's visit, 73–76
    William Randolph Hearst and, 105, 181
    Orville Hodge scandal and, 141–48
    in India Journalism Hall of Fame, 187
    as Indiana Newspaperman of the Year, 173
    Sister Elizabeth Kenny and, 80

on Khrushchev/Garst meeting, 169
John Knight and, 90–93, 105, 172
Lindbergh kidnapping and, 49–50
on Little Big Horn, 28–29
marriage of, 24
member of Indiana Academy, 187
at *Milwaukee Journal,* 24–32
at *Minneapolis Star,* 54–90
New Castle tornado and, 17–18
"new journalism" of, 65–70
newspaper readership and, 40–42, 62
news philosophy of, 8, 29, 31, 43–44, 45, 56, 107
nickname, 15
nuclear energy scoop and, 76–79
printers' strike and, 115–16
on qualities of newspeople, 9, 133
receives honorary doctorate, 137
receives Zenger Award, 124–25
on reporting, 25, 39, 43, 45, 59–60, 110–11, 130–31, 134, 187
retirement, 173–74, 180
Spencer, Iowa, fire and, 45–47
M. Lyle Spencer Visiting Professor, 187
on television, 130–31, 186
tour of United Kingdom, 82–84, 91, 134
traffic safety movement and, 85–87
on typography and makeup, 48–49, 65–70, 78–80, 100–101, 111, 130, 173
Richard Wilson and, 50–51
in World War I, 19–21
on writing, 59–61, 101
Walters, Frederick (father), 12, 13
Walters, Frederick (grandfather), 11
Walters, James (son), 9–10, 116, 156, 162, 180

Walters, John (brother-in-law), 13
Walters, Nancy (daughter), 11, 34, 114, 180
Walters, Nancy (mother), 12, 13
Walters, Paul (step-grandson), 187
Walters, Reah (Mrs. Basil), 18, 19, 24, 34, 53, 55, 63, 64, 71, 89, 93, 94, 137, 152, 163, 182, 188
Walters, Tom (son), 180
Walters, Wilma (sister), 12
Warner, Cliff (Fizzy"), 19
Warner, Raleigh, 103
Weekend Chicago Daily News, 173
Weitzel, Tony, 60
Weller, George, 151, 162
Wells, W. A., 31
Whitney, John Hay, 170
Whittaker, John, 103, 105
Wiggins, J. Russell, 64, 124, 137
Williams, J. H., 77
Willkie, Wendell, 16
Wilson, Charles, 138
Wilson, Richard, 38, 50–51, 70
World War I, 18, 20, 24
World War II, 109
Wright, Warren E., 144

Yates, George, 51, 52
Yost, Casper S., 119

Zeinddine, Farid, 151–52
Zenger, John Peter, 123
Zenger Award, 123–25